Interpreting Nightingales

Interpreting
Nightingales

Gender, Class and Histories

Jeni Williams

Sheffield
Academic Press

To Gwion and Esyllt

Copyright © 1997 Sheffield Academic Press

Published by
Sheffield Academic Press Ltd
Mansion House
19 Kingfield Road
Sheffield S11 9AS
England

Typeset by Sheffield Academic Press
and
Printed on acid-free paper in Great Britain
by Bookcraft Ltd
Midsomer Norton, Bath

British Library Cataloguing in Publication Data

A catalogue record for this book is available
from the British Library

ISBN 1 85075 808 5

Contents

Acknowledgments

I would like to thank the Museum of Modern Art in New York for permission to use Max Ernst's wonderful painting, *Two Children are Threatened by a Nightingale* for the cover.

I would like to thank everyone who has helped me—by discussing or just listening to me work out ideas—but there have been so many over ten years that I am sorry if I leave anybody out.

Firstly I would like to thank Glyn Pursglove, who supervised my first tentative writings on the nightingale, and Francis Warner, my examiner of that time, for his learned comments. Margaret Kenna, Sian Lewis and Adrian Wilmott discussed classical literature with me, while Drs Lewis and Wilmott translated fiendishly difficult medieval Latin texts. Ruth Evans provided useful comments on the medieval chapters. Discussions in the Staff Seminar on *Texts and Theories*, organized by Duncan Large at the University of Wales Swansea, helped to crystallize certain ideas—though any incoherence is certainly my responsibility.

I would like to thank three people in particular: Fern Smith of Volcano physical theatre, with whom I had long and stimulating conversations and who provided me with ideas about space and the body from a very different but equally demanding discipline; Kate Hodgkin who not only read and commented so incisively on the work in progress but proofread the whole manuscript with meticulous care while swamped by her own work; and David Harris, for long and intense discussions, particularly about Chapter 3, and for productive comments and help with ideas throughout.

Finally I would like to thank my two children, Gwion and Esyllt Williams, who soothed my panics. They have grown up listening to nightingales, and, I hope, have not been too menaced by them.

Introduction

Reflecting on the Nightingale

...the nightingale
cannot stop singing
for she sparkles with love in her whole being.
If this were taken from her she would die...[1]

The nightingale that appears so frequently in poetry seems an innocuous figure, a solitary female voice singing unseen, bodiless, her rhapsodic melody swelling through the silence of spring nights, associated with beautiful, melancholy subjective verse. This is the nightingale of the enlightenment subject, familiar as the most romantic of 'poetic' tropes from the most famous of all nightingale poems, Keats's *Ode to a Nightingale*, a figure which speaks of unearthly loveliness, the beauty of the aesthetic experience, its transcendence of earthly struggle and desire. But, as Keats recognizes in that same poem, the flawless voice can also appear dangerous. In an unnerving echo of Keats's vampiric heroines—Lamia and la Belle Dame sans Merci—the nightingale's song calls up masculine fears of impotence, threatening to draw the male listener away from human life into the bloodless world of art, draining him of his ability to act. From this perspective the poetic nightingale shares the power of Spenser's Acrasia, dissolving young men with sensuous delight. Like this nightingale, sirens were always feminine, though their inhuman seduction took a more concrete form: those sailors who listened to them steered to their destruction and were cut to pieces on submerged rocks. Listening to the nightingale seems to have very little danger in comparison. Yet there are dangers in the figure of the nightingale—and not just those seen by Keats. For, from the Renaissance on, the association of femininity with passivity and sublimation seems concentrated with peculiar force in the figure of the poetic nightingale: an association particularly pertinent to the difficulties of the female artist. The nightingale of limpid, lyric poetry can easily slip into an angel of death and paralysis for the female writer or auditor.

It is a problem that Elizabeth Barrett Browning's 1861 poem 'Bianca among the Nightingales' confronts head on:

> —Oh, owl-like birds! They sing for spite,
>   They sing for hate, they sing for doom,
> They'll sing through death who sing through night,
>   They'll sing and stun me in the tomb—
> The nightingales, the nightingales![2]

The power of 'Bianca' lies not in the refusal of past patterns, but in the deliberate and unnerving inversion of them. Bianca's monologue competes and is even confused with the unearthly voices of the birds of love, digging below their immediate symbolism to the roots of their power in death and pain. Yet part of her agony lies in that very confusion: in order to gain the authority and power of art, Bianca's voice is haunted by the voices of the nightingales, and the choral counterpoint they provide to her monologue provides the symbolic boundary against which the massed voices of the past and the past versions of the literary nightingale press, overwhelming and almost suffocating her individual cry even as they figure its enablement. The poem is a *tour de force* of past images and literatures. These nightingales are not merely repetitions of past figures—the classical Philomela or the Romantic bird—but form a kaleidoscope of conflicting meanings made possible only through the immense reading that Barrett Browning, like many other Victorian women excluded from the rigours of formal education, undertook in strenuous attempts to gain access to the charmed world of learning. And only by a reassessment of those forgotten elements—not only the classical Philomela but the medieval nightingale also—can the poem (or the poetic nightingale) be properly understood. The danger for the modern reader is to accept the silencing of received readings which remove the ambiguities of the past.

This book takes the form of a chronological study of the nightingale that opens with Homer and works through classical Greek, Christian Latin and medieval texts before making a huge jump and turning to the Victorians, and, especially, to Barrett Browning. The major focus is on the literary nightingale, whose roots lie in the Greek myth of Philomela, the raped and silenced girl who finds a new voice through art; first through physically weaving her story, and then through the woven notes of song after her transformation into a nightingale, a bird whose Greek name (*aedon*) simultaneously stands for creature, poet and poetry, marking the boundary of the human in the world of nature by singing in the wooded regions outside the walled enclaves of the 'civilized' world. It is not surprising that Jonathan Goldberg's assessment of poetry—'the story in brief: the broken heart, language in place of the lost object'—should draw on the Philomela story as part of its consideration of the significance of loss ('every poet's question').[3]

My own fascination with the nightingale lies primarily in its association with issues of gender. The very fact that the real singing-bird is the male of the species while the female does not sing is itself significant. The transposition of the gender of the literary figure thus implies that it carries qualities that mark it out as 'feminine' over and above the actual sex of the bird and which therefore highlight the constructed nature of gendered identity itself. But the nightingale is not only a symbol of constructed gender identities—of either the perpetual mediation of the feminine voice by sexual desire, or a masculine fear of and simultaneous fascination with sensuality—though this is part of its significance. Nightingales were associated with poetry long before the Renaissance—and in Mechthild's poem the associations which seem so constricting to Barrett Browning are liberating, ecstatic. Barrett Browning may have been driven by a consciousness of 'the woman question', but the mixture of elements in the figurative bird means that at different times different configurations emerge, complicating the 'woman question' with both issues of power relations and major shifts in the very constructions of 'masculinity' and its shadowy other, 'femininity'. Indeed, if gendered difference is constructed through *relations* between the centre and its peripheries, the marginalized status of the nightingale's voice allows it to function as an index of similar relational identities.

In the Greek myth of Philomela, the girl's tongue is cut out to silence her after she is raped. Her first communication (through the woven tapestry) allows for release and revenge, but her transformation into the nightingale, the figure of communication itself, allows for the perpetual remembrance of her violation. For Hesiod the tale of the nightingale equally serves to commemorate the survival of the poet, assaulted by rapacious princes. Despite the apparent differences between the two tales, there are similarities, most importantly that in each case the nightingale expresses—and articulates—her survival in situations of powerlessness. This aspect clearly appealed to the early Christian writers, in terms of both their own victimized status and that of their lord.

Despite the frequency and consistency of references to the myth of Philomela, another, equally significant *literary* role accompanies them. A.R. Chandler notes its age—'the nightingale plays a more important role in European literature than any other bird. References to it are found all along the way from Homer to T.S. Eliot'[4]—while A.T. Hatto points out the enormous geographical spread of references to the nightingale, known 'as the bird of love in the Old World from Japan to the Iberian Peninsula';[5] an astonishing claim even if he qualifies it by admitting that the 'love-bird' does not appear 'in every land' between these two points. Such ubiquity and the consistency of associations with erotic love illustrates more than simple coincidence, and it is interesting that an equally consistent alternative characterization of the nightingale should invert the associations with darkness, victimization, tragedy—and femininity. In medieval lyric poetry especially (including that of Provence and Germany), the nightingale is a vigorous male bird, distinctly different from that of the Greeks, in that he sings joyously in sunlight during a spring characterized overwhelmingly by sexual reawakening; he interacts directly with the human world, encouraging lovers and sometimes acting as a confidant. Though associated with love poetry, he is not a figure of the aesthetic.

Hatto attempts to qualify the difference between the masculine and feminine forms that this figure of love takes by relating them to two distinct contexts, deriving 'Romanic, Germanic and Slavonic nightingales from oral traditions nourished for many years over a more or less continuous stretch of European territory from the

Peninsular over towards the Caucasus'.[6] Hatto sees no other way of explaining such a marked difference between the two characterizations. Referring to the version of the Philomela myth in which the girl's *sister* is transformed into the nightingale and mourns her dead child, killed and dismembered in cannibalistic revenge for her husband's treachery, he questions, 'Why else should a highly literary, tragic mother-nightingale seem to give way to a merry male?'

Oral traditions versus literary ones; the vigorous male set against the tragic female; day against night. The key interest thus seems to lie in gender, but as to be expected in a figure which serves only to reflect the human, its gender is defined through its relation with other terms rather than in any static essential quality. Both in its feminine and its masculine forms, the nightingale's specific qualities are controlled and transformed by wider historical forces, and crossovers occur. Two brief examples will serve: in the first, the change in the representation of the literary nightingale serves to indicate the implications of the spread of literacy from a single exclusive group (the ecclesiastical clergy with their classical/exegetic education) to a range of other, semi-official (or unofficial) groups which brought the values of an oral society into their writing, producing hymns and lyrics rooted in an individual, not hierarchical, experience of ecstasy; in the second, the changing status of the nightingale in poetry points to the association of particular tropes, especially that of romantic love/*fin amour*, with a particular class (the aristocracy) and therefore the appropriation of the symbol of that love by their particular genres. In a thirteenth-century debate poem the nightingale's association with the poetry and values of a refined aristocracy is set against the pedantic cleric figured by her masculine enemy (the Thrush); two centuries later the reification of a more extreme social upheaval appears in the debate between the nightingale and her new enemy: a cuckoo who is characterized as a 'churl', or peasant.

Conflicts about gender cannot be disentangled at any time from those of class: both are related to questions of power and hierarchy. The other interest of this book therefore lies in a fascination with historical change. It seeks to trace what Stephen Greenblatt called 'the deep complicity of our moral imagination even in its noblest and most hauntingly beautiful manifestations in the great

Western celebrations of power'.[7] And the power of the aesthetic—of poetry itself, of the nightingale—is one of the greatest of all. There have been many studies of the literary figure. In 1928, for example, H.W. Garrod attempted the immense topic of 'The Nightingale in Poetry' (though he really meant canonical European and English verse).[8] This book will draw attention to numerous studies of individual symbolic birds, studies which seem so often to be descriptive, detailing the appearance of the trope without analyzing its wider significance. But the richness of the nightingale's song is an insufficient reason for the bird's continuing popularity in literature and I do not intend that this study be descriptive.

The differences between the two traditions of representation are significant in their own right, while the fact that a male singing bird is represented as female in classical poetry and all literature written in that tradition is equally significant, highlighting the cultural associations between femininity and submissiveness (the bird sings hidden in a bush; in the myth she is a victim of rape); between birdsong and the divine voice of the Muse (the Greek word for poetry, poet and nightingale is the same—*aedon*); and between sensuality and the coming of Spring (the migratory nightingale plays a significant part in the *adonia* or fertility rituals). All of these seem to have been carried into literatures far distant from the original Greek and express concern with questions of authority and voice.

The continuing relevance of these associations has led to the frequency with which, under a variety of guises, the Philomelic nightingale has continued to be a moving voice in European literature over centuries: to the extent that the question of the association of authority and authorship and its relation to themes of mutilation, silencing and regaining of voice has become a central concern of much contemporary literature. A fine example of this theme is found in Coetzee's *Foe*, with the silencing of the woman (Susan Barton) and the enslaved black (Friday): in the former the woman's tongue is appropriated by the male writer and her story made exotic and tempting; in the latter the tongue is cut out altogether. Mutilation means that the two are drawn together though the form of silencing differs in terms of overt and covert coercion. A more direct reference seems indicated in *The World according to*

Garp—a text which significantly examines the American polarization of gender identity—in which a girl who has been raped and has had her tongue cut out becomes the centre of a cult whose followers cut out their own tongues and move to live by the boundary of the sea.

These texts seem a long way from the decorous voice of popular sentimental nightingales—and this is one reason why I have chosen to examine literature taken from a wide variety of sources *outside* not only the canon, but also the unspoken canonical period. Focusing on the relation of voice to authority, and on the positive role of art as registering the violations of a violating world—and still being associated with beauty and song—has meant that I wish to question the restriction of the patterns of the enlightenment world. If that world is, as postmodernist critics insist, fragmenting, then the patterns of pre-enlightenment literature are rich sources of analysis. There is no figure more valuable as an index of these fluid boundaries than the nightingale. Looking for the roots of his poetry, the Anglo-Welsh poet Leslie Norris chooses to turn to the nightingale as a figure for both his own childhood and his verse. As a modern Romantic it is fitting that he takes on the role of Coleridge's son as he recalls being taken by his father into

> ...the wood where the nightingale sang
> The unbelievable bird who lived in the stories
> Of almost my every book...[9]

and concludes with a memory of 'the fixed stars reeling:'

> It is the poet's bird, they say. Perhaps I took it home.
> For here I am, raising my voice, scraping my throat raw again.

Chapter 1

Sorrowful Weaving:
Nightingales in Greek and Latin Texts

After resolving a border dispute with the help of Tereus, king of
Thrace (and one of the sons of Ares), Pandion, king of Athens,
rewards his ally by giving him his eldest daughter, Procne, in
marriage. After several years and the birth of a son, Itys, Procne
yearns to see her sister, Philomela, again and Tereus travels to
Athens to bring her back. But on the homeward journey, he takes
her to a wood, rapes her, cuts out her tongue to silence her and
shuts her away in a forest dwelling. He then deceives his wife by
telling her that her sister has died. However, Philomela weaves her
story into a tapestry and sends it to Procne who frees her. Together
they revenge themselves on Tereus by killing Itys and serving him
up to his father in a cannibalistic banquet. When he realizes what
he has done, Tereus snatches up an axe to hack them to death but,
out of pity for their agonies, Zeus turns them into birds: Tereus
becomes a hoopoe, Procne, a nightingale, Philomela, a swallow,
and Itys, a goldfinch.

Philomela's Loss

The *philomel moment* of English poetry is...the postprophetic
moment, when the theme of loss merges with that of voice—when,
in fact, a 'lost voice' becomes the subject or moving force of poetic
song.[1]

As a tale which speaks of the silencing of the violated, the chaos
unleashed by the act of violation and the commemoration of both
elements through the voice of poetry, the myth of Philomela

haunts classical Greek literature, to the extent that, according to
Garrod, 'the nightingale is the stock symbol of unassuaged grief
in Attic tragedy',[2] and Sophocles devoted an entire tragedy, *Tereus*,
to the story. (For a story about displacement and loss it seems
appropriate that this should only survive in tantalizing fragments
wrongly attributed to Aeschylus in Aristotle, or through parody in
Aristophanes' comedy, *The Birds*.) An examination of the myth
suggests why it should have been so popular in Classical literature—and why it might continue to be so—and allows me to make
readings of various Greek and Latin texts. I start by looking at the
fertile transformation at the centre of the myth: the translation of
silenced girl to singing bird.

   One way of interpreting metamorphosis is to see it as effecting
closure on a cycle of compulsively repeated actions;[3] another is to
see it as introducing transformation and thus change into a closed
hierarchical structure. The Philomela myth fits into the latter
pattern by emphasizing the power of passion, violence and song.
In particular it articulates the difficulties of women (either erotic
object or maternal figure, both defining the masculine principle),
draws attention to the complex relationship between eroticism
and victimization, and considers the ambivalent relations of the
aesthetic and the feminine to the political state. It is interesting
that W.R. Halliday should suggest that the Philomela myth is a
fairly late development of a more ancient bird fable, one which
acquired the form and the names by which we still recognize it
during the fifth and fourth centuries[4]—in line with R.M.C. Forbes
Irving's comment that metamorphosis is important in 'the developed narratives of the 5th and 4th centuries' but rare in Homer.[5]
The human story of Philomela and Procne (the two daughters of
the king of Athens) thus emerges from an Athens destabilized
both politically, by protracted war, and ideologically, by the questioning and doubt of fifth-century rational philosophy and the
insurgence and development of the oriental cult of Dionysus, the
god of excess and drama.[6] The fifth-century interest in transformation stories can be related to the ideological uncertainties that
these contradictory impulses seem to articulate. Metamorphosis
blurs and questions the defining boundaries between the mortal
and immortal worlds, the human and the animal: both metaphorically and spatially it interrogates the limits of the civilized. In

this reading the story of Philomela can be seen to illustrate the spectral shadow that haunts fifth-century rationalism and gains its immediacy by emerging out of a society whose boundaries are in crisis. Once crystallized in this form the pattern provides a potent literary myth, a metaphor for the relation of the aesthetic to the political through the victimization, silencing and recovery of the feminine voice.

Because of the sheer volume of material it is impossible to do justice to all texts I mention here, so I restrict myself to brief discussion and focus on only a few: commenting on the significance of the mythic nightingale in the *Agamemnon* and *Oedipus at Colonus*; glancing at the role of the wooded place of the nightingale voice in the pastoral; and comparing Ovid's mythological narrative to the scientific 'objectivity' of Pliny. (Texts are given in Appendix I).

Voice and Silence: The Myth of Philomela

The figure of Philomela illustrates the loss of individual and social identity that accompanies the act of victimization, and throws light on the coercive nature of both formations of identity. Reading the myth as a structure of meaning indicates that Philomela appears to lose her place in the defining structures of family or social grouping: she is neither married nor unmarried; she is a rival to her own sister; she is shut up in a forest hut, away from the 'civilized' world of the polis. Her ambiguous status uncovers the artificiality, and hence the arbitrariness, of the structures themselves. Roman myths are more concerned with punitive closure than Greek ones. Martial's epigram replaces the social structures challenged by Philomela's anomalous status with a rigid (and equally arbitrary) aesthetic closure, seeking to contain the arbitrary transformation by flippantly reducing the girl to a mere element within the fixed pattern of the poem: 'she who was a silent maiden is acclaimed as a bird of song' (14.75, see p. 233). Writing at a time when the social and political structures of his contemporary world were under threat, and the festival of Dionysus provided the cultural frame to contain and explore dangerous ambiguity, Sophocles is less interested in containment and, in fact, multiplies the story's ambiguities by expanding it to tragedy. Precisely because of its metaphoric ambiguity, the resonant phrase, 'the voice of the shuttle' (a fragment from his *Tereus*), has led to fascinating analyses of both the artifical voice of literature—Geoffrey Hartman, 'The Voice of the Shuttle: Language from the Point of View of Literature'[7]—and the repressed voice of woman—Patricia Klindiest Joplin, 'The Voice of the Shuttle Is Ours'.[8] Each interpretation can be accused of omission—Hartman of the voice of woman; Joplin of that of art; both perhaps of history—but it is testimony to the extraordinary suggestiveness of the myth that such varied interpretations should emerge.

Perhaps the extraordinary potency of the myth lies in its concern with the voicing of the silenced. Central to the tale is a double concern with the nature and the different forms of communication, the relationship of the excluded, the powerless to those in power. The voice of the nightingale thrust into the wood endlessly resonates with the human tale that has led to her metamorphosis, the woven images on the tapestry springing to life in the inhuman commentary of the tale itself as it weaves poetry out of a human story of violence and lost innocence. Of all Greek transformation stories, the Philomela myth seems the most suggestive: R.M.C. Forbes Irving considers that 'none of the others [display]…the same richness of detail or such elaborately developed themes'.[9] This richness and ambiguity provides the ground for immensely varied interpretations of its narrative: a narrative which operates on many levels as a study of complex power relations out of which the related issues of aesthetics and gender emerge.

With so many resonances, it is unsurprising that the nightingale and its shadowy myth should erupt so consistently into the drama of an Athens whose empire, and hence authority, were falling apart. There are many political reasons for the Philomela myth to be relevant during the Peloponnesian war. Philomela is a victim of the dismemberment of social order as much as of the individual moment of rape, and as such serves to illustrate the spreading horror of social anarchy. Tereus's link with Ares, the war-god of brute violence, is crucial. He violates all social bonds, starting with those that hold allies together in the face of a common enemy, betraying masculine pride and solidarity when he betrays his

father-in-law, undermining the family through his deception of
both Pandion and Procne. In this context Philomela's rape is not
an isolated act of violence, for it is incestuous at the same time as
it is adulterous, and it leads to further distortions, the accumulated violations turning in on Tereus's own self as the women he
has betrayed unite to destroy the child, Itys, and, in an inverted
'family' meal, feed him to his father.[10] Seen from this perspective
the myth acts as a warning. It polices the ordering of society by
depicting its unravelling, the chaos following the breakdown of
accepted patterns. The symbolic victim, Philomela, is a scapegoat,
shut up in the forest, away from both polis and family, dislocated
and therefore potentially, and actually, disruptive of an order that
displaces the violence inherent in the civilized world onto her
suffering.[11]

Yet the myth is more than a fable of politics. Its focus on the
symbolism of rape and on the vengeful inversion of traditional
women's roles that follows indicates the centrality of gender to
the story. The two sisters can be seen as aspects of the same figure
(woman), for if Philomela's rape transforms her into her sister's
rival, it also points to a duplication of roles: both are possessed by
Tereus, Philomela sends and Procne receives the woven message
which lays bare the truth of their double betrayal and the lies of
their betrayer, while Philomela's rape and mutilation is visited on
her sister's child. The confusion of identity is reflected in the
metamorphoses: in Greek stories generally the nightingale and
swallow are often confused with each other. In the hypothesis of a
tragedy thought to be *Tereus* itself, it is unclear which woman
becomes which bird, and in the Latin version of the myth it is the
raped girl who becomes the nightingale rather than the mother.
But the myth is not interested in the precise meanings of individual, separate figures within the structure of the myth, rather it
investigates the *relations* between them. What is central is the definite association of the nightingale with betrayed women and poetry: the Greek word *aedon* is used for the bird, poet and poetry.
In addition the link with Philomela and/or Procne points to a
general background of pain, loss and lamentation associated with
the feminine, whichever woman becomes the bird: a conclusion
which bears out Joplin's emphasis on the intimate connections
between social and gender hierarchies in the myth. Indeed, bear-

ing in mind the barbarian nature of Tereus, she concludes that

> ...both barbarian and virgin daughter are proverbial figures of the
> Greek imagination. They are actors in a drama depicting the neces-
> sity for establishing and keeping secure the boundaries that protect
> the key figure, that of Pandion, the sympathetic king who disap-
> pears from the tale as soon as he gives up both his daughters....
> What the myth reveals is how the political hierarchy built upon
> male sexual dominance requires the violent appropriation of the
> women's power to speak.[12]

Joplin sees the myth as caught within a cycle of 'violation-revenge-
violation'[13] which assures the continued 'appropriation of the
women's power to speak' by seeing any rebellion in terms of the
murderous conclusion of the tale and the dismemberment of the
child Itys. Attempting to read against this didactic message and to
recover 'women's power to speak', Joplin turns to the metaphoric
voice of Philomela's woven message to her sister. But this communication remains locked within the story: by omitting Zeus's
refusal to allow Tereus to dismember the women, the suspension
of violence through the final transformations and the creation of
the voice of art, commentating from outside on the manipulations of a political world, Joplin similarly cannot move outside the
boundaries of the tale. Her concentration on the woman's
weaving at the centre of the plot, on the 'the voice of the shuttle',
omits the ambiguity of an art which is gendered and thus caught
up itself in the power structures of its society[14] and leads to a
silencing of Joplin's own: that of the nightingale, of art. By translating the vindictive oppositional frame she sees inscribed in social
relations directly into the structure of the myth, Joplin seems to
attempt to verify its relevance through a 'kind of reality testing'
which denies the fictional construction of the tale as a whole:[15]
the fact that Philomela is a woman means that, from Joplin's point
of view, she is always a victim, even if her experience allows her
access to a special sense of her potentiality. She can thus only be
given a metaphoric voice, and her freedom of expression can only
take the form of a traditional women's art: weaving. Philomela
remains locked within the story, not given access to the voice
through which the story is *transmitted*: the voice of poetry, of words
that connect and allow difference, of the communication that articulates the story of violent silencing. As a woman she is denied

the voice that Joplin employs in order to speak for her.[16]

I would argue that the human story caught within the myth may point towards a 'deadly' structure but the very *inscription* of that myth points outwards to other readings and possibilities.[17] The nightingale's voice in the woods is not the fearful voice of violence, but the voice that commemorates the expulsion of each of the figures from the human world, ensuring the suspension of the cycle of 'violation–revenge–violation', and simultaneously holds them in memory through symbolic representation. Each of the other birds takes on symbolic meaning—the hoopoe is associated with treachery, the tongueless swallow chatters around the eaves of houses, warning women of masculine betrayal, the goldfinch comes to signify the maternal breast in the iconography of medieval paintings of the Virgin and Child[18]—but the nightingale has a more particular significance. The treacherous hoopoe is shunned,[19] but the nightingale sings of the loss of her child—Joplin's final innocent victim—and though, like Philomela, she is banished into the realms of the inhuman, her liquid commentary calls up the whole story of violation and makes the women's final revenge explicable rather than arbitrary.

Joplin argues that Philomela's ambiguous status after being raped creates a 'redundant or equivocal sign' which spills over the confinements of a closed system of signs: 'once she can no longer function as sign, she wrests free her own power to speak',[20] and is able to cut through Tereus's deceit with the truth of her woven expression. Yet the ultimate art of equivocation is not weaving—which as 'women's art' *has* a place within a closed system of signs—but poetry. Both are art of different kinds though one *speaks* and the other gestures through image. Jane McIntosh Snyder's work on weaving imagery[21] indicates a pertinent coincidence of vocabulary between the two activities.[22] It is a coincidence which bears significantly on the nightingale: a figure which, especially in the Philomela myth, is associated with both weaving (within the tale/human society) and poetry (outside/in the woods). Where Joplin sees the act of weaving as expressive of 'woman's voice'—and does not consider the 'singing' of poetry—Snyder shows their creative connection:

> ...references to weaving in Greek literature have an immediacy and vividness which we should not overlook...weaving was closely

> linked in the Greek mind to singing, and...this link led naturally to the Greek lyric poets' use of metaphors derived from the art of weaving to describe their own art as a 'web of song'.[23]

Though Snyder sees the use of weaving imagery in Homer as split between women's work (descriptive) and intellectual process (metaphoric),[24] Homer's description of Penelope, famed as a woman who uses the process of weaving as a wile to avoid social pressure into marriage and thus into containment, seems to gesture towards a closer association of the two. By night pulling apart the threads that she had woven together during the day, Penelope laments her fate and compares herself and her weeping to that of the nightingale ('Pandarus's daughter'[25]) (see p. 226). The depiction of looms and lyres on vase paintings show structural similarities both between the stringed 'instruments' and between their respective tools, shuttle and plectrum, a similarity which is exploited in representation.[26]

In line with the mythic association of the nightingale with both weaving and poetry, perhaps the description of Anakreon as one 'who once wove songs of womanly melodies'[27] can be interpreted as implying the close work of woman's art rather than any general effeminacy. The association of poetry with women seems confirmed by linguistic echoes. Not only does the word *aedon* summon up poet, poetry and nightingale, but it also evokes similarly sounding words: those for 'regarded with awe' and 'deserving of respect' (for women; for the genitals, especially the pudenda; and for the adjective describing 'the hidden' or 'the unseen'). The mere voicing of any of these words would unconsciously evoke the others.[28] The mystery, the hidden nature of the sexual voice that must be respected, speaking outside the civil community but referring to that which is within it: all these refer to both poetry and the feminine. Yet if the myth of Philomela is considered as in part about the regaining of the lost voice, it need not be the voice of women alone—for the child Itys is also a victim. Instead it may be seen as part of the construction of a special arena where the feminine (but not female) voice of art may tell the forbidden, the violations of a violent world: first through weaving, transforming a material object into a gendered communication (one whose truth overcomes the lies of the powerful), and then through the woven notes of the nightingale who laments her murdered boy-child.

Noting the association of both the nightingale and the swallow with the mourning rituals of Adonis, D'Arcy Wentworth Thompson[29] believes that the nightingale's mourning of a dead boy is significant. Like the hoopoe, the nightingale and swallow are migratory birds.[30] Such birds, in their sudden and almost magical reappearance in spring, attract particular attention in those cultures which are dependent on the cycle of the seasons, and they are frequently associated with rituals of seasonal change.[31] Thompson suggests that the customary melancholy of the nightingale is a residue of its place in a ritual which also concerned women wailing a dismembered boy:

> ...the innumerable references to the melancholy lay of *aedonis* or *aedon*, and to the lament for *Itys*...[are] for the most part, veiled allusions to the worship of Adonis or Atys...the mysterious and melancholy ritual of the departing year when women 'wept for Tammuz'...This conjecture is partially supported by the confusion between [the nightingale and the swallow], by the mythical relations between [them], and by the known connection of both with the rites of Adonis.[32]

Thompson's suggestion reintroduces the question of history. The fertility cults of the *adonia* did not originate in mainland Greece but arrived there from Syria and the east during the second half of the fifth century. The reference to the *adonia* in *Lysistrata* suggests that the cult was a threat to accepted patterns. If war threatens the state from without, religious cults and the restive women who practise them threaten from within. Aristophanes depicts a world in which the destructivity of war (Ares) is set against the fertility and voluptuous sexuality of the women, and the men are distracted from their war preparations by women wailing for the dead Adonis on the rooftops (ll. 387-98). Though the nightingale itself is not mentioned, the structural ambiguity that lies at the heart of the Philomela myth is evoked in Lysistrata's manipulation of an 'oracle' drawing on the husband and wife relationship of hoopoe and swallow, and the transgression of gender roles caught up in the myth.[33] Hearing the oracle, the women question 'shall *we* be the upper?' (see pp. 230-31).

The references to the nightingale in Hesiod's *Works and Days* (see pp. 226-27), and Aesop's *Fables* (see p. 227), draw on structured relationships that recall the patterns inscribed in the

Philomela myth even though the named *human* figures do not appear. In both cases a female singing nightingale is attacked by a powerful male hawk: in the former the bird is pierced by the talons of a vicious predator who drags her out of her element; in the latter the nightingale's status as a mother bird is reinforced as the hawk (like Tereus) devours her offspring. The parallels between these stories and that of Philomela seem even more striking when Greek confusion over the relation between hawk and hoopoe—seen as different stages of the same bird[34]—is taken into account. At the same time it is the testimony of the *poet* (the nightingale) which exposes the violations and allows them to be remembered and condemned, clearly indicated in Hesiod's political gloss, in its address to the 'princes who themselves understand', and in the punishment imposed on the hawk in Aesop (he is captured by hunters).

The victim-status of the female nightingale is not, however, to be sealed off in the past. Its tenets continue to be taken for granted in A.R. Chandler's descriptive survey of the nightingale in Greek and Latin poetry,[35] in which Hesiod's passage is seen only in terms of a personal predicament, without considering the role of convention. But the parable's poignancy is created through its dependency upon tropes which Chandler does not question: the nightingale as female victim, the association of poetry with sadness, the place of personal tragedy within an arena dominated by political machinations. I want to argue that whenever the mourning Philomela is evoked, in Greek drama and elsewhere, this very complex of politics and fragmented order is associated so closely with the nightingale that it need not be expressed directly but exists in a shadowy subtext of associations which are all the more powerful for being unspoken.

Ambiguity and Violence: The Notes of the Drama

To an unstable Athens the nightingale's mythic background had a tremendous suggestive power. It emerges with particular force in the *Agamemnon* of Aeschylus which shares the myth's concern with disruption and chaos, conveyed through linked themes of treachery, incest, past cannibalism and mutilation, Above all the deceitful manipulations of the powerful are set against the true voice of the victimized girl, Cassandra, torn away from her Trojan home and forced to become Agamemnon's concubine. Like both Philomela and Procne, both her body and her voice are violated. The boundaries of the Greek community were defined through language: those outside the civilized world were barbarians and, like Philomela, they babbled as incomprehensibly as swallows: a metaphor which silenced them by denying the human characteristic of rationality. It is no surprise that Clytemnestra, mistress of deceiving words,[36] should employ the conventional trope when she remarks that Cassandra speaks with a swallow's tongue. Like Philomela, Cassandra has had her ability to communicate wrested from her. Her voice and her visions of butchery prophesy the coming carnage: that which the audience both knows and awaits. But within the twisted world of the play the Chorus, echoing the Trojans before them, cannot understand her plainest statements. The play as a whole testifies to the truth of Cassandra's vision of the tragic future—just as the nightingale sings of past tragedy—and thus Cassandra, like the nightingale, speaks a truth which is accessible only to the spectator who stands outside the momentary linear unfolding of the plot. Simultaneously the pathos is heightened by an irreconcilable confrontation—itself within the confines of artificial form—of the abstractions of art with the pain of experience, as Cassandra pointedly compares her agonies, so clearly echoing those of the myth, with the thoughtless existence of a real bird (see pp. 227-28).

The myth seems to have been most popular during the fifth century when it provided the plot not only of Sophocles' *Tereus* but also of (at the least) a tetralogy, the *Pandionis* of Philocles, of which no fragments remain. Elsewhere it appears in Sophocles' *Ajax* and *Trachiniae* (see p. 228). As with Aeschylus's references to the bird (also in *The Suppliant Maidens*) (see p. 228), and with the later references in Euripides' *Hecuba* (see p. 229) and *Helen* (see p. 229), the Philomela myth seems to lie beneath the surface plot, conveying a sense of victims, of violence and of twisted and impossible communication which problematizes the boundaries and hierarchies of the polis. Sophocles' references throw up the Philomela myth in particular: in *Ajax*, the agonies of the hero's mother are compared to those of the mother Procne, while the entire myth resonates throughout *Oedipus at Colonus*.

The metamorphosis in the Philomela myth—as in other trans-formational stories—creates a place outside the boundaries of the human and the social, an ambiguous place with a double role. It functions both in addition to the civilized (providing its defin-ing boundary) and as that which completes, makes whole (the 'civilized' needs a contrasting value to give it meaning).[37] What is special about the Philomela myth however is the place it provides for a *voice* which articulates that supplementary place, the voice of poetry that records the place outside of which it stands. The special ambiguity of the supplementary place of poetry, which, as the place of the nightingale, is both violated and whole, wonder-fully illuminates Oedipus's arrival in Colonus in *Oedipus at Colonus*. It is a play intimately concerned with boundaries and definitions, as the defiled and mutilated Oedipus seeks wholeness outside the boundary of his birthplace, Thebes, the polis which has ejected him for the second time. As the birthplace of Sophocles, Colonus—and its nightingales—is associated with the birth of his individual poetic voice as well as with poetry itself. If the nightingale's voice speaks to the political world of its viola-tions, the place from which it sings is a place outside these corrup-tions, a place that enables both the recognition of mutilation and the construction of harmony. Thus the singing birds have two meanings for Oedipus depending on where he stands in relation to the defining boundaries of polis and wood. Travelling towards Colonus, but still outside its sacred place, the nightingales that sing there speak to his past, with shared themes of incest, mutilation, displacement. Yet when he arrives, Colonus becomes the place of golden flowers and fertility, the place outside the boundaries of the violating world, the place of art and wholeness: 'white Colonus' glowing with beauty. To move outside of the closed economy of violence in the political world allows for free-dom, and, just as Procne/Philomela, transformed into the night-ingale, sings from a place outside society though her voice refers to the tragedies within it, so Oedipus too may leave the past behind, no longer the scapegoat for his manipulative world. It is instructive that once he has entered this place of redemption he should resist the calls of his uncle-brother Creon and his brother-sons which try to take him back into the polis—and that he should be protected in the place of the nightingales.

Themes of manipulation and betrayal, of the boundaries of the human and the animal, of true and false speech, are evoked through parody and farce throughout Aristophanes' comedy, *The Birds*, a political satire loosely based on *Tereus*.[38] Tereus becomes the treacherous leader of the birds while Procne, beautiful, sexually attractive and sad, sings of the fragility and transience of human life (see pp. 229-30), though, suspended in the artificial world of comedy, there is no agony, no pain. Forbes Irving's comment about the metamorphosed human figures of Greek transformation stories is significant, seemingly aimed directly at *The Birds*:

> [they] are now free from any further human tragedy, in comparison with which neither the suffering of birds nor any further evil that they do among each other needs to be taken seriously.[39]

Chandler's assessment is similar if more sentimental:

> ...the most charming tribute to the nightingale that has come down to us is in Aristophanes' *The Birds*. The hoopoe and the nightingale...remember their human stories, but no bitterness remains in their hearts.[40]

But the comedy of *The Birds* is rooted in a bitter reality and its riotous laughter conceals a sharp edge at the expense of political mismanagement and public deception. The bitterness lies in the artefact of the play in its entirety, not in the individual characters. Indeed, the fact that these figures are distanced from human tragedy only serves to define their symbolic status more precisely for the audience. Aristophanes' comedy emerges out of the discrepancy between art and reality by retaining both sides of the equation: the mythic pattern and the depiction of a ludicrous reality. Avoiding the tragic confrontation of abstraction and experience in Aeschylus's Cassandra, the comedy rests on the playfulness of ambiguity and doubled meanings.

Footnotes

This is not to argue naively that the nightingale always has the same meaning, but to suggest that her voice is characterized by ambiguity, expressed in the drama in the harmonious lament for violation and the chaos that violation unleashed, but sometimes in the mixing of sorrow with joy as the voice of poetry that sings

from the freer space of the woods. Of the early lyric poets, it is
interesting that the nightingale should appear in a number of
fragments by Sappho, a woman poet. These passages seem to
depict the nightingale in terms of a spring or erotic symbol which
seems untouched by Philomela's lamentation (see p. 227). On the
surface this seems to be in line with the way the masculine nightingale is presented in oral/medieval tradition. But it is neither
simple nor merry. It is significant that Anne Carson's study of the
Greek perception of desire should draw its title from a line by
Sappho[41] which presents erotic love in terms of 'the bittersweet',
always pursued and never achieved. Sappho's other love poetry
expresses the same ambiguous mixture of sadness and joy, rather
than singleness, robust merriment: her depiction of 'eros' takes
the form of an excessive desire for the unobtainable.

In the pastoral interest shifts from the *voice* of the nightingale as
that of poetry, to the *place* from which the nightingale sings. It is
as if, like Oedipus, we move into the wood instead of listening
from outside. In pastoral the voice of the woods takes over, silencing that of the city, for the nightingales still sing outside the
boundaries of a corrupted, civilized society. Though it is reductive
to try to interpret the nightingales that sing in the pastoral poetry
of Theocritus and those writing after him in the same way as those
that sing in the woods of Colonus, their association with poetry
insistently throws up questions of definition and place, voice and
silence. Despite the absence of both personal violation and the
power struggles of the political world in the pastoral's nostalgic
depiction of a rural world, the nightingales that sing there continue to carry the poetic burden of a raped innocence. This time,
however, the violation, the silencing, is made present not by the
nightingale, singing of the past, but by the reader whose experience supplements the utopian harmony. The very simplicity and
completeness of utopia, of an idyllic world,[42] throws the (omitted)
corruptions of the town into relief. Pastoral poetry is a sophisticated urban product: able to manipulate the defining boundaries
between the civilized and the wild, choosing to locate its voice
within the wild (the uncivilized woods), as a means of criticizing
the civilized. It is unsurprising therefore that the nightingale, as
the pure voice of both poetry and the wood, should become a
prominent part of the pastoral apparatus. Writing as an exile of

his native Sicily, Theocritus summons up the lost countryside of his youth from within the corruptions of urban Alexandria: his idyll, *The Women at the Adonis Festival* (see p. 231), similarly depicts the rituals of the *adonia* in terms of their simplicity, a quality notably absent in his contemporary world.

The pastoral's evocation of lost perfection means that it provides the perfect vehicle for elegy, the lamentation of lost perfection on a personal level: the purified voice of pastoral lament speaking self-reflexively of the loss of the perfect poetic voice. Violation and reconstitution thus form a shadowy backdrop to the elegy and it is unsurprising that references to the *adonia* should be central to what is often seen as the first poem recognizably in this genre. This is *The Lament for Adonis*, in which Bion, one of Theocritus's followers, constructed a form for mediating loss which was imitated in the (anonymous) *Lament for Bion* (see p. 231). In the former the effect of Adonis's death on Aphrodite is central; in the latter the issue is personalized, with attention turning to the effect of the death of a poet on an idealized nature. The nightingales that appear in this poem retain the traditional associations, though these are split into three aspects: representing the art of music/poetry ('dead is music...likewise the Dorian poetry'); the grief of the Philomela myth ('never so woeful the song of that nightingale...or the dirge of that swallow'); pupil poets ('the nightingales and swallows...which once he taught to speak'). It is significant that two of the greatest of English elegies, *Lycidas* and *Adonais*, should be written by poets who directly associated the art of poetry and their own poetic voice with that of the nightingale.[43] On the other hand connections with pastoral and elegy provided a vehicle for early Christian Latin poetry, for—as I discuss in the following chapter—the nightingale that appears sporadically in these poems sings from the uncorrupted wilderness of a divinely created nature and is not defined according to human gender. Later Christian poems trade directly on the nightingale's mythic associations with suffering and silence transformed to transcendent voice, and associate the nightingale with the unsexed human soul.

Plato implicitly understands the political critique lying within the lyric voice, that associated with the nightingale, for it is this type of poetry that he wishes to ban from his republic.[44] Unsurprisingly, the references to the nightingale are not significant in Plato and Aristotle, though those that do appear reinforce its associations with poetry, lamentation and song (see p. 231), as does Pausanius when he uses the bird to indicate both poetry and immortality, mentioning the fable that nightingales sang on the lips of the lyric poet Stesichorus as a child (see p. 235).

As I note above, there is frequently a confusion between nightingale and swallow in Greek and this confusion is carried through into the changed form of the Philomela story in Latin literature. Considering the frequency of references to the nightingale in Greek poetry, it is significant that so few occur in Latin, perhaps indicating that its association with a recognizably unstable social identity—so potent for Athens during the Peloponnesian war—is no longer relevant in the authoritarian Roman state. Among the few references to the bird, Virgil and Catullus retain the Greek version of the tale: Virgil referring to the nightingale as Procne in his sixth Eclogue (see p. 232) and fourth Georgic (see p. 233); Catullus referring to her 'elegies of loss' (see p. 232). Elsewhere however the far more satisfying conclusion—in that the references to seasonal change are no longer central in an urban society—is that the mutilated girl should become the singer of poetry rather than the betrayed mother. This is the form of the story touched on by Martial and, most significantly, Ovid (see p. 233). Despite the paucity of references in the literature, however, the two passages on the nightingale which dominate the European representation of the bird for centuries are Latin: those of Ovid—whose version of the Philomela myth throws up questions about the nature of the Roman state—and Pliny—whose rational 'scientific' description cloaks his narrative's collusion with imperial ideals.

Ovid's version in the *Metamorphoses* is the most well-known and bloodiest of all. One of the major changes that Ovid introduces is the association of the sisters with the rites of Dionysus, god of drama, fertility and vegetation, associated with irrationality and the ecstatic rejection of discipline. Primarily worshipped by women, his rites included the orgiastic dismemberment and devouring of a sacrificial animal though stories also refer to the sacrifice of children.[45] In Ovid's version of the Philomela myth the inner room drips with gore and Philomela taunts Tereus with the bloody head of Itys. Ovid's extremity focuses on individual figures at the expense of the political context, emphasizing violence and the breakdown of both social order and related personal identity that such unleashed violence instigates. The horror is rooted in the perversion of stability on every level: Tereus imagines himself as his father-in-law, 'and if he were,/He would be as wicked a father as he is husband' (ll. 483-84); the graphic description of his rape of Philomela mingles the blood of her mutilated tongue with that of the sexual violation itself; Procne viciously appraises her son's likeness to his father, cold-bloodedly assessing her now fractured duties; while the once-demure Philomela erupts into the tale, splattered with blood, swinging Itys's head by its hair. Joplin's analysis of the effect of rape on Philomela is, despite her emphasis elsewhere on Greek literature, taken straight from Ovid: 'the transgression of all bonds, oaths, and unstated but firmly believed rules initiates a radical loss of identity, a terrible confusion of roles'.[46] But to conflate accounts taken from two linguistically and geographically differentiated cultures further separated by four hundred years is to remain locked within a conceptual structure in which woman is always a victim and always a victim in the same way: in such circumstances there is no possibility of change—and thus it is impossible to speak outside the hierarchical structures that endlessly define and contain individuals in the same way, impossible to recover 'women's power to speak'. If such accounts silence the voice of art, of the nightingale, they also silence that of history which relativizes the forms that structures take. Whereas the Greek versions of the myth focus on the relationships between the figures, and turn Procne, the mother, into the nightingale, Ovid is interested primarily in the individual figures, competing and attacking one another in fierce and agonized revenge. Ovid contains this chaos, not by achieving any balance, but by shifting to another unstable situation. The world of the *Metamorphoses* is one of continuous and violent flux: there is no place, no order to turn to. If fifth-century Athens crumbles under the pressure of its wars, Augustan Rome crumbles from within: for Ovid there is no wished-for place, the only resolution lies in the witty verbal artifice of his text which visits its rejection and violation of the world of experience onto the figure of Philomela while simultaneously recording the violations expressed in the myth itself.

As a final note, the scientific description of Pliny combines natural history with myth (see p. 233). Thompson considered that this was the *locus classicus* for literary representations of the nightingale's song,[47] for this detailed description of its construction reappears constantly in later poetry. If Plato ejects lyric and epic poetry from his ideal polis, fearing its ability to contaminate rational and political control, Pliny simply silences the voice of difference by the implicit assumption that there *are* no boundaries, that this *is* no narrative, that there is only 'reality'. Yet for all its appearance of calm rationality, Pliny clearly does construct a narrative about the nightingale. Though placed within a codified and explicable world (his nightingales are 'good' mothers), it is one which, like Ovid's, promotes traditional associations of the feminine with death and song. His fiercely competitive mother birds may assiduously teach their offspring to sing, but they would rather die than stop singing and lose a contest. As to be expected, Pliny's narrative contrasts with the mythic representation of Ovid, for his description articulates the values of his urban society and its espousal of a defining reason rather than questioning (as does Ovid's metamorphosis) its boundaries and their arbitrary nature. Pliny's 'rational' description excludes any notion of its own constructed nature: it masquerades as the truth, as reality itself. The wooded places of the Philomela myth, of *Oedipus at Colonus*, of the pastoral—all of which play upon the limits and limitations of the civilized world—are all subsumed in a rational discourse which draws nature into its own framework, denying boundaries and seeing only things. With Pliny competition is no longer between the nightingale and an aggressive representative of political or gendered power structures but between a group of undifferentiated individual birds. This competition becomes inextricably woven into the melancholy text of the nightingale, and the silenced voice of art is set against that of rationality, much as elsewhere it is set against political power or a violating masculinity. The voice of the nightingale and the place from which it sings illuminate the boundaries of society and change. It is caught up in ideological subtexts whose meanings conflict at every level save one: that of the feminine nature of a symbol associated with death and poetry.

Chapter 2

Christian Nightingales: Transforming the Classical to the Christian; the Sacred to the Erotic

Sweet Bird, that sing'st away the early Howres,
Of Winters past or comming void of Care,
Well pleased with Delights which Present are,
Faire Seasons, budding Sprayes, sweet-smelling Flowres:
To Rocks, to Springs, to Rils, from leauy Bowres
Thou thy Creators Goodnesse dost declare,
And what deare Gifts on thee he did not spare,
A Staire to human sence in sinne that lowres.
What Soule can be so sick, which by thy Songs
(Attir'd in sweetness) sweetly is not driuen
Quite to forget Earth's turmoiles, spights, and wrongs,
And lift a reuerend Eye and Thought to Heaven?
    Sweet Artlesse Songstarre, thou my Mind dost raise
    To Ayres of Spheares, yes, and to Angels Layes.
—William Drummond of Hawthornden[1]

Though William Drummond of Hawthornden's lovely sonnet to the nightingale was written in sixteenth-century English it has unusually close relationship to earlier Latin poems on the nightingale in which the birdsong draws the Christian soul to appreciate both Creator and creation. There seems to be no connection between this 'sweet' redemptive bird and the tragic Philomela of classical literature. The differences between the Greek and Latin versions of the Philomela myth—quite as much as the different ways that it can be used to interpret diverse literature from tragedy to the pastoral—provide timely warnings about the danger of reading the detail of the story as 'archetypal', universal in its application across cultures and times. The myth remains valuable, however, when it is read in terms of its structure, stressing the movement of voices from a central political/masculine space to and from the aesthetic/feminine/natural spaces at its margins.

Despite the conceptual difficulties currently raised over the existence of crucial 'turning points' in history[2] I accept that they exist and argue that the slow accumulations that produce them can be traced through markers of cultural and personal identity which occur within a specialized discourse such as poetry. Poetry foregrounds the various relations of the 'feminine' to a changing 'masculine'; of the 'natural' to what is seen as 'human'; of the ambiguous literary voice to the discourses of power. These are clearly areas in flux for the early Church as it attempted to construct a coherent institutional identity which was separate from the secular states through which it operated. Though individual aspects of this complex of relationships may be examined in a number of ways, a consideration of the nightingale (both as a classical figure which touches on all of them and as a figure of poetry itself) seems particularly fruitful.

The study and emulation of classical literature by Christian writers ensured the shadowy presence of versions of the Philomela myth in early Christian writing which continued to associate the bird with both poetry and the ambivalent boundaries of human— here translated to specifically Christian—identity. But this specification alters the terms of that identity. Halliday and Forbes Irving suggest that Greek beast and bird fables became stories of human transformation during the fifth century—a time of political and ideological instability—and focusing on human identity involves the problem of human gender. On the other hand, by locating itself within a non-human space of 'nature', the pastoral is uninterested in human gender. As in the pastoral, the nightingales which appear in early Christian Latin poems exhibit no human characteristics, for they sing from a divinely created nature: human gender is not a significant issue. By the twelfth century, however, the nightingale is once more associated with human suffering and the pathos of human existence. I will argue that this return is related to a time of massive economic and social change, resulting in a profound cultural and psychic dislocation. The simultaneous growth of emotional—irrational—responses in both religious and secular arenas (the subject of this chapter) and the increasing interest in Aristotelian rationalism among the clerical classes (the starting point of the next chapter) is reminiscent of developments seen in the fragmenting Athenian polis of the fifth century BC with its fractured foci on the body and the mind. With human characteristics centre stage the nightingale—yet again voicing multiple and shifting boundaries—repeats her role as the lamenting Philomela: the female victim who, in mourning the murdered Christ, dies in an ecstasy of sorrow.

Yet such an argument runs the risk of oversimplification, of being a reductive approach which assumes a linear and homogenous development of ideas throughout a homogenous culture. The nightingale may provide an index of changing relationships between the polis and its peripheral spaces which can be used to address the problem of Christian writing in a pagan state, but as the situation changes so the relations between church and state shift: culture cannot be isolated and frozen into these pockets. If the concepts of 'nature' and the 'feminine' are seen as constructed positions then these concepts will vary not only over historical time but also within it, according to the interests of different social groups. As the chief singer of the spring chorus the nightingale has a clear connection with the natural world and hence serves as an index of the shifting relations of different categories. Running alongside the literary tradition is an equally potent oral/folk poetry in which the nightingale's spring voice *links* the human and the natural by expressing the passion of physical desire. As a vigorous daytime singer, a male bird which actively interacts with the human world, the nightingale of oral verse is almost a mirror image of the lamenting Philomela. This difference reflects different class evaluations of the role of sex, for, in contrast with those who produce written literature, oral traditions emerge primarily from those groups excluded from power. Folklore concerns itself with neither the construction of the state nor the ideological significance of the literary space, so it is unsurprising that the folk nightingale should be more concerned with the problematic moment of individual desire than with those aspects significant to those in power within the authoritative political world.

Once in written literature, of course, contexts are lost and this division between two nightingales (female, lamenting; male, joyous) and two traditions (literary and oral) becomes more fluid. The extension of literacy and the reassertion of the body in Christian teaching, through emphasis on the physical suffering of Christ, meant that though poems appear in which the nightingale of the oral tradition appears to have filtered directly into the written texts, in practice the two strands became entwined. Both the devotional poems of the *béguines* and the secular love poetry of the troubadours and minnesingers—the poetry of mystical women and powerful aristocrats—concern the body of the beloved object. Both groups mark aberrations in terms of gender relations, whether through the freedom of the *béguines* or the servitude of the courtly lover, both are written in the vernacular, and both thus evoke debates over gender and class.[3]

The vernacular debates form the subject matter of my next chapter, in which I seek to complicate Joplin's analysis (the establishment of political power through the silencing of the female voice), by relating the 'feminine' to complex and shifting subtexts of power politics and class. This chapter is centrally concerned with the nightingale in Latin, primarily Christian Latin, poetry written during and articulating a period of immense change, but attempts to avoid oversimplification by drawing on and discussing oral poetry from the same period. Because I want to cover so much ground I am forced to follow a pattern of linear development, but it is clear that there is a great deal of overlap within the text as I approach the same period from different angles. The chapter falls into four main sections. I start by examining the relation of the literary voice to that of the polis in the Christian community of the fourth century; trace changes and developments over chronological time into the twelfth and thirteenth centuries through detailed discussion of individual texts; examine poetry of the twelfth century and after (including oral, secular, Latin and vernacular); and finally discuss religious poetry after the thirteenth century with reference to Pecham's *Philomena*. I conclude with a footnote on the fifteenth-century rewritings of Pecham once attributed to Lydgate. (Because these texts may be inaccessible, the poems or passages discussed in the second section are given with translations in Appendix II.)

Early Christian Latin Poetry: Contexts and Implications

When occasional poems within the body of extant Christian Latin texts praise the nightingale as the voice of a God-given nature, the focus appears to lie on a fresh, created world which, like the pastoral, simply omits the political order of the state and the gender politics that underpin its workings—central issues of the Philomela myth. But the issue is more complex. Though the utopian politics of the pastoral gives this early poetry generic shape, the fact that the genre has been appropriated by a group that deliberately sets itself outside the polis as a whole means that new meanings emerge from the existing form.[4] Greek nightingales illuminate the boundaries of an unstable polis; Ovid and Pliny draw on the mythic bird to explore their relations to their state ideology: in both cases, the literary voice is directly related to a concrete, existing situation. In early Christian Latin poetry, however, the nightingale's voice is associated with boundaries that *literally* exist in the imagination, boundaries associated with the active construction of a Christian identity—a project which required ideological coherence if it were to disentangle itself from the control of the dominant group.[5]

As the meanings and relation of polis and nature have to be renegotiated when the character of group and individual identity changes, representations of the natural world have particular significance in such changes. The nightingale's appearance as the voice of the natural world in Christian Latin poetry is thus significant in its own right—quite apart from the separate matter of the bird's characterization as mythic victim, its association with poetry or its role within the specific genre of the pastoral. If the nightingales that appear in Christian Latin literature seem to depict an objective nature (as in the poems by Paulinus of Nola or Fulbert of Chartres), both her femininity and her association with lamentation as well as with joy (present through denial in Eugenius of Toledo's praise poem) reveal the shadow of classical literature and invite more complex interpretation.

The psychological significance of the sexual violations and mutilations inscribed in the Philomela myth seems clear in the way that they are uncannily enacted in the tortures suffered by the early Christian martyrs: torn apart by wild beasts, dismembered or, concentrating particularly on the female genitals, mutilated.[6] As in the myth such violation leads to transformation, and movement into a new space; in this case the victims accepted their sacrifice as a preliminary to their movement into Heaven.[7] But in accepting martyrdom as a mark of Christian identity, the place of transformation is literalized, no longer that of poetry, of the imagination reflecting back on the previous existence, but separated and named as the place of the blissful afterlife. This literalization and appropriation has two major effects on art. Firstly, though both classical and Christian places of transformation are characterized by music and song, the latter attempts to divorce itself from—and deny—the political and social world and to relate music and song to the Christian God. Secondly, non-Christian art becomes doubly marginalized, doubly treacherous as like and unlike the Christian space. Its attraction must be denied: conceptualized as the voice of devils practising on the true Christian with sensual and seductively feminine wiles.[8]

Primarily Greek-speaking for the first three centuries, the Christian Church did not need initially to differentiate its writings from that of the Roman state: its separate identity lay in martyrdom and rejection of the status quo expressed in a different language. Even if the prison diary of the second-century martyr, Perpetua, was originally written in vulgar Latin, it was immediately translated into Greek.[9] But with Constantine's conversion, his peace with the church in 313, and the special marks of favour he showed to the Christian community,[10] everything changed. Without persecution, without an ethnically differentiated background, and with its language and liturgy increasingly rooted in Latin, the language of the state,[11] the expanding Church was no longer marginalized to the same extent and urgently needed to differentiate itself from the state for fear of absorption. This need for self-determination was in part addressed by the construction of a distinctive culture.[12]

That language and poetics provided a crucial site for this struggle for a distinctive identity is evident in the vehemence of writers such as Augustine and Jerome against the literature they had learned in the schools.[13] Torn between passionate rejection and obsessive attraction, they seem unable to achieve a secure place and a separate literature from which and with which they can counter the almost physical desire for classical texts which, in their frustration, they perceive as both feminine and seductive. Both Jerome and Augustine seek to establish themselves as those in control rather than as victims, as active, not passive (as were the Christian martyrs).[14] Both writers are tortured by the need to communicate directly, to speak with a clear and separate voice, struggling with an imposed secondariness, an imposed relation to pre-given boundaries: a struggle which again recalls the terms of Philomela's mythical struggle for voice. As speakers for the emergent Church they wish to achieve the voice of authority, to avoid the mimicry forced upon the disempowered. Hence though they draw on the powerful rhetorical training of the schools, their language is marked by a violent ambivalence towards it, for they fear that they mimic the expression of unbelievers, rather than speaking with the voice of God.[15]

The nightingale that appears in the small poem by Paulinus of Nola articulates great anxiety about the form of expression. Together with the poet Prudentius, Paulinus has been credited with establishing the form of Christian lyric poetry in the West,[16] so a poem in which he wishes to sing like the nightingale whose song he describes so carefully, a figure whose links with the literary voice would have been quite clear to him as a highly educated patrician, is a significant composition and more self-referential than it initially appears (see p. 236). On first reading the poem appears unsophisticated, yet its anxiety about form is evident in the technical description of the *kind* of song that the nightingale sings, that the poet wishes to emulate.[17] Links with earlier literature are evident in the way that the voice is characterized by lamentation though the bird represents joy, and by the nightingale's femininity, and status as poet. But the choice of both a new Christian poetics and a rural setting implies a break with convention: a rejection of social verse and the politics of the urban centres. Paulinus's attempt to align his own voice with that of the bird is far from an emulation of a purely 'natural' voice, for he sees it as expressing the unqualified voice of God—in clear opposition to the partial truths of the unbelievers of the city. Appealing for divine inspiration to *fons verbi, verbum deus* (1.1) (the fountain of the Word, the Word of God), he desires to sing like the spring bird, implicitly comparing the voices of poem and nightingale (*ales*), a comparison which is carried through to the end of the poem. Both voices are placed at the boundary of the merely human world (*avia rura*) in attempts to gather all signification into the one perfect harmonious place (the divinely created nature/the divinely created song), that arises, like the nightingale's voice, from the hidden depths of the wood. Yet the fragility of that world is equally indicated in the violence of the poem's sudden closure—which coincides with the sudden cessation of the nightingale's voice (*rupta*)—a strategy which recognizes the ease with which the fragile Christian vision can be threatened by disharmonious (i.e. non-Christian) elements. Though this fresh voice articulates a different world to that of the Philomela myth, it remains sad (*flebile*), while associations with the literary voice in general, and individual poetic genres in particular, indicate the bird's significance as a voice of problematic boundaries, a voice which illuminates the desire to stabilize Christian identity during the fourth century, and which continued to illuminate it on these terms until the twelfth century.

Changes and Developments: Christian Latin Nightingales before the Twelfth Century

If the nightingale that sings in Paulinus's poem articulates both the problems and the expression of his contemporary Christianity, that of the seventh-century poem by Eugenius of Toledo (see p. 236) is equally concerned with problems central to his contemporary faith. The earlier text espouses the fragile beauty of the nightingale's song in its attempt to construct a coherent identity for the church as a whole, one which was differentiated from that of the political state. This particular issue had been resolved by the seventh century and Eugenius's poem is more relaxed, stressing an easy balance and harmony at all levels—human and natural; human and divine—the poetry of the nightingale is available to all. The emphasis on balance and harmony is characteristic of Christian art of the seventh century; to the extent that Gervase Mathew suggests the possibility that 'painting and mosaic were in some fashion apprehended as music and the colour combinations seen as harmony'.[18] Similarly the concern with melodious sound reflected the Neoplatonic belief that the purified

Christian ear was able to hear the divine harmony of the spheres, Creation's original and perfect melodies,[19] and that Christian music and poetry should attempt to replicate it.

Neoplatonic veneration for harmony and music magnified the significance of figures such as the nightingale, associated with poetry and song in classical literature, while the femininity of her voice could be seen as responding to God's masculine authority, essential within a balanced, symbolically gendered and fertile universe.[20] Paulinus's description of the nightingale as *fons verbi, verbum deus* and his attendant anxiety as to the form of expression becomes, in Eugenius, less a question of authority and the construction of new forms and more one of emotional response within an accepted order—especially within a monastic movement held together by the written word of the Bible. By locating itself through emotion and writing, Christian ideology appropriated areas traditionally seen as disruptive of politics—Plato's desire to eject the lyric form of poetry associated with the nightingale from his rational and ordered ideal *Republic* has already been mentioned. But the written communications of friendship that connected far-flung communities indicate the positive role accorded emotion and writing in the Christian community—in deep contrast to the formal hierarchies and fiercely contested geographical boundaries of the secular state.[21] In line with the centrality given to emotion and writing, Christian ideology also took over those traits of gentleness, softness and humility marginalized within a power structure and conventionally gendered feminine.[22] Even if actual churchmen did not necessarily demonstrate these attributes, Christian ideology built them into its identity. This linking of the Christian with the literary, the feminine, and the natural points to an ideological investment in the asocial, the apolitical, the individual.[23]

In line with this it is the emotional and personal associations that are most striking in Eugenius's poem. Where Paulinus uses technical language to describe the voice of the nightingale as that which emerges from the leaves, her single tongue weaving together many voices into a fragile and lovely music, Eugenius's bird sings unproblematically out of a divinely created nature. Whereas Paulinus wishes to emulate the nightingale's song, to reach *into* her non-human world, the world of God from which he is so easily sundered, Eugenius's poem is full of space, his nightingale moving among flowers, meadows and branches, in the company of swans, swallows and parrots, its openness inviting everyone to enter it—everyone can become a singer in a world characterized by ease and harmony, a world which does not exist in *opposition* to the human. In this later poem the human relation to God's creation does not rest on a technical analysis of the beautiful voice but on an emotional response, of gratitude, of praise for a divine gift, with the nightingale representing the qualities of Pliny's good mother, soothing pain and feeding with delicious song. The torn and agonized martyr, the vicious political world out of which the bittersweet voice emerges marked by pain—these are washed away as the voice rings out like honey, healing and tender, taking on aspects of the religious communion by nourishing the Christian soul, teaching all to praise, all to sing. If Paulinus's poem equates the realm of art with that of the divine— and sets this arena apart from that of the human, sundered from it—then Eugenius's poem registers an ideal which has left this divisiveness behind, which has established a coherent ideology that allows for the incorporation of the human *within* the divine. Modern historians of philosophy seem to lament the lack of interest in logic and metaphysics over the next few centuries[24]— the attempt to categorize and define; yet Raby (as a Christian Romantic aesthete) celebrates it, suggesting that this rhetorician's meditation on the nightingale may be prophetic, tentatively considering whether it expresses 'a slight trace...of a new note, of a new feeling, [that of] the new world of medieval emotion and mysticism'.[25] Its later popularity—there were many direct imitations, such as the three by Paulus Albarus (one of which is given in the appendix, p. 238)—indicates the possibility that it was at least read in this way.

Eugenius's poem on the nightingale can be seen as illustrating an ideal Christian identity for the seventh-century Church: one that rested on mutual responsiveness rather than analysis, a fusing of the human and the natural worlds in place of a concern with order.[26] It is an ideal that reflects multiple anxieties ranging from the instability of the political world within Europe, to European insecurity on the political stage in the face of growing Arab power. That it did not accord with the individual agenda and practice of the church authorities in alliance with the closed world of the nobility from which they drew their members, is in some way irrelevant: the markers point to the appeal of harmony as one of the factors by which the ideology claimed ethical supremacy.

The early Christian concern with aesthetics and language proved an important means of sustaining the community over distance through the practice—adopted from the classical aesthetes—of writing intricate verse letters. It was a practice in which the material of language was adapted into wordgames which could be fully appreciated only by the specially educated initiate, a shared taste which proved far more binding than the mere communication of information.

Such cohesion is a valuable resource for a political community and Charles the Great's educational reforms in the face of a hostile nobility can be related to a desire to effect a similar sense of shared values throughout his restive eighth-century realm. He appointed Alcuin of York to oversee the establishment of an educational system which stretched—at cathedral, monastic and even parish levels—throughout a growing empire. Alcuin's love of pattern was not restricted to the language games of verse but, unusual amongst his peers in his interest in mathematics,[27] he applied it far more widely. Mathematics fascinates because of its ability to quantify and control flux through coded abstractions: it is a significant passion for men committed to institute rules and to control disruptive variation. Involved in a central role within the political state, Alcuin was equally concerned to bring order to the institution of the church through texts and writing: instrumental in standardizing the Christian liturgy, collating a definitive Bible and perfecting the Caroline miniscule script from which modern Roman typefaces derive.

I want to read Alcuin's didactic poem on the nightingale (p. 237) in this context, stressing the emphasis on control and order in a poem taking the form of lyric. A major difference lies in the poem's depictions of the poet. In the two previous texts the figure serves to register and reflect the song of the central figure, the nightingale; in Alcuin's poem, however, he is subjectively central, analyzing and interpreting information. In addition, the nightingale is evoked through an absence explained in terms of theft and envy. Nature is not to be wondered at here but is used instrumentally within an intellectual puzzle, shrunk from the joyous inclusive countryside of Eugenius's poem to the diminutive body, the tiny throat. The poem is neat, controlled, playing with paradox, placing the scale of the divine against that of the physical material world; the richness and depth of musical harmony set against the humble throat from which it emerges. Figuring both scorned body and praised voice, the bird has no place in the poem, transformed to a symbol of lost happiness, a symbol caught within labyrinthine time schemes. The poet refuses the present moment, the moment of sadness caused by the deprivation of past joy (itself created against past sadness), and sees his past happiness as prefiguring the future joy of heaven. The greatest paradox rests on the nightingale's Latin name, *Luscinia* (of light), which provides the base upon which a series of paradoxes are built, illustrating the metaphorical depiction of Christ as a light in darkness:[28] her song 'lightened' the poet's sorrow, she sang through the darkness of night. The creation of a Christian community is most clearly articulated in the poet's desire to bring together other birds in a communal lament for the lost bird, the lost happiness. Despite the closing remarks which draw parallels between the nightingale (as the transient voice of nature) and the cherubim and seraphim (singing perpetually in heaven), the real focus of the poem lies in neither the nightingale nor the place of nature/of art from which it sings, but on the Christian self. This is a self (unlike that of Eugenius's poem) that resides in Christian doctrine rather than emotional responsiveness. Hence the nightingale is not important in its own right (it is not even there), but serves to trace the boundary between the material and the divine, simultaneously expressing both as a minor reflection of Christ, prefiguring the poet's own loss. Though apparently located in the natural world, and discussing a feminine bird, the poem employs these aspects only to indicate future bliss, subsuming both within the deductive frame which concludes the poem (*si... dum/* if...when), which makes the imaginative space subservient to the ordering intellect.

Alcuin's poem is successful on its own terms: far from aiming primarily at aesthetic excellence,[29] it is the aesthetic itself, with its disruptive possibilities which Alcuin seeks to control by simultaneously silencing the voice of poetry itself, and that of the material natural world (i.e. the nightingale) at the heart of a poem supposedly on the nightingale. The poem thus illustrates how the need to order, to assume the central voice of authority, is rooted in the control of its marginal areas; here the slippery quality of poetry which denies closed and exclusive categories—beautifully encapsulated in the absent Luscinia's dual associations with light and darkness. Yet by naming the site of such ambivalence and shifting the seasonal implications of time passing onto the movement towards the heavenly, Alcuin indicates the grounds for future elaboration, future ambiguities, which were to be taken up in later Christian poetry on the nightingale.

Aldhelm had already constructed a riddling poem (see p. 237) which associated the nightingale's song with the processes of death and rebirth in a way strongly reminiscent of the *adonia*—even without direct influence an understandable association for a spring bird.[30] But her associations with light and dark, with life and death, with the human and the natural are beautifully elaborated in the lovely ninth-century poem by Sedulius Scottus (see p. 238).[31]

Like Eugenius's poem it is a celebratory text; unlike Alcuin's it does not conclude in a logical proposition but in the openness of a greeting—*ave*—which is aimed at both the resurrected Christ and the arrival of spring. This inclusiveness is conveyed by the title (*Carmen Paschale/Easter Song*), and the narrative voice. Omitting the personal pronoun, the speaker associates his song with both the praises of happy congregations and the spontaneous songs of the natural world—and thus emulates the voice of the nightingale.

The *Carmen Paschale* is the first of extant texts to translate the nightingale's association with light and dark to the fearful boundary between life and death.[32] Christ's resurrection is presented metaphorically as the rising of the true (*verus*) sun during the night of the soul, his reassumption of the body prompting a sudden fragile spring in the physical world, one whose bees, flowers and birdsong blossom into careless and unconscious being. As Philomela—simultaneously the voice of poetry, of spring and of light—the nightingale provides the pivotal connection between the different levels of interpretation. Quietly weaving together irreconcilable realities, the poem's individual voice presents itself and its vision *as* reality itself, a song of praise built on connecting rather than controlling the natural and the divine spheres by introducing a human sacred place *within* nature: that of the church whose happy praises themselves reflect the songs of both bird and angels. Philomela's mythic status as victim parallels that of the murdered Christ, while the traditional sadness of her night-time song provides a shadowy lament to fill the time before the rise of the new sun; yet this sadness is deliberately inscribed within the poem in order to be assuaged. The nightingale's song smooths the anxiety and fear associated with death by weaving mortal and immortal worlds together, by placing the nightingale's song in conjunction with the coming of a spring associated with the resurrected Christ, and, echoing the sacred place of the church, the poem also draws on the *joyous* implications of the place of art. Though appearing only in one line, the nightingale's place at the boundary of so many worlds—life and death, light and dark, winter and spring, human and natural, mortal and immortal—thus reflects the voice of the poem as a whole, the literary voice which turns anxiety over death to a final celebration of liminality (*limina lucis*) and to the open declaration of greeting with which the poem concludes.

In later texts the nightingale's association with Easter and, by singing during the darkness of night, with the Passion of Christ, is narrowed to an emotional identification with the Passion alone. As in the *Carmen Paschale*, her voice serves to illustrate the body of a material church (itself increasingly conceptualized as the 'Bride of Christ', and therefore feminized) which replaced the realm of nature as an expression of God's place on earth. But if the natural world in its entirety no longer expressed the conjunction of the place of art with the place of the divine, it was free to be seen as human again. Traditional folk tales of anthropomorphic animals reappear in religious literature, the first beast epic to be recorded[33] being the anonymous tenth-century *Ecbasis captivi* (see p. 238). For the purposes of this study this is a significant text because, in a tale within the tale, the nightingale and the blackbird attempt to charm a restless lion king to sleep by singing of Christ's Passion. Raby's interest in tracing lines of tradition points this passage out with sober excitment: 'This is the only poem before Pecham's *Philomena*...in which the song of the nightingale is associated with the Passion of Christ.'[34]

When nature is used directly to express the human instead of providing the defining boundary of the political society (as in the pastoral or the early Christian lyrics), it becomes the vehicle for fables, where interest lies in the narrative line rather than in investigations of poetic ambiguity or philosophy. This is clearly what happens in the beast-epic, for the structures of the human world are replicated in the animal, seemingly without political implication.[35] The *Ecbasis* is crudely put together from different sources, a patchwork of texts written in a confused Latin which is very difficult to understand. Its greatest interest lies in its form and its exploitation of the figure of the nightingale; the suggestion, as Raby points out, that not only is the nightingale associated with the Passion, but that 'the singer wishes to die for very grief'.[36]

A similar humanization of the natural world with a corresponding interest in narrative marks another tenth-century poem, possibly by Eugenius Vulgarius (see pp. 239-40), but this is both more complex and more overtly political. Considering the chaos of the church at this time,[37] it is unsurprising that the poet does not openly question the boundaries of his world. Instead he displaces its envy and sectarian competition into the comic bird contest which disrupts the leisured human world concerned to 'love thy neighbour' (*amor petens finitima*), which takes up the first three stanzas. As part of its avoidance of the political it foregrounds its technical virtuosity, in the chiming rhymes and stressed rhythm of the sequence—short lines, here of eight syllables, a single sustained rhyme throughout, rapid connected movement around a strong narrative thread. Here the single rhyme, made more insistent by its frequency within such short lines—not counting additional internal rhymes—produces pleasure through its play with sound rather than stressing content, echoed in the fact that sequences were sung to accompaniment.[38] Yet though these characteristics appear to divorce it from political commitment, its content is surprisingly interesting: where previous Christian Latin poems had either considered the nightingale's voice in isolation or seen it as a voice of harmony within divine nature, this nightingale provides the focus of a competition which *disperses* the gathering of birds. As in Pliny she is a mother bird who teaches her offspring to sing and to compete, but this time the competition is not restricted to other poets (other nightingales)—apart from the humorous reference to Codrus—but takes place at the heart of the natural world facing the hostility of predatory birds (stanzas 12-13) who are vanquished by her beautiful song. Political implications lie in the polished aesthetic form, the word-play and the recall of earlier texts rather than in direct comment. Echoes of Hesiod and the moral fables of Aesop seem inescapable, while the delight of the verse recalls the political significance of Ovid's disruptive playfulness.

Despite the great differences between them, similar political implications can be seen in the poem on the nightingale by Fulbert of Chartres (see p. 239). The poem reflects an innate conservatism. Emphasizing the role of music and the imagination in contrast to contemporary philosophical rationalism, the poem recalls Eugenius of Toledo's open and inclusive vision of the natural world. Yet there are major differences. Where Eugenius's poem creates a natural world which was part of the divine world and equally accessible to all, an open world centring on the second person address, Fulbert's nightingale sings within a world set apart from the human. His bird may, like that of Eugenius, be envisaged among flowers, grass and branches, but her voice is part of the physical regeneration of the earth, prophesying spring and summer—not the afterlife—in a celebration of the natural world as a place of harmony in its own right. As in the previous poem, the pattern of sound is centrally important, emphasizing the importance of harmony throughout in its composition—in leisurely fifteen-syllabled trochaics—and its intended accompaniment to the lyre, the monochord and the organ.[39] Like that poem too, the depiction of a harmonious natural world expresses covert political aims.

Whereas the two previous poems humanized nature, allowing in the second the possibility of hidden political commentary, Fulbert goes to the other extreme by distancing the natural world. This creates a slight unease in the reader/auditor, for, by referring in the third person to the nightingale that sings so passionately there, the poem provides no place for either poet or reader within that world. Indeed the human role in nature seems restricted

to that of a predator (Latin *anceps*, l. 16; English snarer, l. 10), for
the only other reference to human activity, that of music making,
omits human players; a significant omission which conceives of
music and the musician/poet as both creative and connective, to
be set against the intrusive destructivity of the appetitive human.
Denied a personal relationship with the nightingale (as in
Eugenius), the reader's interest is directed to the narrative of the
seasons: that which confers order and hence meaning on the
beauty of the nightingale's song. But this order too excludes the
reader, for it is an order rooted entirely in the autonomous
natural world: an exclusion which the poet remedies in the sudden reversal of the final two lines when he moves outside this
narrative frame to address the nightingale directly (*voci tuae*/your
voice). He allays anxiety by bypassing the divisions of the physical
world for a larger frame of reference (that of God) within which
there *is* a possibility of connection with the lovely song and the
ideal world it articulates. The unexpected change in the narrative
thread thus serves Fulbert's purpose in highlighting the significance of harmony at all levels of the created world, and playing
on the fears of an isolated reader faced by exclusion from the rich
intricate world of nature. It works by quickening an emotional
response to the bird's song and binding that response to a
hierarchic heaven.[40] Though this divine force is hinted at in the
stilling of the three arenas within the poem—the human hunter,
the natural world and an abstracted music which can cross the
boundary between the two previous categories (Latin: ll. 11, 12,
13; English: ll. 10-11)—it is only made explicit in these last two
lines. It is possible that Fulbert's individual entanglement in the
bitter politics of his contemporary church[41] created this vision of
the natural world, but the text is more significant than as an
individual utterance. Haunted by anxieties about the relations
between human and natural, it looks forward to the anxieties of
twelfth-century humanism. Emotion not logic provides the primary force in this poem—a very different conclusion to that of
Alcuin. It is unsurprising therefore that both Raby and Arch-
bishop Trench should associate this piece—if uncritically—with a
growing emphasis on an emotional, rather than a mystical, response to nature,[42] while Waddell sees its interest in spring as a
significant indicator of the humanism of the next century.[43]

The stress on harmony in Fulbert's poem points to one pole of the debates between the sensual and the ascetic, the emotional and the intellectual, that emerged with the growing interest in an increasingly isolated individual during the twelfth-century Renaissance. The verbal artistry of the sequence form illustrated in the poem by (?)Eugenius Vulgarius marks the other, with an emphasis on intricate verbal play. Peter Dronke notes that the very fact that Latin was now taught as a dead language stimulated such wit and wordplay: 'However well it had been learnt, it always remained in the last resort a learnt and not a native language, and therefore a language in which from the outset the intellect was used.'[44]

From the eleventh century the spread of literacy into the secular world fundamentally altered the way the nightingale was represented in Christian poetry. As is to be expected, questions about identity and power relations reappear directly in the literature of this period—a result partly due to the destabilizing presence of an increasing mercantile class, a class which by funding the enormous Gothic cathedrals made a claim for respect and status but which lacked a coherent identity within a social structure dominated by the aristocracy.[45] Indeed the very movement away from a Romanesque art which bound the individual to the fixed pattern of creation, towards the Gothic pathos of the isolated individual has been interpreted as in part due to the aspirations and mobility of this merchant class.

The Twelfth Century and after

The Re-emergence of the Body and of Gender
The focus on a dislocated individual led to the re-emergence of the body as a topos in both religious and secular verse. Nowhere is this more evident than in Franciscan writing with its anguished focus on the physical suffering of Christ and the duty of the Christian to think on it constantly:

> Have always the eyes of the mind towards Jesus crucified, crowned with thorns, having drunk the vinegar and gall, spit upon and abused, blasphemed of sinners, wearied with the multitude of scourgings, consumed with death most bitter, pierced by the sword, buried of mortal men... The flower of all flesh and all human

nature is filled with bruises and broken. That royal blood flows on every side from every part of his body.[46]

Early Christian Latin poetry on the nightingale conceives of the natural world as a space outside the boundaries of the human, where the boundaries of life and death, of the cycle of the seasons and, through the symbolism of light and dark, the boundary of the mortal and the immortal realms meet and are voiced by the symbolic bird. Because this poetry was not concerned directly with the human boundary between masculine and feminine, the night-ingale's primary association was with nature and art rather than with the feminine. But the enormous social changes of the twelfth and thirteenth centuries, reflected in and bound up with art, philosophy, numeracy and the extension of literacy, forced a crisis in the Christian identity, attended by attacks on heretics, Jews and lepers.[47] Even within the church the literary voice became both more concerned with the physical world and more alienated, tor-tuously outside of the mores of society—and in both religious and secular verse the central difference within the human world, gen-der, reasserted itself alongside the focus on the body.

The Franciscan emphasis on the physical suffering of the fleshly Christ was seen as part of a double, gendered passion: the blood of Christ and the tears of the Virgin mother. Thus the female victim, weeping her dead child, metaphorically pierced to the heart by the spear thrust into Christ's side, reappears at the same time as the interest in the body. The religious nightingale is no longer depicted as singing in a space outside the human but illustrates an internal division within it through its association with the weeping Virgin. The most poignant of these poems is John Pecham's *Philomena* in which the bird senses her coming death and, as a Christian soul accepting her fate and remem-bering the sufferings of Christ, sings her heart out in the divine service before dying in an ecstasy of compassion at nones.

If the religious verse of the twelfth century and afterwards focused on the physical body of Christ, secular poetry increasingly focused on the erotic body of the beloved. One way of inter-preting the changes in religious verse is to trace the effects of the wide-reaching social changes and the emergence of a new social class: similarly it has been argued that the verse of the troubadours and the minnesingers reflects an aristocratic response to social change.[48]

Yet not all changes took place within the existing dominant group: as literacy spread, groups previously excluded from power drew on oral folk traditions with very different ideas of nature and the erotic.

The Sensuous Oral Voice

> Lo rossinhols s'esbaudeya
> Josta la flor el verjan,
> E pren m'en tan grans enveya
> Qu'eu no posc mudar no chan;
> Mas no sai de que, ni de cui,
> Car eu non am me, ni autrui.
> E fatz esfortz, car sai faire
> Bo vers, pois no sui amaire![49]

The ideological boundaries of the dominant class both police their own group in order to retain power and exclude others from its benefits. Though it is clear that one of the ways that a dominant ideology seeks to secure its continuity lies in attempts to naturalize its own cultural norms and negate those of subordinate groups, this practice is never wholly successful.[50] Long-established groups such as the peasantry (as opposed to the clerisy which after the twelfth century increasingly sought to challenge the aristocracy for positions of power[51]) have a culture in their own right, one with different boundaries, and hence different constructions of nature and the feminine. The space at the boundaries of a polis in which they have minimal investment does not carry the same ambivalent value as to those who discipline themselves in the pursuit of authority. It is no surprise that the nightingale's seasonal role is interpreted differently in an oral tradition in which the nightingale has no connection with the literary voice, but is the voice of pleasure signifying the sexual delight of spring. In that the natural world is not perceived as a space that defines and threatens identity it need not have a feminine voice—and the nightingale that sings in folklore and oral poetry is, like the real bird, a male. Singing during the day (rather than the darkness of night) this bird is closely identified with the erotic pursuits of human lovers.[52]

During the eleventh century new amalgams started to appear between the two kinds of poetry—the written and the oral—as the balance of power between them shifted, and as the authoritative Latin with its European dimensions and intellectual wordplay was increasingly offset by the vernacular of particular regions[53] which was more likely to be influenced by oral traditions. The oral lyric celebrates the physical body rather than the intellect and the emergent poetry was characterized by a new rhythmic poetics, by style as well as by its emphasis on the body. Rejecting a fixed, rational world it moved inwards, focusing on the subjective and voiced a world in which experience was fluid, intense and internalized. This influenced the development of genre, and as Dronke points out: '...henceforth the creative achievements in religious lyrics occur, almost without exception, in the poetic, not the hymnic tradition; in the subjective and mystical modes, not in the objective.'[54]

One of the most prominent of the new voices appearing during the twelfth century is that of women: and Dronke considers that 'it is to women that we owe some of the highest flights of mystical poetry in the Middle Ages'.[55] Earlier women writers had tended to produce highly subjective and sensuous verse—characteristics associated with the feminine as a constructed identity, an association reinforced in practice by women's traditional exclusion from education and formal training in rhetoric and the patterns of past literature.[56] But change affected gender roles. On the one hand the interest in emotions and the body softened conventional ecclesiastical hostility towards physical and sensuous pleasures and led to new attitudes towards love *within* marriage which changed the woman's role within the home.[57] On the other, shifts in the value accorded to the subjective and the physical led to an increase in women's writing—despite the fact that female advocates of women's education faced papal disapproval.[58] Women sought new freedoms with the rise of heretic groups like the Cathars or semi-monastic groups like the *béguines*,[59] groups in conflict with a church increasingly attempting to create and sustain a central and centralized authority through the systematic persecution of heretics.[60]

Influenced by a folk tradition with place for a feminine speaker,[61] literacy, heresy and sensuality combine in the devotional poems of Hadewijch of Brabant and Mechthild of Magdeberg, women poets based in German *béguinages*. Mechthild adapts the sensuous symbol of the erotic nightingale to convey her passionate adoration of Christ, though aspects of the classical bird—its femininity and its association with death—also seem present. The two strands combine to produce the poetry of ecstasy, this speaker seeking to lose her individual self in the natural voice, flooding her whole being with song, ecstatically longing to dance with her beloved, identifying wholly with the nightingale as one fated to sing of the pain of love—

> The nightingale
> cannot help singing,
> for she sparkles with love in her whole being.
> If this were taken from her, she would die...[62]

The dance, song, and passionate desire of these poems display links with oral poetry associated with the *fêtes de mai* of contemporary France, Italy and Germany,[63] as much as with the more frequently evoked ecstasies of the Song of Songs. The rest of this section will be devoted to poetry influenced by this oral tradition—its erotic *jouissance* seemingly erupting into the controlled arena of the written text from a utopian natural world, one in which the values of the political community are irrelevant. Though David Lampe, considering what he sees as two nightingale traditions (secular and religious) behind the nightingale figure of *The Owl and the Nightingale*,[64] characterizes this nightingale as the 'secular' bird, I believe that it is the oral/folk background rather than any fixed 'secular' tradition (which Lampe divorces from any ideology of class) that creates the surge of erotic energy within these poems—and that the nightingales of the later religious poems I have been discussing act as vehicles for this intensity.

Secular Erotic Poetry: Politics and Transgression

Lampe's assessment proves useful in that he draws attention to literatures outside the confines of the church. This section thus uses his definition of 'secular' but attempts to complicate the term by relating it to class politics and the erotics of transgression of both gender and class.

Few examples remain of secular verse: texts are more or less restricted to odd fragments[65] or the 'snatches' or burdens of popular love songs retained to indicate the popular tunes appropriated by the church as it sought to discipline the populace with more spiritual words. Amorous nightingales tellingly appear among these fragments: an unsexed bird appearing early (thirteenth), a female one appearing later (fifteenth century):

> Do, do, nyghtingale singes wel mury;
> Shal y neure for thyn loue lenger karie.[66]

> The nightingale singes
> That all the wood ringes;
> She singeth in hir song
> That the night is too long.[67]

As in the *béguine* songs mentioned briefly above, the passionate nightingales singing in these songs demonstrate a mixture of pleasure and pain, a complicated erotics similar to that described by Dronke as characteristic of early love songs with women in active, sexually provocative roles and very different from the more straightforward songs associated with male voices.[68] The issue of gender is thus caught up with that of class and further complicated when the strong feminine voice of these popular forms is appropriated by the aristocratic class. As long ago as 1907 E.K. Chambers traced a line of development behind the recognisably modern love lyric, sung by a male poet, by examining the eavesdropping and reporting techniques of the *chanson d'aventure*,[69] to the verse of the troubadours and the parallel male and female voices in German Minnesang.[70]

What appears to be happening is the slow colonization of the 'feminine' voice of the folk song by that of a courtly—and masculine—literary elite. Both Chambers and F.L. Utley see the *pastourelle*, with its seducing courtier and clever peasant girl, as a more complex form of the *chanson d'aventure*, one in which the passive male auditor moves from semi-voyeur to participant. R.T. Davies's tentative rule for the folk roots of ballad and carol, 'a kind of poetry distinguished by its style—e.g. advance by repetition with partial variation;—or by a content similar to folklore',[71] points to the same conclusion: a folk background to the *pastourelle*,[72] an oral form appropriated by a literate courtly elite.

The economy of this poetry is very complex, playing off two different constructions of power: those of class and of gender.

Being both female and lower class the peasant girl is doubly associated with the physical world and with physical desire (elements marginalized within an ideology of power). She thus exerts symbolic power within the arena of nature, in part *because* in class terms she is inferior to the aristocrat, the cultured, masculine figure. It is interesting that the nightingale—expressing both class and gender affiliations—should feature in a Langue d'Oc example. In the pastoral the natural world constitutes a utopian realm of harmony, outside the urban, political world, one which reflects back on the insufficiencies of that world; in the *pastourelle* however, the courtly figure, the knight, invades the rural idyll, in erotic pursuit of its female inhabitant. In this example he suggests that he take on a rural identity (here 'un gardaire'/a shepherd), a suggestion which involves its own transgression of social definition and categories. She responds by turning back to the natural world to put him in his place, equating his words with the song of a lascivious nightingale, the erotic voice of her own world, and banishing both man and voice to a distant patch of shade. Impossible in the political world, this assumption of authority on her part transgresses both class and gender lines and is only possible here, in a place which provides the erotic supplement to the regulated and ordered court. There are clear indications that such transgression is itself titillating for an aristocratic audience:

> 'Lougarias bous un gardaire, pastrouletto?'
> 'Ne garderai be prou sualetto, chibalie!
> Ne garderai be prou souletto, rossignolet!'
>
> 'E nous sieiren o l'oumbretto, pastrouletto?'
> 'L'oumbretto n'es enrousodado, chibalie!
> L'oumbretto n'es enrousodado, rossignolet!'
>
> 'Obal la fouyeir' es seco, pastrouletto!'
> 'N'i cal ana per un'ouretto, chibalie!
> N'i cal ana per un'ouretto, rossignolet!'[73]

Immediately recognizable as the love messenger of folk tales,[74] the erotic charge of the nightingale as the voice of the natural world is here transferred to the courtly invader, who is thus given a central role within that world even if he does not gain his desire there. The poet's skill is evident in the fact that this transference of power is effected through the voice of the shepherd girl, whose transgression—rejecting the sexual offer of a social superior, she refuses to acknowledge his (masculine) power—works as a covert recognition of his disruptive presence within her world and thus eroticizes the whole exchange. In this exchange the nightingale's role is crucial to the balance between the two figures and their respective domains: nature and the feminine; the court and the masculine. Yet again the nightingale functions at the ambiguous boundary of a number of conflicting areas: court/nature; masculine/feminine; active/passive. What is most interesting, however, is the association of the erotic messenger of popular oral poetry with the amorous male aristocrat, an association which is further developed in both troubador and minnesinger poems.

That these folk associations continued to operate in parallel to the aristocratic lyric, however, can be seen by a brief discussion of a fifteenth-century version of the Holly and the Ivy carol which turns on the gendered symbolism of the two plants[75] and the *querelle* that they imply. In this text the birds popularly associated with the paradisal otherworlds of such divergent texts as the Thomas Rhymer romance[76] or the vicious satiric sermon[77] on *The Adulterous Falmouth Squire*[78] cluster around the spiky masculine representative. If the *pastourelle* noted above illustrates a class appropriation of a 'feminine'/'natural' space through the significance of the voice of the nightingale, in this text the quarrel takes a different form. Here the nightingale is not characterized by her song but serves only as a counter in the gendered debate, a desirous figure associated through shorthand with masculine virility. The feminine ivy is associated with the colour black and with the appetite of a single and predatory night bird, the owl; while the masculine holly is presented during the day, populated by elysian birds. The ivy's berries imply winter—a frozen, infertile season to contrast with the spring of the masculine holly:

> Ivy hath beris
> As blake as any slo:
> Ther com the owle
> And ete hem as she goo.

> Holy hath birdes,
> A full faire flok:
> The nightingale, the poppinguy,
> The gayntil laverok.[79]

The carol illustrates a clear victory *within* nature for the masculine values that the holly embodies, a victory achieved by an association of the feminine with darkness and cold, with singleness, appetite and cruelty.

The poverty of references to this tradition and its inaccessibility to later writers means that I prefer to concentrate on the *written* secular poetry after the eleventh century, poetry which is both well documented and—because written by those involved in active change—more clearly expressive of ideological change. In this poetry the new topics were spring and spring love:[80] the nightingale's song, appearing to slip into the lyrics from folklore, retained its masculinity and association with the erotic moment in both vernacular and Latin poetry. Chambers 'explains' the male nightingale's role in troubadour poetry[81] by deriving it directly, if contentiously, to a geographically restricted folk tradition, again divorced from any consideration of ideology or class:

> His song is the symbol of amorous passion, and he himself is appealed to as the confidant and adviser of lovers, the go-between who bears messages from heart to heart. He has a right to his place, for in France his coming, like that of the swallow in Greece, the stork in Germany, and the cuckoo in England, is the signal to the folk that summer is at hand.[82]

It is not to be expected that Chambers would consider ideology or class—at least not in my terms—but his comments provide useful starting points. The nightingale is not restricted to Provençal poetry but is popular in German Minnesang,[83] while the new Latin love lyrics turned on the same topics, employed the same nightingale. Indeed Chambers's contemporary, Arthur Symonds, considers that the 'frequent references to linden-trees and nightingales...indicate a *German* home for the poems on spring and love' (my emphasis)[84] in both the eleventh-century songs in a Cambridge manuscript and the group of twelfth–thirteenth-century lyrics in the *Carmina Burana* (discussed below).

Both Chambers's and Symonds's readings are complicated by T.A. Shippey's belief that this poetry rests on classical precedent, not folk traditions. He thinks that the popularity of the nightingale poem in this period is rooted directly in the tale of 'Philomela and Tereus'.[85] He sees the myth as satisfying 'the demands of a love-story for the men of the early Middle Ages...as

in Tristan and Isolde, or Lancelot and Guinevere, love comes suddenly, overpowers all obstacles of honour or morality, and ends
unhappily'.[86] The resurgence of interest in the myth is of course
significant: direct references to 'Philomela's ancient wrong', to
her lamentation and to the mixed joy and pain of love abound.
But whereas in the original myth (as far as there can *be* an
'original') the violating Tereus was vilified and punished, in this
love poetry Philomela's rape is translated into a cipher for erotic
male desire that may lead (as in the paradigms of Lancelot and
Guinevere or Tristan and Isolde) to masculine destruction.
Despite these allusions to the raped girl, it is significant that the
name of her violater, Tereus, does not appear. Shippey unconsciously elides this issue when he places Philomela and Tereus in
the company of Lancelot and Guinevere, and Tristan and Isolde,
and comments in a matter-of-fact way that the resistance of the
woman was totally unimportant. It is, of course, significant: if
desire is self-destructive, conceptually inseparable from violent
rape, it surely indicates ideological difficulties with the containment of desire. A different interpretation might point to the need
for self-authorization within an aristocratic ideology that sup-
presses the self (see the discussion of the debate in the next chapter). This interpretation of the love relation marks another, and
violent, side to the willed subordination of courtly poets in love: as
Warner reveals by drawing attention to Bernard de Ventadour's
reference to wife-beating. [87]

Shippey sees courtly love as essentially the unconsummated love
of another's wife and as uniform throughout Europe: an analysis
challenged by many, including Ferrante and Dronke.[88] By selec-
tive citation he undervalues the folk tradition, not mentioning the
fact that there are many more nightingales in German poetry
than in that of Provence. Just a few of the varied nightingales in
The Cambridge Songs, or the more robust ones of the *Carmina
Burana*, give another picture, illustrating a folk background in
which the erotic moment is far less painful. In the poem 'Letabun-
dus Rediit',[89] it would be wrong to see the lovers dancing to the
pipers as tragic just because 'the nightingale more sweetly sings /
A descant to their caperings'—associations with the *fêtes de mai* are
more pertinent. The figure cannot be divorced from its class-
determined context, and be given a single 'medieval' profile. To

do so is to silence the variety of meanings accorded to the defining categories of nature and the feminine within different groups, to stabilize and therefore impose the master narrative of the dominant group. Though the nightingale in the aristocratic romance does indeed convey an intense doomed love there is a deeper significance to this interest in tragic, violent love. The value of Shippey's study is that it highlights the strain within a particular class, a strain that is devolved onto the sexual arena where it can be safely acknowledged.[90]

The nightingale's place in the new love lyrics (and that other late developing genre, the romance, with its equal love interest)[91] is confirmed by its absence from other genres: the bird in the Holly and Ivy carol I quote from is the only one in Greene's comprehensive *Carols*. Similarly, Eleanor Hammond's anthology of conventional secular poetry between Chaucer and Surrey, a volume which excludes Romance, Ballad, Lyric and Drama, also excludes the nightingale. At least three of these genres—Romance, Lyric and Drama—explore relationships and hence deal in some way with both desire and identity. That the nightingale with her associations with the natural, the erotic and the feminine should appear in these genres and not in those concerned to police social mores (such as satire) is yet another indicator of her function as a marker of identity within the specialized discourse of poetry.

Latin Love Lyrics: The Cambridge Songs, *the* Carmina Burana

The first major collection of Latin love lyrics consists of forty-nine songs, a few from France and Italy, most from Germany, which appear in the eleventh-century Cambridge manuscript now referred to as *The Cambridge Songs*. They reflect the miscellaneous nature of the later *Carmina Burana* so faithfully that Dronke remarks that 'the range of these forty-nine songs shows us in little the lyrical repertoire of secular as well as clerical medieval Europe'.[92] The correlation between this collection and larger collections of European poetry is illustrated by the inclusion of three poems in *The Cambridge Songs* which match the description of three of four songs sung to a worldly priest in a contemporary German satire: how the

> Swabian cuckold tricked his wife in turn;
> how wise Pythagoras discovered octaves;
> and how the nightingale sings with flawless voice.[93]

That one of these three songs features a nightingale is unsurprising, for it reflects the wider popularity of the bird as topos within both this collection and contemporary Latin and European vernacular poetry. But if, as I argue, the appearance of this nightingale is related to an oral tradition then its appearance is more significant than that of a fashionable topos. I believe that it is both too widespread and long-lasting for that. I suggested reasons for the intrusion of oral traditions into written texts related to the spread of literacy outside the church. This is not however sufficient: if I continue to argue that the nightingale's role as a voice of nature, of the feminine, and of desire, gives it the status of a marker of identity within a particular discourse, then when that discourse changes by according a different value to such a marker, wider shifts within the construction of meaning must be implicated.

As I point out in discussing the Langue d'Oc *pastourelle*, the mixing of oral and written conventions involves transgression of class as well as gender lines. I would argue that this is the case with any generic change, and not just where the erotics of such a transgression are openly used. A discussion of one of the songs featuring the nightingale from *The Cambridge Songs* illustrates what I mean. Though the poem is a religious text, it plays on both the classical associations of the nightingale as poet and its status as a bird of love in oral poetry. By doing this the nightingale is given a double identity: both an instantly recognizable symbol of pleasure and unstable earthly love and the voice of a divinely created nature. In refusing the former, the jealous narrator excludes himself from the latter and the poem can ridicule the sterility of jealousy—especially of a bird. By drawing contrasting meanings together the poem plays upon the nightingale's inherent ambiguity as well as her different functions within separate ideologies. The text works through a recognition and exploitation of the very different traditions associated with the nightingale and the irreconcilability of the identities implied by each. The ambiguity expresses itself in the poem's generic instability, shifting from comic lyric towards debate, itself a form closely allied to the self-identity of a rising clerical class (see Chapter 3). These few stanzas demonstrate the knowing ironic tone of such self-aware textual play:

> (v)
> O tu parva, cur non cessas
>   clangere, avicula?
> Estimas nunc superare
>   omnes arte musica?
> Aut quid cum lira contempnis
>   sonora dulciflua?
>   (ix)
> Iam cessato laborando,
>   non premitit brachia,
> ... te cuncti auscultant,
>   nemo dat iuvamina
> nisi ipse, qui te fincxit
>   propria spiramina.
>   (xi)
> Illa vero stringens pauca
>   modulorum garrita
> in estate stupefacta
>   pro natorum gloria.
> Bruma tegit nebulosa
>   corpus sua funera.[94]

This text provides a fascinating counterpart to the poem by Alcuin discussed earlier in this chapter, foregrounding the very qualities which the eighth-century text seeks to control. This narrative voice dramatizes its subservience to the text, its aggrieved tone offset by the complex patterning which contains it and which, like the nightingale against which it directs its complaints, balances ambivalent differences into a harmonious whole. Set within the complex flux of conflicting demands—the variety of a world which includes rather than rejects desire—the clerkly narrative voice appears comic and querulous. It is threatened by variety, demanding silence instead.

Such generic changes and hybrids, reflecting the social upheaval of the twelfth and thirteenth centuries, can be fascinatingly tracked through the ambiguous voice of the lyric nightingale. Yet the irreconcilability of conflicting demands can equally be expressed through a dramatic situation: in the case of the nightingale the importance lying on what is *heard* in her voice. This is the

situation described by Shippey as the 'laüstic situation' of 'listening to the nightingale'. Shippey draws on Marie de France's *lai de
laüstic*[95] for his name. The *lai* is rooted in a Breton tale in which
an aristocratic wife who gazes nightly at her lover in the neigh-
bouring house pretends that she is listening to the nightingale.
The erotic significance of the bird is evident in the emphasis that
it is no other: 'ceo est russignol en Franceis /e *nihtegale* en dreit
Engleis' (ll. 5-6).[96] The husband understands the implication of
passionate desire, and has the bird killed. Wrapping the corpse in
an embroidered cloth, the woman sends it to her lover as a token
of their doomed love. Equally aware of its significance, he places it
in a jewelled reliquary and keeps it forever. The story and situation are interesting on a number of levels: the woman/listener is
punished for her transgression, her desire to move *out* of the
symbolic enclosure of the house, her wish to move *into* the natural
world outside of her window. The use of the potent figure of the
nightingale transforms a conventional *fabliau* situation (the old,
jealous husband, the adulterous wife and her young lover) into a
far more significant and poignant encounter: the wife's desire is
associated with an external, undomesticated figure, her husband
wishes to destroy it, her lover understands and in some way shares
it. The husband and wife depict an oppositional relationship
while that between the wife and her lover allows for reciprocation.
The situation can be understood in class terms, an older order of
isolation and aggression (masculine versus feminine; human
versus nature) confronted by one which is interested in shared
action, one which negotiates its own boundaries (masculine associated with both feminine and natural). The husband is characterized by force and possessiveness, his actions transferring the
publicly sanctioned violence of the knight into the domestic situation, his murderous actions deflected onto the defenceless bird at
the periphery of his world. Destroying the bird which symbolizes
both the love relation and the space of love outside the boundary
of his perception, he attempts to destroy his wife's desire—also
beyond the boundary of his control. Yet by turning the nightingale into a corpse he binds the lovers together, providing them
with a concrete figure of their shared love, all the more potent
because it brings the figure of nature within the boundary of the
house. In this reading the *lai* dramatizes the clash between an

older aristocratic culture of violence and rigid control and one which lays emphasis on a blurring of boundaries, on exchange and interiority: values that Eugene Vance sees as marking mercantile ideology, experienced as a threat by the aristocracy and appropriated in symbolic terms in new literary genres. Marriage and, crucially, the issue of feminine desire provide the symbolic site for this conflict, for the representative figures of the competing orders (warrior versus lover) are defined in relation to its institutional boundaries and the elements (nature and the feminine; the nightingale and the woman) which they seek to control.[97] Nature, femininity, desire and loss—all the elements of the conflict—coincide in the magnetic figure of the victimized bird. The popularity of the story over the next couple of centuries[98] testifies to a shared understanding of the nightingale's fetishistic meaning—and hence, I would argue, a continuing conflict between older and emergent ideologies, symbolically devolved onto the site of the marital debate and its relation to the external natural world as that which is excluded in the relationship.

As a footnote to this discussion it is interesting that, as the bird does not cross the 'nightingale line' into Wales, there is little traditional use of the nightingale in medieval Welsh poetry[99]—yet Dafydd ap Gwilym, the fourteenth-century Welsh lyric poet, was known as '*eos Dyfed*', or the Dyfed nightingale. If my analysis of the association of the bird with particular genres, themselves linked to shifting conditions of class, is seen to be valid, this name conveys more than a mere compliment on the sweetness of the poet's verse. Instead it may serve to indicate the *type* of poetry he wrote, to recognize his links with the troubadours, his subject matter (nature and desire), and his conflict with traditional 'praise poetry' composed in support of a rigid warrior-based hierarchy.[100] After all the bird itself has little status within Dafydd's poetry. Apart from the use of the nightingale in a Birds' Mass—an extension of the idea of Eugenius's chief singer which occurs in various versions throughout Europe[101]—there are very few.[102] The most interesting of these occurs in his elegy to Gruffudd ab Adda, a fellow-poet. This poem draws on the Greek Bucolic lament in its vision of the nightingale singing in a fair fruit grove: the poet bird is Gruffudd; the grove, Powys. Though the material fruit may remain, when the nightingale has been killed the orchard becomes

merely a *place* without significance, losing its vitality as a defining
space of otherness, hence its magic and its soul. In this text's
relation of the nightingale to both the defining natural space and
the poetic voice, the structural similarities with Marie de France's
lai are striking[103]—even more so when the absence of an erotic
interest (supposedly the focus of the *lai*) is noted.

Humility to Vengeance: The Nightingale's Links with the Passion

Humility: Nightingales of Delight

> With notis cleer, and vois entuned clene,
> Lyk the ravisshyng marvelous armony
> Off Jherusalem, I hard the phylomene
> In derk December syng melodiously,
> The curious sownyng of whos melody
> With such delyt so in myn eris rong
> That evyr me semyth I her her blisseful song.[104]

The merging—or transgression—of received boundaries between
the natural and the human, the masculine and the feminine; the
revaluation of emotional qualities previously devalued as feminine
weakness: all these aspects become increasingly evident in religious movements after the twelfth century, and are caught up in
the figure of the nightingale within religious poetry, both in Latin
and in the vernacular. Lampe and Walberg consider the Christian
Latin tradition of the nightingale as separate from that of the
vernacular love bird throughout the medieval period:[105] a position
I accept for the early Middle Ages. However, after the twelfth century this is no longer tenable. As this chapter has demonstrated,
the conjunction of secular and religious, oral and literary—all of
which employ the figure of the nightingale—resulted in the emergence of new genres which disrupt any settled 'tradition'. The
various nightingale figures of these disparate elements seem to
converge in Pecham's *Philomena*, a text which marks a new voice,
that of the passionate Franciscan, focusing on the physical body of
the tortured Christ and the Passion he shares with his mother.

The fact that two religious poems called *Philomena*, by John of
Howden (d. 1278) and John Pecham (d. 1292), remain from the
thirteenth century points to the nightingale's continuing resonance within Latin devotional poetry. Discussing Pecham's poem,

Raby sees the bird as figuring 'the type of the devout poet or meditative soul, singing the praises of Christ without ceasing'.[106] The existence of contemporary French versions of these poems indicates the popular comprehension of the motif,[107] while Otto Glauning remarks on the 'great popularity of Pecham's poem during the Middle Ages' in the introduction to his edition of the pseudo-Lydgate's two nightingale poems.[108] In view of Raby's critical affiliations, it is unsurprising that his analysis omits any consideration of the relation of the soul and poet to the feminine. Yet this is exactly the sort of conjunction that texts like Marie de France's *lai* appear to illustrate in a wholly different sphere.

Raby's study on Pecham's poem concentrates on two aspects: an unproblematic association with the vernacular love messenger, 'the joyful harbinger of spring',[109] and the Franciscan's intense personal experience of Christ's life (presentment) and deep devotion to Mary as Mother. In addition he recognizes an alternative Latin tradition of the nightingale singing Christ's Passion. The thirteenth-century emphasis on individual experience through the significance of the body, of emotion and of nurturance, indicates an emphasis on individual subjectivity in terms that had previously been allocated to the feminine. The linkage with the feminine is particularly evident in this nightingale, for she characterizes the feminine 'soul' (*l'âme pieuse*), who, especially in the Nativity scene, yearns to care for the Christ child.

Though Raby does not consider gender as significant in the construction of the poem, Rosemary Woolf's discussion of this particular section of the poem[110] sets it in the context of contemporary religious lyrics featuring the nightingale as a motif and sees its power as resulting from the transgression of earthly boundaries expressed through the Incarnation: the spiritual within the physical, the most powerful submitting to the meekest and humblest. Though she does not use this terminology, Woolf is clear as to the association of the nightingale with the characteristics conventionally assigned to the feminine, the poetic and the religious. A measure of its representative significance lies in the fact that, according to Walberg, the passionate crux of the French version lies in the sweetness and humility of the Nativity passage, clearly rooting this in the structure (which can be translated to another language) rather than in the arrangement of particular words.

The more closely the nightingale became associated with these three qualities—the feminine, the poetic, the religious—the further she moved from the rules of a world increasingly constructed in rationalist terms: as in Greek literature, her voice sings outside the polis. But when Douglas Gray associates the nightingale with the scheme of redemption, discussing the symbol under a chapter devoted to 'Christ and the Virgin Mary', he too omits any consideration of gender. Like Raby, he claims only that these poems employ 'the nightingale, the traditional messenger of love, as a figure of Christ…a remote and mysterious voice to whose service the poet has devoted himself'.[111] Yet the lyric to which he refers (which opens this section) clearly depicts a *female* bird, the spiritual voice of the soul. Appearing as a bird of spring in 'derk December', her song takes on the aspect of a miracle: spring unfolding in the depths of winter/of the wintry soul.

In line with this chapter's concern with the voicing of boundaries, Murray's discussion of the changing medieval understanding of the concept of the miracle is pertinent here. He points out that miracles are an integral part of a world conceived as perpetually created by the deity, a world in which they function as a gift and not as a transgression of fixed rules. Yet by the close of the eleventh century this conception of the universe, like so many other things, was changing, and if nature itself is no longer understood as arbitrarily controlled by the divine will, but is thought to be ordered and comprehensible, miracles take on a wholly different status: that of transgressing universal rules. The conceptual problem raised by biblical miracles was resolved for the thirteenth century by Aquinas, who qualified miracles as proofs of God's ability to intervene in a rational universe.[112] At a different level miracles do not only testify to a divinely sanctioned transgression of an ordered nature, but serve to unite human class differences through shared religious beliefs. This point is illustrated by Murray's comment that contemporary mendicant friars (such as the Franciscans) noted that 'an enthusiasm for a miracle-worker will include not only the unschooled populace, but "many noble women". A miracle working statue will attract not only the common folk, but "some of the best people in Florence".'[113]

From this perspective, belief in miracles appears to indicate a desire to accept the possibility that boundaries (on the one hand,

those between nature and the divine, and on the other, those constructing class and gender)—those aspects illustrated so variously
in the figure of the nightingale—can dissolve. In the case of this
particular poem, the miracle is translated into an inward event by
allowing the divine intervention into the natural world—the nightingale's expression of the 'marvelous armony / Off Jherusalem'
reaching out from that world into the separate, painful being
where it is incorporated as the 'blisseful song' that echoes within
the self without regard to time. The divine voice is not the creative, harmonious voice of earlier verse but takes on the authority
of a masculine intervention. By abandoning themselves to the
'ravisshyng' voice, both poet and reader (jointly the 'I') suffer
metaphoric rape; the feminine nightingale voice being internalized as a 'feminization' of the very self as the text celebrates subjective experience in the face of an objective, and objectifying,
world.

Gray considers that Pecham's nightingale with its links with
spring love lies directly behind these redemptive nightingales.[114]
The acceptance of connections between seasonal change and
individual desire is certainly clear in the French version, in which
the nightingale both announces the departure of cold weather
and gives hope to faint hearts. The poet cries out:

> Roussigneul, qui repaires quant le temps assouage,
> Pour noncer le depart du froit temps yvernage,
> Tu qui par ton doulx chant esbaudis maint courage
> Vien a moi, je t'en pri, si me fai un message.[115]

The particular significance of this configuration of nature,
emotion, femininity and religion for the thirteenth century
becomes sharper when the brittle fifteenth-century adaptations of
the *Philomena* once attributed to Lydgate are considered.

Vengeance: The Pseudo-Lydgate's Nightingale Poems

I shall discuss these poems in some detail for two reasons. The
first is that they illustrate the hardening of religious attitudes
along feudal lines, and the second is that they are roughly contemporary with the two debate poems with which I am most concerned in the next chapter: *The Cuckoo and the Nightingale* and *The
Floure and the Leaf.* Both the pseudo-Lydgate and the debate

poems explore the problem of individual desire within an ideology which denies the individual; a comparison of the two indicates how this problem is, itself, a product of unstable times. Where the debate poems foreground a doubting subject, the pseudo-Lydgate suggests the rigorous suppression of such doubt.

The two vernacular pieces long attributed to Lydgate may be based directly on Pecham's poem and echo the earlier explicit references to *l'âme pieuse*, but they express hugely different values. Though the nightingale is still female the characteristics associated with that position are closer to the mannerisms of an imperious courtly lady—a figure defined by her social position—than to the feminine soul who expresses the desire to abandon a class-bound world. In line with this move, there is a shift from the domestic arena to the public and social realm. The poems may differ in the degree to which they vary from their shared original, yet both change significantly the biblical scenes which they see the canonical hours as representing. There is no place in either for the homely reference to the scene which is so strikingly emotive in the original: the nightingale/soul's wish to help the Virgin wash the Christ child's rags. Though Glauning claims these differences as indications of Lydgate's originality,[116] this attitude imposes an anachronistic aesthetics on the text and fails to address the changing construction of religious attitudes illustrated within it. These changes express a consistent and coherent move away from twelfth-century Franciscan ideology, moving from a religion associated with subjective understanding, with the unclassed human soul, pierced by the pains of compassion, accepting the overwhelming authority of a paternal God.

This reading is borne out most strikingly by the change in the bird's cry: where Pecham's nightingale calls out 'oci! oci!' (a cry conventionally associated with the bird; at the time understood to be taken from the French verb *ocir*, to kill), she expresses her desire to be killed in a surfeit of grief at Christ's agonies. The Lydgatian birds are far sturdier. In *A Sayinge of the Nightingale* the poet falls asleep listening to what he thinks is an erotic nightingale and fondly imagines that her call 'ocy, ocy' refers to the vengeance to be taken on false lovers. He is visited by an angel who pours scorn upon his solitariness and reflectiveness:

> Whiche to me sayde: 'Foole what dostow here
>   Slepyng allone, gapyng vpon the mone?
>   Rise, folowe me, [and] thow shalt se right sone
>
> An vnkowth sight, If thow list to speede.
>   The briddes song I shal to the vnclose. (ll.47-51)

The lesson he learns is that the heart pricked 'with fyry remem-braunce' may pour out a *love* song but

> For hir synggyng—who-so takith heede—
> Nothyng Resownyth vnto flesshlyhede. (ll. 83-84)

Love in this context is a piercing and violent desire seen either as erotic or devotional: there is place for neither nurturing mater-nal care nor shared compassion. Like the disapproving angel, this nightingale is fierce and unforgiving. Her cry, '"Occy"—considre wele the woord!' is a far more sinister demand than the agonized cry of Pecham's bird. It expresses no internal distress but is directed punitively away from the self at those who are ungrateful for Christ's sacrifice:

> She cryeth: 'Sle al tho that bien vnkynde
>   And can of loue the custom nat ob*serve*!
>   Why list the lord for mannes sake sterve
>   ...
>   But for to pay of fredam the Raunsoun,
>   His hert[e]-bloode, for theyr redempcioun?' (ll. 106-12).

Where the earlier poem emphasized the pathos of the situation, this text stands upon *duty*: its Christ is both self-righteous and self-pitying:

> For mannes sake with me ful hard it stoode:
>   Forsaken of alle and eke disconsolate;
>   They left no drope, but d[r]ewe out al my bloode.
>   Was neu*er* none so poore in none estate! (ll. 169-72)

To read this nightingale poem after reading so many others comes as a shock. There is no ecstasy, no loveliness, no humility, no sense of a generous and all-powerful God—all aspects com-mon to earlier texts. What the poem evokes instead is a brittle class-defined self, to which the nightingale's song serves only as material to be deciphered rather than revelatory in its own right. If the function of the literary/feminine/natural voice is in some sense to *supplement* the political and social world, by providing the defining spaces at and on its boundaries, that function cannot be fulfilled here. This poem articulates an obsessive desire to control, restrain and define, and registers a deep anxiety about the ambiguity of the nightingale and the ambivalent boundaries it voices. It is striking that the problem lies in the relation of the sacred to the erotic, recalling the narrator's ridiculed stance in the comic nightingale poem of the *Cambridge Songs*. Here, however, the insecurity of the clerkly voice takes over the entire poem, and it is deadly serious. This obsession with control and explication is reflected in the choice of genre.

By encasing his version in a courtly form, the dream allegory, the poet complicates the simple conception of the earlier poem.[117] Though the dream vision indicates a movement inwards, within the self, which could introduce a personal vision at odds with the social ideology—as I argue happens in *The Cuckoo and the Nightingale* —in this version what is found there (the fierce bird, the admonitory angel) replicates the punitive, repressive pattern that exists in the social world. This dream poem denies rather than explores the different possibilities of the spiritual and the feminine by presenting them as aspects of a centrally ordered social and class norm and attempting to punish any deviation—as in the poet's idleness and thoughts of erotic love. There is hardly a mention of the actual birdsong, which is disposed with as fast as possible, clearing the way for the laboured explanation.

The poet no longer overhears and responds emotionally as an individual to the nightingale's 'celestial music',[118] but has it interpreted, turned into unambiguous meaning for him by the impatient angel. Similarly the piercing of grief is 'explained' by an emblematic object, a thorn. These new factors serve to abstract and rationalize Pecham's religious ecstasy, and, as part of this, the nightingale's song is reduced to the opening move in a sermon. Didactic argument replaces melody as a means of persuasion to repentance. Instead of the simple relation between an auditor and a bird, clarified and made comprehensible through individual emotion, the introduction of the angel creates a small, hierarchic society within the poem to mirror the numerous courtly audience and match the more corporate version of the Bible that takes the place of scenes from a simple 'life'.

Though the poet draws on the traditional sensuous nature of the bird, he makes it equally explicable, relating it to the courtly figure of the lovers' rose and its erotic thorn—thus denying the bird itself the ambiguity of its traditional place at the edges of the social and political world. Though the early fourteenth century French *Chant* had introduced thorns in the tree on which the bird sang—

> L'arbre espinoux ou chante et fait sa demourance
> Cest oisel vers sa fin, c'est vivre en penitance
> Et l'arbre de la croiz avoir en remembrance,
> La courronne d'espines et les clous et la lance. (ll. 89-92)

—they had referred back to the central allegory of Christ on the cross and not to a peripheral, and distracting, explanation of the nightingale's song. *This* use of the thorn suggests, on the other hand, a class affiliation rather than a religious experience constructed at its boundaries. The nightingale's associations with the rose and its thorn may derive ultimately from Persia,[119] but their rapid assimilation into English poetry (especially that of the later Renaissance) indicates the Rose's allegorical significance in the poetry of the aristocracy. In the *Philomena* the nightingale figures the desire to step into a freer world of spiritual rather than social relations, but in this text the nightingale is drawn back into and contained within a punitive class ideology, one that determinedly crushes alternatives.

The other pseudo-Lydgate nightingale poem, *The Nightingale*, with its male aristocratic audience (shown more by the topical reference to the dead Lord of Warwick as someone known personally, than by a possibly rhetorical address to 'lords and princes'), is also marked by this rigidity, a polarization of the Christian community around issues of class interest. Here again the nightingale appears a mechanical symbol. Despite sugared opening references to delight, her song similarly provides, though in a more developed way, a preface to a sermon which concludes with dire warnings of

> The fende, youre enmye, lying in a-wayte,
>   Goth fast a-boute, your soules to deceyue,
> Leying hys lynes and with mony a bayte
>   Wsynge his hokes, on theym you to receyue. (ll. 302-305)

Where Pecham concentrates on a *personal* identification with intimate scenes from Christ's life, 'Lydgate' provides a synopsis of the Bible to address the *class*-identification of his auditors. This corporate approach is mirrored by the switch from the individual address of the Latin and its near-contemporary French translation—

> *Te* caelestum musicum faciet repente. (l. 20, my italics)
> La celestel musique *t*'ensaignera sans doute. (l. 52, my italics)

—to the plural and formal address ('youre') favoured by Lydgate. Though it goes without saying that there is no celestial music.

By articulating a didactic demand for vengeance, these poems express the anxiety of the fifteenth-century upper classes—including the merchants benefiting from the existing systems of patronage and who themselves patronized poets such as Lydgate. Religion in both of these texts is highly socialized and political. Swerving from the model of tender nurturance in the thirteenth-century poem, it marks a paranoid breakdown of a carefully constructed religious identity. Yet the humanized nightingale and the feminized reader of Pecham's *Philomena*—despite the attractiveness of its vision—is as much a response to unstable times as is the fifteenth-century reaction demonstrated in these poems. If the first attempts to flee from class, the second clings to it to the extent that, paradoxically, the pseudo-Lydgate's religious poems on the nightingale actually mark the final absorption of the utopian Christian figure into the hierarchical political world. The following chapter considers this period of change between the twelfth and fifteenth centuries from a different perspective: that of secular poetry written under the influence of the scholastic debate. The nightingale appears frequently in these texts, entangled with shifting subtexts of class and gender; making the same transition from a sensual voice to one associated with the aristocracy. The difference between the two kinds of texts, however, is that where the religious poems are concerned with doctrine and hence seek to deny opposition, poetry influenced by the debate has difference incorporated within its fundamental structure. It is in this secular poetry that a recognizable literary space, one which incorporates opposition, emerges as the forerunner of a humanist tradition—one in which I shall argue that two outcomes are possible, dependent on the varying places assigned to gender.

Chapter 3

Debating Class and Gender: Medieval English Nightingales

A comparison of early Franciscan verse with the debate poem—a genre that emerged during the same period—usefully demonstrates the interrelation of formations of class and gender. Pecham's poem, together with the translations, adaptations and lyrics that it generated, expresses a deep emotional identification with the bodily Christ and the passions of Jesus and Mary, and articulates a fascinated mystification of the material world. The debate, on the other hand, practises disengagement and looks to logic as a means of understanding the world. Though the nightingales that appear in both religious lyric and formalized debate are associated variously with love and lyric poetry, with women and with nature, these associations are used differently to construct particular readers. As a measure of the gulf between the two it is only necessary to note that Abelard subordinated the divine to secular principles by systematically applying logic to theology[1]— a move unthinkable before the twelfth century and very far from Pecham's emotive verse. Logic developed in relation to the study of rhetoric: even at its most abstruse it was a means of attempting to understand the workings of language and hence aimed to *interpret* the world through the exercise of reason, not to mystify it.[2]

The development and huge popularity of debate poetry accompanied the growth of the secular clerisy in the burgeoning universities of the twelfth and thirteenth centuries: as part of the study of logic students were expected to debate issues by constructing

opposing arguments around a basic situation or set of information. The poetic genre worked in the same way by concretizing
value systems into oppositional symbols (body and soul, water and
wine, owl and nightingale), abstracted out of the social and political world to be set against each other in binary opposition.[3] After
reading the contemporary Mechthild of Magdeburg's impassioned lyrics, Pecham's gentle *Philomena* or even slightly later
troubadour poetry such as that of Bernard de Ventadour, the
distance and shock of medieval debate poetry is instructive. Yet
the debate can only be seen as a system of binary oppositions if
the reader or audience are passive receptors, and I do not think
that this is the case: the dyadic system is predicated on a third
term, the interactive reader or audience. The university student
learnt to perceive the world in clearly rational terms, for placed
within the parentheses of a formal structured argument, the
debate was conducted in an abstract space outside the human
sphere:[4] the reader of the debate poem was similarly dissociated
from the issues at hand and learnt to assess them as arguments.
The academic debate thus channels its readers into an acceptance
of its ideological presuppositions: that conflict (difference) can be
resolved through reduction to rational argument and that rational argument leads to the achievement of truth. This is most
revealing in the vernacular debate: in some ways the classical
debate text extends the intellectual bias Dronke detects in the
acquisition of a literary language such as Latin,[5] but there was no
such inclination in the vernacular. As an alien genre imported
into a mother tongue literature, vernacular debates demonstrate
the exercise of logical patterns more clearly than their Latin coun-
terparts. This is one reason for focusing on the English vernacular
debate in this chapter; the other is that, having been written in
English, they formed part of the body of texts which continued to
be read and therefore to influence later writers both directly and
in terms of the generic possibilities they offered. Individual texts
discussed here were translated and adapted by writers as diverse as
Richard Niccols,[6] Milton,[7] Dryden,[8] Wordsworth[9] and, eventually,
the subject of my final chapter, Elizabeth Barrett Browning.[10]

The twelfth-century debate poem, *The Owl and the Nightingale*,
which provides the basis of my discussion of the medieval debate,
is a perfect illustration of the role accorded to rationality in the

debate. The text is ordered by legal procedure[11] but staged in the non-human/non-legal space of nature. This strategy suggests that a nature conceived as fractured, split equally between the two female bird voices, serves to define the 'human' as *un*divided and—in opposition to them—as 'masculine'. As 'he' assesses the value of the irreconcilable partial arguments allocated to the vituperative birds, the reader's human status is defined by a capacity to judge this fractured feminine world. The debate constructs a 'masculine' reader whose 'masculinity' is simultaneously equated with a class value: the philosophic rationalism of the secular clerisy.

In the previous chapters I argue that, repeatedly characterized as the voice of nature in literary texts, the female nightingale acquires a significant role in the various ideological constructions of the human sphere. That the bird associated with erotic desire and the aristocratic poetry that celebrates and idealizes that desire should appear simultaneously in both religious verse and the rationalist debate of the twelfth to fifteenth centuries not only points to the significance of her role in cutting across social and political boundaries but also indicates ideological struggles over the definition of the human through a feminine figure of the natural. Yet though this analysis appears to explain the frequency with which the nightingale appears in the various literary texts, it is insufficient to explain its special significance in the debate poems which provide the material for this chapter. As a feminine figure, the nightingale has a relational identity that fluctuates with differences within the dominant value of masculinity. The major difference here is between ideas of masculinity in clerical and aristocratic terms[12] which themselves involved the establishment of class differentials. I consider that this is one of the functions that the nightingale acquires in the debate. Because the debate foregrounds conflict as a way of achieving truth it provides a fascinating arena for investigating problems of identity[13]—and the nightingale's simultaneous associations with desire, femininity, nature, and, of course, voice indicate its significance in such an arena. It may also suggest why the aristocracy should be so interested in the nightingale—as demonstrated in the previous chapter and exemplified by its role in these debates. Genres such as the romance, the epic and the lyric were closely associated with the aristocracy and its need to define its identity.[14] The lyric, in particular, was in Patterson's phrase, a genre 'relentlessly concerned with staging subjectivity'[15]—and the lyric was equally closely associated with the nightingale. I want to argue that the association of the nightingale with nobility is in part due to an aristocratic rejection of rationalism and an attempt to appropriate the birth-space of nature as part of its legitimating self-identity: their cultural power lay, not in merit (reason), but in blood lines (nature).

The three poems on which this chapter focuses are the thirteenth-century 'The Thrush and the Nightingale', the late fourteenth-century *Cuckoo and the Nightingale* by John Clanvowe and the anonymous early fifteenth-century *Floure and the Leaf*: all texts in which the female nightingale is characterized as an aristocratic voice. My interest in these debates lies in the changing nature of her opponents, as expressed through their language, and the way this reflects back on the meaning and implications of the nightingale. In the first poem he is a scholarly thrush; in the second, a churlish cuckoo mediated by the consciousness of a narrator; in the third, an insubstantial but aristocratic goldfinch. The modulation of the issue at the heart of each debate further indicates problem areas in the aristocratic ideology with which the nightingale seems increasingly associated. In the first the debate is a *querelle*—a debate specifically about whether women are disruptive of male identity, or whether they nurture and sustain it (hence the emblematic significance of chastity);[16] in the second, the debate concerns the place and value of love (whether disruptive or the root of (masculine) virtue); I shall argue that, far from being a poem in which 'the Virtues ask the Vices to a picnic'[17] the third is a text in which an aristocratic anxiety about its own substantiality is worked out through an internal debate about the value of harmony, pattern and hierarchy. In each case changes in the subject matter and structure of the debate demonstrate shifts in the ideological subtext of the genre. The fact that the two later poems are firmly linked to a courtly way of life—in Clanvowe's case possibly spoken from the absolute court of Richard II—indicates the specific problems of the subject with an ideology which denies the personal and rests on wholly public definitions of the self. In both these cases the resolution of the textual problem through increased complexity simultaneously marks the estab-

lishment of a personal space (hedged around with difficulties)
through the ambiguity inherent in the act of writing.

  Though linguistic echoes in 'The Thrush and the Nightingale'
indicate that it is modelled at least in part on *The Owl and the
Nightingale*, the change from open-ended legalistic debate to the
closure of the arguments of the *querelle* imposes a quite different
and more passive role on the reader. I consider this to be part of a
covert aristocratic appropriation of the debate, one which redefines rationality as materialism and then devalues it as gross physicality, a move which simultaneously degrades the rational reader.
As part of this shift, 'The Thrush and the Nightingale' allocates
different genders to its two protagonists, vanquishes the masculine thrush, and concludes by ejecting him from the symbolic
place ('lond') of the debate. Whereas the debate in *The Owl and
the Nightingale* follows the rational procedure of the ecclesiastical
courts, with female birds that have natural features as well as
functioning as abstract figures, in the later poem the debate
expresses conflict by opposing the poetics associated with different social groups—the aristocratic lyric of the feminine nightingale and the masculine thrush's scholarly argument. In the first
the victory lies in the establishment of reason and language as a
way of reaching truth; in the second, this achievement is subtly
subverted, the argument translated into a hierarchy which benefits those in power. In this second case the reader is no longer
required to exercise judgment but is coerced by the appeal to the
Virgin (who exists beyond reason) into supporting the arguments
of the nightingale, a figure who thus naturalizes her class position
into that of moral superiority.[18] The complex interpenetration of
class and gender both in this debate as a whole and in the figure
of the aristocratic nightingale in particular is the reason why I
choose to focus on this poem rather than on *The Owl and the
Nightingale*.

  Language is never innocent, and the language used by the
protagonists in these debates is particularly marked by class.[19]
During the twelfth to fifteenth centuries class struggles developed
between the secular clergy, on the one hand, educated in the new
universities, insisting on reason and merit, and the aristocracy on
the other, who rested on the 'irrational' notion of birthright
buttressed by abstract concepts of 'honour' and 'virtue', and ac-

cused the literate class of vulgarity and self-centredness. Rational clerks and chaste nightingales are thus significant symbolic figures—whether filtered through the *querelle* or appearing in two fourteenth-century debates between clerks and nightingales. I want to argue that these last two texts lack the ideological coherence which can appear as aesthetically pleasing because they were written by representatives of a group stigmatized within the very genre which they were struggling to appropriate. My reading suggests ways of relating changes within the literary form to those issues of class (courtier, aristocrat and writer) I see dramatized in the late fourteenth-century *Cuckoo and the Nightingale* and the early fifteenth-century *Floure and the Leaf.*

Differences between these late debates and the contemporary didactic religious texts are explicable on the one hand by reference to the issue of agency—these poems are written by a Lollard lord and an aristocratic woman respectively and thus, unlike Lydgate's, derive from places located by religion and gender at the ideological periphery of the dominant group—and on the other by a literary structure which foregrounds conflict as an (unstable) means of achieving stability and consensus. The result is that both of these texts display characteristics of self-reflection on the part of their narrators (mirroring the disrupted subjectivity of their authors) while this reflexiveness is further replicated in the debate structure; disrupted by these narrators in terms of both the expected conduct and closure of the argument, and by the intrusion of an alternative genre—the dream vision—which places the consciousness of the narrators at the heart of the debate itself and thus leads to new possibilities in terms of both structure and possible resolutions.[20] Where the dream-vision in Lydgate's nightingale poems summons up personal desire and questioning only to quash it with the authoritarianism of the interpretative angel, in these poems it produces an exploratory complexity—and a subjective engagement on the part of the reader. The creation of complexity beyond the singleness of individual genres and ideologies through the interpenetration of debate and dream, of class and gender, thus evokes the richness of the literary itself as a space in excess of the class-informed discourse. Not only is the problem of the subject within ideology broached—the subject as 'written' by the intersection of conflicting ideologies—but also the subject as 'writer', central to both texts, in excess of these individual ideologies: a risky excess that mirrors the excess of the reader and his or her delight in the text, a subjectivity denied by the dual manipulation of material and reader in earlier debates. In his study of 'Tradition and Discontinuity in Medieval Culture' Stephen Nichols pointed to the desperate desire for fixity seen as knowledge: 'Not *to knowe* was to be lost, like Dante pilgrim in the *selve oscura* (dark wood) of *Inferno* I. The alternate reality of the Middle Ages was a slippery and dangerous world of motion.'[21] This is the dangerous world hidden below these final debates, for to exceed the careful categories of the scholars, or the regulations about lineage and marriage of the nobility,[22] was equally to risk that changeable world and to invite the reader to participate.[23] It is thus with a consideration of the rational reader implied by the twelfth-century *The Owl and the Nightingale* that I begin my discussion.

Abstracting Arguments: Stealing the Debate for the Aristocracy

Many modern studies of *The Owl and the Nightingale* assume a passive reader, one with the skills of a detective who is required to process information in order to reach a predetermined conclusion. But, as Atkins points out, this approach questions neither the significance of the genre's popularity at this time, nor the mechanics of how it operated. This issue is usually resolved by referring to twelfth-century academic training and the emphasis on logic as an apolitical accomplishment—yet it was clearly part of a wider cultural movement which stressed rationality and decision-making as part of personal advancement.[24] Murray points to the political implications of the schools' emphasis on rationality:

> Professional rationalism and private interest... merged to cast the growing ranks of the literate as critics of the hereditary ideal. Literature and philosophy had scarcely entered their medieval renaissance before both were engaged in a campaign, to swell with them and ultimately to outlast the Middle Ages, against the social rights of birth.[25]

The Owl and the Nightingale displays strategies devised to develop the skills and underlying assumptions of rational argument by positioning the reader as an active participant in the debate, but

confining his role to that of an assessor. The opening lines present an individual, an unqualified 'ich' who finds the hidden spot
where the dispute takes place in an undefined natural world
distant from 'his' own. As both non-human and non-male, the
debating voices are doubly qualified to speak from this space;
each bird establishing her case by continual repetition of her own
points and vilification of her opponent's. Neither accommodates
the other's point of view, so the reader is confronted with equally
valid but irreconcilable mores, something pressed home by the
fact that the poem's conclusion does not mark the close of the
debate, which is deferred to the judgment of a (male) human
figure outside its formal structure. The poem concludes with the
two birds agreeing to submit their arguments to the wisdom of a
Nicholas of Guilford (ll. 191; 1746–47), a figure who mirrors the
role of the reader as a figure outside the frame of the poem but
intervening and actively interpreting it.

For the purposes of this study the issue of how and why the
debate is conducted is more productive than the question of its
subject matter. Various interpretations attempt to reduce the
argument to one between various pairs of historical factions,[26] to
arguments which set polyphony (the nightingale) against mon-
odony (the owl), or to an argument between religious orders,[27]
but this approach isolates the poem and treats the genre as a
transparent vehicle for a specific occasion: it questions neither the
structures and presuppositions of the debate nor those of its own
reading practices (which in traditional criticism assume a passive
reader) as themselves historically determined. Though individual
interpretations can be fascinating (the information in Janet
Coleman's study was footnoted in the last chapter in relation to
the changing status of women in the twelfth century), such
approaches tend to reduce the poem to information and 'explain'
the nightingale by deriving it from a particular source—troubadour poetry, the *fêtes de mai,* the allusion to Marie de France's
laï—rather than discussing issues such as the construction of
notions of nature, of gender or of relation to authority: in short,
the poem as a function of its historical context.

Neither situations nor genres remains stable and by the thirteenth century the debate registers attempts by the aristocracy to
grapple more satisfactorily with increasing social and ideological

instability.[28] *The Owl and the Nightingale* is an open-ended debate which invites the reader to participate as the third, defining term, outside the frame of the text but drawn into and implied within it; in contrast in 'The Thrush and the Nightingale' the answer is already inscribed within the textual frame because the argument is weighted in favour of one of the parties. The gendered distinction between form and content is thus blurred and the active masculine reader is placed in a passive (feminized) role in relation to the text, accepting the authority vested in the poem itself and equating textual closure with that of the issue at hand. Secondly, irreconcilable ideological positions, themselves dramatizing class disruption and subservient to legal procedure, are reconceived in terms of a gender struggle between two protagonists, seen from the perspective of the aristocracy to articulate different class positions. The question of 'woman' is reduced to one of chastity and feminine desire: a stance previously equated with a religious rather than a class perspective.[29] My discussion of the poem seeks to indicate why this should be important.

'The Thrush and the Nightingale'

When a love-lyric contemporary with 'The Thrush and the Night-ingale' opens with the nightingale song—

> When þe nyhtegale singes þe wodes waxen grene,
> Lef & gras & blosme springes in aueryl, y wene,
> ant loue is to myn herte gon wiþ one spere so kene,
> nyht & day my blod hit drynkes, myn herte deþ me tene,[30]

—the passage is immediately recognizable as a *Natureingang*: an escape from the political world into one characterized by sensuality and physical pleasures and hence love; at the same time closely associated with courtly verse and therefore simultaneously an expression of a class-defined appropriation of the natural space. As expected the nightingale is the voice of this naturalized aristocratic world. A fourteenth-century example is longer and more elaborate: the nightingale's voice is still central to the love message, but it is associated with the daisy and has been joined by the song of a thrush:

> Lenten ys come wiþ loue to toune,
> wiþ blosmen & wiþ briddes roune,
> þat al þis blisse bryngeþ;
> dayes-eȝes in þis dales,
> notes suete of nyhtegales,
> vch foul song singeþ.
> þe þrestelcoc him þreteþ oo;
> away is huere wynter woo,
> when woderoue springeþ.[31]

It is unnecessary to detail every instance, but it is obvious from these poems alone that the similar opening lines of 'The Thrush and the Nightingale' announce that this poem too is concerned with the sensual world and with love, and that the nightingale's voice is the most potent force in that message:

> Somer is comen wiþ loue to toune,
> Wiþ blostme, and wiþ brides roune
> þe note of hasel springeþ,
> þe dewes darkneþ in þe dale.
> For longing of þe niȝttegale,
> þis foweles murie singeþ.[32]

Yet despite this opening, 'The Thrush and the Nightingale' is not a love-lyric. The lines therefore have a different function: they are emblematic, indicating the poem's conclusion before it has properly started. A major difference from *The Owl and the Nightingale* is immediately apparent: where the earlier poem employed the *rational* procedure of the ecclesiastical courts, this one mimics the *sensual* introduction of the lyric, thus aligning itself with an aristocratic interpretation of the natural world. The dispute within this poem is traced through conflicting discourses set within a literary lyrical space, with the human difference of gender central to both structure (the allocation of masculinity and femininity to the protagonists) and content (the debate over women). This marks a major shift from the position in the earlier debate in which the two figures were associated directly with the natural world by being given characteristics and habits of real birds (i.e. of the non-human), while form and content were separated and gendered masculine and feminine respectively. In this poem the voices are human, in that they are constructed through class-determined language and gender. The female nightingale is the voice of a sensual natural world, and of the aristocratic lyric associated with that world; the male thrush is the voice of a human clerk, scholarly and out of place in a world in which the birds that sing everywhere do so 'for longing of þe niȝttegale'. Despite similarities therefore between the two poems these very opening lines serve to indicate a division into two spheres: femininity against masculinity; aristocracy against scholarship—and finally, a faith that rests on the control of the sensual, against a reason that denies it.

Where *The Owl and the Nightingale* weaves description and narration together without any subjective presence on the part of the narrator (a 'rational' figure simply reporting what he has heard), and draws the reader into a fluid text which mingles different experiences which 'he' (replicating the narrator) then assesses, the text of 'The Thrush and the Nightingale' is more obviously ordered and controlled, proceeding in a linear fashion, opening with argument and subject matter rather than passion and rage. The opposing stances of the two birds are outlined, immediately after the *Natureingang*:

> þat on hereþ wimmen þat hoe beþ hende,
> þat oþer hem wole wiþ miȝte shende. (ll. 10-11)

This patterning is kept throughout the poem and only broken to emphasize a point in the nightingale's favour. The thrush opens and closes the debate and the poem tracks his rise and fall: an intruder who is forced to leave. Apart from the first three stanzas, which set the scene, each bird is allocated two stanzas in which to develop its arguments. The turning point comes midway through the poem, marked by the nightingale who, increasingly frustrated at the thrush's 'false mouþ', breaks into one of the thrush's tirades, cutting him short half way through his second stanza and continuing for a further two stanzas.

This structure makes for a very different reading experience to that of the earlier debate. The reader is passive, responding to patterns within a masterful text, waiting for the outcome which—as I point out—is inscribed in the very opening lines. Attention is drawn to the skill with which these positions are managed and the way in which the thrush is made to overreach himself to lose the argument. Yet below the debate about women lies another in which the question of gender both hides and enables the discussion of class.

In text after text the nightingale's ambiguity places her at a defining boundary: feminine, natural, poetic. And as such she is caught within competing definitions—attacked by aristocratic hawks in Hesiod and Aesop, like Philomela, subject to a male attack, acting as a figure of Christ and competing amongst other birds in Christian Latin poetry. The sort of conflict within which she is found is therefore a significant guide to wider issues of definition. Though the nightingale is not a victim in *The Owl and the Nightingale* and not subject to a violent male attack, she is defined by the slipperiness of her 'wise tunge' while the owl's physical threats echo those of the Greek hawks. What is missing is the gendering of the confrontation with its subtext of tyrant and victim: this is no hierarchy but an irreconcilable confrontation which must be determined outside the text by reader or monk. In 'The Thrush and the Nightingale', however, the conflict is both contained and resolved within the text. The fact that there is a resolution means that one of the figures gives way to the other's arguments—not to threatened violence. This is a change that incorporates aspects of what Eugene Vance would call the methodology of the market-place, moving from a culture of violent confrontation to one of words and of accommodation.[34] And, as in Vance's argument over the appropriation of this methodology by the aristocracy in the lyric,[35] in this debate it is the aristocracy that appears to win the arguments by setting the poem on the ground of the lyric itself. To be more precise: an established confrontation between nightingale–female–victim and predator–male–aristocrat shifts as the nightingale becomes associated with the aristocrat, that is with a position of power, while the role of the victim, the loser, is projected onto her opponent the thrush. Retaining the pattern of a male attack on women and on the place of women, the conflict hides an aristocratic attack on a figure whose intrusion into its lyric space is presented as a frustrated attempt to despoil—to rape.

Stating his *auctors* and attacking women for deceit and inconstancy, the thrush is immediately recognizable as a representative of the medieval clerk, the literate class which increasingly gained positions of authority during the thirteenth century and which was perceived as a threat by the aristocracy.[36] English debates between 'town' and 'gown' appear frequently during the fourteenth century[37]—the time of the greatest expansion of English universities[38]—but they were responding to a clerkly careerism established during the twelfth and thirteenth centuries. As Murray points out,

> ...the arguing, job-hunting scholars of the twelfth and thirteenth-century schools were bound to question [the] principle [of noble succession]... In so far as scholars aimed at government office, the principle was...a threat to their hopes of livelihood.[39]

In this poem the class debate is sublimated into the *querelle* as the aristocracy appropriates traditional Christian arguments about chastity, and hence their ethical force, for its own purposes: morality (conceived as aristocratic virtue) overcomes textuality (construed as clerkly misogyny); virtuous faith overcomes materialist reason.

Resting on birth in place of merit, aristocratic power could not be legitimated through the exercise of reason. 'The Thrush and the Nightingale' thus places the aristocratic nightingale, associated with the non-physical/spiritual/irrational simultaneously, against the rational thrush, a figure devalued by the accusation of materialism. This makes for a complex relationship with nature: the aristocracy's power is legitimated through the 'natural', yet nature is also the space at the defining boundary of the civilized.

One answer is to transform nature into images, emblems divested of their sensual physicality—as in heraldic devices[39] or the imagery of the courtly lyric, as in the cult of a love denied consummation; and finally, of course, in the centrality of the cult of chastity, in which the conventional figure of the irrational— feminine desire—is rigorously policed (here clearly the nightingale). The irrational thus provides the ground upon which virtue must be constructed (in the non-material) but it also threatens that abstract and emblematic value system through individual desire: this ambivalence towards nature is formalized in the nightingale's claim to authority in the invocation of Mary—the impossible conjunction of virgin and mother—as the spiritual equivalent of temporal authority yoked to irrationality.

Because the relation of female victim and male attacker is rewritten from the perspective of the ruling class, it is impossible for the nightingale's opponent to be the customary hawk or eagle: on the one hand these birds have powerful aristocratic associations[40] which the thrush must be denied, and on the other, by conducting the debate with another spring bird, the nightingale wins the debate through her traditional musical pre-eminence while the thrush is devalued as a discordant element in the symbolic 'natural' harmony. Yet at the same time the retention of the feminine gender allows the nightingale to trade on associations with vulnerability and the traditionally 'feminine' qualities of nurturance and healing that she herself claims as women's special province.

In *The Owl and the Nightingale* the nightingale's opponent faces criticism of her nesting place and the habits of her young (ll. 625-54); in this dispute however her descendant, the thrush, is a dislocated male individual with no association with homes or off-spring. The experience he claims is drawn from books, serving simultaneously to place him outside both the natural world and the literary space of the lyric which is associated with that world. Though the thrush insists on the pain of 'real life', of real situations, this is mediated through other texts. He insists that women's

> ...þout is fals, and ountrewe
> Ful ȝare ich haue hem fonde (ll. 41-42)

—though he is given references only to classical pagan (Alexander), Old Testament (Adam and Samson), and Arthurian (Gawain) sources, not to the New Testament.

Where the nightingale denies both reason and feminine desire to espouse a disembodied nature, the thrush denies nature and espouses reason, rooting his arguments on feminine desire. These conflicting economies indicate the significance of the issue of chastity, for if the thrush is given arguments that express a deep antipathy to the natural world in which the argument is conducted, one of the major motives in his attack on women is his belief that the natural is the sensual, that beauty and love are deceitful masks. Crabbily evaluating the creation of women in economic terms—

> Hit is þat worste hord of pris
> þat ihesu makede in parais
> In tresour for to holde (ll. 142-44)

—the thrush is made to criticize his maker, to overreach his position, arrogant and out of place. It is a perfect dramatization of aristocratic anxiety about aspiring clerks.

Subtly undercut on all levels, the thrush's alignment with realism—basing his account on documented evidence, he insists on the treachery and pain in human relations—further indicates his class affiliations. Realism foregrounds the physical world and in the thirteenth century it was a mode associated with the depiction of clerks, priests and peasants in the fabliau: an aristocratic genre which rooted the lower classes in the sensual physical world, with scatological humour and sexual exploits. Though the thrush's arguments are neither funny nor erotic, they rest on a perception of women's sexual infidelities and thus express the reductive meanness of spirit by which the nobility stigmatized those inferior in rank. Caught in a reductive materiality, the thrush thus argues that without women the world would be a happy place. The nightingale's response appropriates what is left out of the thrush's account—the non-material—for her class position, so that the key issue (the nature and value of women) is redefined in *ethical* terms, not in those of the material world, resting on culture (conceived as 'above materialism') rather than the economy:

> Hy beþ briȝttore ounder shawe
> þen þe day wenne hit dawe
> In longe someres tide. (ll. 124-26)

As in the earlier poem, there is no discussion between the two birds: the nightingale merely sets her vision against his. Set against the physicality of the thrush, she draws on the Christian ideology of an already fallen world of necessary pain within which women act as havens and healers:

> In þe worlde nis non so goed leche,
> So milde of þoute, so feir of speche,
> To hele monnes sore. (ll. 151-53)

Thus the nightingale appropriates the high moral ground, not in opposition to her adherence to social mores, but in order to legitimate them. In her vision the aristocracy is intrinsically virtuous: rationality is merely the mode of blinkered materialists.[41]

That the thrush's link with the physical world is intended to be reductive is clearest when *he* attempts to introduce the concept of nobility. He refers to King Alexander, claiming to

> ...take witnesse of monie and fele
> þat riche weren of worldes wele,
> Muche wes hem þe shonde. (ll. 46-48)

But here again he is made to condemn himself through his own
words (his 'false mouþ') by confusing goods and rank with gentility. In contrast the nightingale does not consider the physical
world, turning to faith in an emblematic and idealized essence
when she discusses the value of women:

> I-maked hoe wes to *mones* fere,
> Nis no þing al so swete. (ll. 35-36, my italics)

The thrush, on the other hand, is locked into *individual* examples,
mainly men—or women qualified only by their relationship to
men ('constantines quene'; 'saunsum['s] wif')—to prove his reasoned case. As a cleric he speaks for the church establishment,
making traditional scholarly accusations in condemning women
as fornicators and deceivers:

> Hy willeþ for a luitel mede
> Don a sunfoul derne dede,
> Here soule forto spille. (ll. 64-66)

The thrush's animosity towards women includes the nightingale:
though he calls her 'gentil fowel' (l. 61) he makes his sarcasm
evident by dropping the adjective denoting her aristocratic birth
to insult her with plain 'fowel', and accusing her of lying ('les') at
the beginning of the next stanza, only a few lines later. By shifting
the ground to that of truth perceived through reason, the thrush
sets himself against aristocractic patterns which refuse these
categories.[42] Though discussing the ideological background to
Chaucer's 'Knight's Tale', Patterson's comments on aristocratic
ideology are equally pertinent to this discussion:

> ... chivalry must be understood as the central form of self-
> definition by means of which the noble class situated itself within
> medieval society... Insofar as the nobleman restricted his self-
> understanding to a chivalric identity, to that extent he excluded
> from his view the economic, social, and political forces that were
> challenging his dominance.[43]

The nightingale's response (backed by her appropriation of the
religious ethical ground) is one of exclusion and refusal, culmin-
ating in her twin accusations of madness and a lack of virtue:

þrestelcok, þou art wod,
Oþer þou const to luitel goed. (ll. 73-74)

But the nightingale is not restricted to a refutation of the thrush's
arguments: where he believes that 'ich holde wiþ þe riȝtte' (l. 87),
her frequent references throughout the poem to 'shome', 'cor-
teisy' and 'shende', reveal more openly the chivalric basis of her
world. Her reproaches are equally class-determined: she accuses
him of dishonourable behaviour: the very fault that Gawain—the
first witness that the thrush calls upon, 'þat ihesu, crist ȝaf miȝt
and main / And strengþe for to fiȝtte' (ll. 89-90)—is so desperate
to avoid.

The thrush tries to rest on rationality—'þou hauest wrong'
(l. 85), 'ich holde wiþ þe riȝtte' (l. 87), 'þou art ounwis' (l. 157),
'soþ ne seist þou ene' (l. 68)—but rationality itself is defeated by
the Virgin who combines irrationality and chastity in a potent
spiritual equivalent to the chivalric nightingales. Faced with this
single proof, he no longer questions the nightingale's right to 'me
senden of þis lond' (l. 86) and is forced to accept her earlier
judgment:

Niȝttegale, I wes woed,
Oþer I couþe to luitel goed. (ll. 181-82)

The thrush is left only with the example of Jesus 'þat soffrede
wundes fiue' (l. 186) for the deceit, not of woman alone, but of a
treacherous mankind. His rationality proved insufficient, there is
no place left for him and he is forced to give up everything by
which he has defined himself, opinions and books, to leave the
symbolic space within which the debate has taken place:

Hout of þis londe willi te,
Ne rechi neuere weder I fle,
A-wai ich wille driue. (ll. 190-92)

So far my analysis has mainly concentrated on class, reading the
argument about the place of women as a means adopted by the
aristocratic figure in order to *dis*place the clerical thrush. But this
process cannot be disentangled from that of gender: the ground
on which this debate is conducted after all. It is a ground which
sees the physical in terms of the feminine—as either non-desiring
nurturance or uncontrollable lasciviousness—and defines the
masculine by its relation to that given quantity.

The conflict between the thrush's realism and the nightingale's lyricism is focused by a confrontation between a degraded physical world and an idealized non-physical one. There is no place for a positive evaluation of physicality: the non-physical *is* the ideal. In an echo of the aristocratic appropriation and redefinition of the erotic nightingale of oral tradition, the issue of women's chastity is not only central to the poem but reflects back on the larger significance of the female nightingale as an aristocratic voice.

Women's chastity had always been an important issue in the church, but in the thirteenth century it became increasingly significant for the aristocracy. Warner's fascinating chapter on the troubadours sets the issue of matrilineal succession at the heart of the change from an eleventh-century celebration of sensuality to the later veneration of chastity: 'By the early thirteenth century, lyric poets no longer sang of the joy or agony of physical love, but accepted without demur that their lady was worthy of their love precisely because she was too pure to reciprocate it.'[44] As she points out, such a schizophrenic split between body and soul—precisely the split expressed in class terms in 'The Thrush and the Nightingale'—could only be resolved by the Virgin Mary. Warner comments that by the thirteenth century the growing fervour for the Virgin Mary was useful as 'an establishment prop':

> ...as a woman who won her position through her son she did not confirm the feudal authority of an heiress who enjoyed her rank and property in her own right. Instead she lent symbolic support to the figure of a mother, and as the model of virginity she challenged all justification of carnal love.[45]

From this perspective the class conflict voiced in the *querelle* serves to reduce women to the ambiguous state of non-physical physical beings, idealized figures on whom the ideological justification of a class position may be pinned. Further, by conceptualizing female self-determination in terms of lasciviousness and projecting that idea onto a lower-class figure, aristocratic control of both their own women and a class anxiety which was not openly acknowledged are confirmed in the thrush's defeat. As a victory for 'women' it can only be seen as Pyrrhic for it marks a reductive perception of women ventriloquized by a emblematic female bird: the chaste, virtuous and aristocratic nightingale.

Moving away from the aristocracy, Ferrante points out that the

thirteenth century was a period of very great disruption—not just
among an aristocracy threatened by social mobility and attempting to tighten control of inheritance laws. She points to
widespread anxieties, economic depression, social discontent and
rebellion.[46] In this context, all social identities appear unstable:
'only mystics and lyric poets still attribute any positive powers to
women'—and these positive powers are limited to the chaste or
the female intercessor with God. Not just for the aristocracy
therefore but across classes the Virgin becomes the ideal woman:
'but as a real woman she is unique, hence even further removed
from womankind than the personifications and symbols of the
earlier period'.[47] As in 'The Thrush and the Nightingale', class
and gender operate as interwoven subtexts: class disruption en-
genders arguments about the place of women while the *querelle*
hides anxiety about class.

Generic Problems: Affinities between Class and Literary Form

There are interesting differences in the way that these topics
resurface in two (unconnected) fourteenth-century satires against
women which are both entitled 'The Clerk and the Nightingale'.
In these poems the clerks appear to aspire to the moral ground
implied by the aristocratic belief in the value of women (through
chastity), while the bitter misogynous tones are unexpectedly
provided by male aristocratic nightingales. Both poems reflect the
reduced perception of the debate form itself—presenting irreconcilable ideological divisions in terms of gender—but whereas 'The
Thrush and the Nightingale' is written from the perspective of the
aristocracy, these poems appear to reflect the interests of the
clerks. If this is the case it is interesting that neither is as aesthetically satisfying as the previous poem, for they are unbalanced,
there is a sense of disorder: the arguments are not so evenly
distributed and the nightingale's voice loses its courtly idealized
veneer and is left to speak uncharacteristically of a bastardized
love. These poems lack both the rational patterning of the early
debate and the chaste lyricism of the later.

Though one of the clerks tries to defend women against the old
charges of lies, deceit and lust, repeating the arguments of the
earlier poem's nightingale—women 'bryng men owt of woo'
(l. 35); although one woman brought about the fall, 'a-noþer... /

broʒt vs alle to game' (ll. 47-48); 'wymmen be fayre & hende' (l. 66); 'were a man in sorow broʒt, / wymmen myʒt out hym bryng' (ll. 69-70); and, finally, 'How sholde men be forth broʒt / ne wymmen ware?' (ll. 87-88)—the debate is inconclusive. The citation of the Virgin, the crowning stroke of 'The Thrush and the Nightingale', is thrown away in the middle of the poem and even discounted when the nightingale points out that she is unique among women.

Similar problems of balance occur in the second 'Clerk and Nightingale' poem: the overall ordering of the debate—so masterfully controlled in 'The Thrush and the Nightingale'—is missing and the number of stanzas allocated to each speaker ranges from two to four with no set pattern. The poem advances in a stilted manner, lacking the even distribution of speeches of 'The Thrush and the Nightingale', while the syntax of the lines is ragged and uncomfortable. The clerk appeals to the nightingale's nobility :

> And as thou art hend and ffre,
>> And comyn off good blode—
> How schall I, tell thow me,
>> To know the trew and the good? (ll. 35-38)

The impression is that the genre is being twisted; the fact that it is no longer a debate between two birds in the lyric space of the nightingale points to disruption in itself, while the introduction of a human figure disturbs the abstract quality of the debate. Though it is necessary to do this because the lyric/natural space is one already marked as aristocratic and in this arena only an aristocratic predator can overcome the nightingale, entry into the human world immediately invokes class and gender, marks of the (real) social and political world in which the clerk lacks authority. Despite this, when the clerk speaks he is forced to attempt to draw the nightingale into his terrain. Yet this attempt by a group already stigmatized within the debate to appropriate the genre and claim the moral advantage implied by victory is highly problematic. Like the text, the reader is caught between different ideological demands: there is no clear role for him/her, the effect is of confusion and dissatisfaction. It is difficult to change the ideological bias of a particular genre without damaging its delicate balances, and this is what appears to happen in these two debates. It is hard for the male clerks to achieve the high moral ground of chastity—which rests on emotional identification—when the dispute is conducted, not in the place of the lyric, but in that of the rational and scholarly clerk. Ideological confusion thus feeds directly into aesthetic dissatisfaction.

Other factors are present. The clerk checks his own attempt to challenge the aristocratic nightingale because his social aspiration leads to a partial acceptance of the aristocratic equation of merit with birth: he believes that the nightingale's 'good blode' indicates knowledge of the 'trewe and the good'. Because of this the poem avoids direct confrontation: the clearly defined positions of the earlier texts are replaced by a discussion which leads to a particularly lame conclusion:

> Haue good day, clerk ffre,
>   ffro the wyll y wende;
> Take hede what þat I haue seyd þe
>   ffro the bygynnyng to the ende. (ll. 75-78)

The silenced term in these final *querelles* is the feminine, for the four protagonists are all male and the function of the quarrel over gender in mediating class relationships is transparent in these texts. Female chastity is part of a strategy of aristocratic legitimation that transforms the physical into the non-physical, that translates nature into emblem, reason into materialism.

The fractured and inconclusive debates between the clerks and the nightingales indicate ideological problems which the genre itself cannot accommodate without radical structural change— and this is what happens in the poems that comprise the material for the final two sections of this chapter. This change also influences the aesthetic satisfactions offered by these texts, allowing for greater pleasure through a more complex hybrid. In these poems the difficulties detectable in the two 'Clerk and Nightingale' debates are resolved by incorporating a different genre—the dream vision—at the centre of the text. It is a move that places the interior space of the human subject centrally within the 'natural' space of the lyric wood, translating the debate from a conflict between wholly differentiated classes into an internal argument that reflects psychological conflict between aspects of the self. In addition the introduction of a mediating observer—a figure familiar from the courtly *chanson d'aventure*[48]—incorporates aspects of reflection and self-reflection which create a subjective presence

within the text. This figure is dramatically involved first as com-
mentator and then as actor, in *The Cuckoo and the Nightingale*, as
watcher of an external procession from within a hidden bower in
The Floure and the Leaf. Thus by developing and complicating the
literary *form* new meanings are allowed to come into play. The
meanings that emerge through the elaboration of a complex
literary text—rather than one which is more clearly rooted in an
abstract debate tradition—are those that the dominant ideology is
intent on repressing: aspects of the silenced self, in particular the
role of *pleasure* within both text and reader.

As both lyric and dream vision channel the potentially disruptive experience of love into recognizable aesthetic forms,[49] what
happens in these two poems is a consideration of the place and
meaning, not of *women* in life, but of a love which simultaneously
affirms (as the site of veneration and idealization) and disrupts
(as the site of individual desire) the ideology of the nobility,
unconsciously clarifying and exposing the significance of the insistence on womanly chastity as part of the aristocratic policing of
desire within a 'feminine' nature in 'The Thrush and the Nightingale'. With links to both erotic love in oral poetry and violent
victimization in classical literature, the nightingale serves as an
emblem of aristocratic identity and its relation to nature in both
texts—but it is the desire of the unsettled narrators that is central
here. These narrators are not only created as emblems, 'written'
by particular class ideologies, but dramatize their instability as
writers, summoning up a complex subjective response from the
reader as part of their status as determinedly literary texts.

Both narrators dramatize their identities as writer and insert
references to the fact within their texts, satisfyingly complicating
the text with a sense of self-reflexiveness and richness which is
markedly different to the response generated by the debate
poems considered so far in this chapter. The very abstraction of
the argument and structure of the debate deflects the reader away
from emotional identification and towards a consideration of
argument and pattern. The history of critical discussion of these
debates appears to bear this out. Despite pleasure at the descriptive passages of *The Owl and the Nightingale*, enormous energy
seems to have been expended on trying to work out which bird
wins, on what *exactly* each figure is 'meant' to represent in a kind

of intellectual puzzle. These two later poems are different, however, invoking a response of delight, sympathy and appreciation as
part of their highly developed textuality. The titles by which the
poems are known—'The Cuckoo and the Nightingale' is also
known as 'The Boke of Cupide',[50] while *The Floure and the Leaf* not
only implies an allegorical debate but also refers to a courtly May
game—further serve to illustrate this complexity, for in both cases
the implied identity conferred by a title, even one retrospectively
imposed, appears unstable, unconsciously undermined by the textual ambiguity of name and word.

Debating the Literary: The Cuckoo and the Nightingale *and* The Floure and the Leaf

> In the Middle Ages many of the texts we now call literary carved
> out for themselves, without the benefit of a theory of the literary, a
> space of ideological opposition.[51]

Though the texts to which Patterson refers in this comment are
texts such as *The Canterbury Tales* and *Piers Plowman*, seen as
'literary' in the sense that they have been placed in a separate
category of canonical writing, comment is equally pertinent to *The
Cuckoo and the Nightingale* and *The Floure and the Leaf*. By drawing
both on aspects of other genres and on a multitude of textual
voices from beyond their own textual frame, the relation between
the debate and a specific class ideology is complicated even when,
as in *The Floure and the Leaf*, the text attempts to align itself with
the dominant ideology.

Neither text opens in the aristocratic lyrical space of the wood—
even though *The Floure and the Leaf* appears to do so. Both open by
mediating the very entry into the textual world through another
text: *The Cuckoo and the Nightingale* opens with a direct quotation
from 'The Knight's Tale'; *The Floure and the Leaf* rewrites the
opening passage of 'The General Prologue' to *The Canterbury
Tales*. The poems are therefore located in a determinedly literary
space, their textual boundaries blurring with the questions summoned up (in both cases) by implicit references to the issues of
language and identity examined throughout *The Canterbury Tales*.
In different ways both poems engage with aristocratic ideology.
Within *The Canterbury Tales*, 'The Knight's Tale' provides the

aristocratic paradigm against which the narratives that follow with their competing values and resolutions are set. By choosing to begin his poem from inside another's text, Clanvowe engages in an implicit debate with Chaucer's subject matter that runs parallel to the double debate within the poem: between the two birds as symbolic figures and as aspects of the dreamer's subjectivity. If, as Patterson argues, 'The Knight's Tale' is a tale of 'chivalry's interior',[52] *The Cuckoo and the Nightingale* indicates the chaotic interior of the individual (masculine) subject caught within that stern ideological frame.[53]

As an accepted figure of the courtly lyric, the nightingale is central to both poems, set first against the vulgar love of the churlish cuckoo in Clanvowe's poem, and then against the insubstantial and showy playfulness of the goldfinch in *The Floure and the Leaf.* Language itself falls into conflicting patterns related to class in the comic debate of the first poem and the subjectivity of the 'olde vnlusty' lover; in the second, however, the poem is delicately balanced within a consistent courtly discourse, its decorous narrator avoiding all hints of desire as she attempts to speak as an ideal: one recognizable as that articulated in earlier texts by the nightingale. Significantly the dreamer/protagonist of *The Cuckoo and the Nightingale* is an active masculine figure riven by opposing impulses, while that of *The Floure and the Leaf* is a passive feminine observer. Because of these differences in emphasis I shall discuss the poems in turn, seeing *The Cuckoo and the Nightingale* in terms of its relation to class and subjectivity, and *The Floure and the Leaf* in terms of issues of gender and interiority.

The Subjectivity of Class: The Cuckoo and the Nightingale

Even without reference to the wider context of the issues considered in 'The Knight's Tale', the opening couplet of *The Cuckoo and the Nightingale* indicates the poem's interest in the nature of power and its relation to the individual. The god of love is represented as an absolute lord with power over 'everich herte', a power defined in the following couplet as an ability to invert accepted oppositions: 'For he can make of lowe hertys hie, / And highe lowe, and like for to die' (ll. 3-4). The experience of love thus confirms established social hierarchies by depicting disruption in terms of inversion. This indication of an interest in public values is reinforced by the exposition of formal and measured antitheses that takes up the next six stanzas—before the focus shifts to a genuinely disruptive personal voice, expressed through a confusion of tones and registers. Linguistically the narrator is neither 'hie' nor 'lowe', but both, and the lofty antitheses of the primary authoritative voice disappear with the advent of the narrator's self-depreciation and colloquial phrases. When these categories reappear, embodied in the emblematic quarrelling birds of the narrator's dream, their standing has been transformed from abstract universal principles to aspects of a complex self, articulated in the interaction of the voices of nightingale and cuckoo, voices defined through class affiliations with the 'gentil' and the 'churl' respectively. Thus from the very start of the poem, language provides the material—not just the means of expression—out of which authority and disruption, class and subjectivity arise and through which they are shown to be intimately connected.

My emphasis on the interaction of class, language and subjectivity is a very different approach to that taken in traditional evaluations of the poem which concentrate on its evocation of the country and its 'freshness'. C.S. Lewis provides a pertinent example of such analysis, assessing *The Cuckoo and the Nightingale* as 'a bird-debate of the familiar kind, written in an unusual rhyme scheme, and pleasantly full of country sights and sounds'.[54] This assessment looks to the debate at the centre of the poem, and disregards the frame, leaping over the introductory lines to normalize the text's relation to other debates and separating its formal textual innovation from a content seen to 'pleasantly' and simply reflect a real countryside. But where Lewis perceives repetition and security I see exploration and self-reflection: this is not a simple bird-debate but a dream poem in which the dreamer both drives off and takes the place of the cuckoo in the debate with the nightingale. The dreamer's internal conflict is mirrored in his contradictory words and actions. He is a figure who wishes to hear the nightingale but hears the cuckoo instead, who draws on folk proverbs rather than classical learning, who desires love but is fated to disappointment by his character and age: individual characteristics which all exclude him from the literary construction of the noble lover. The introduction of this figure, drawn to both nightingale and cuckoo rather than impartially standing back from the argument in judgment, or simply aligning himself with one of the figures—the roles of the narrators in *The Owl and the Nightingale* and 'The Thrush and the Nightingale' respectively—marks a major change in the debate, one which addresses the problems raised in the two clerk and nightingale poems, and uses the genre to investigate those aspects it seems designed to repress. And in all the cases so far what is consistently excluded from the abstract debate poem is the individual desire of the self which would disrupt the ideological conflict embodied in the emblematic birds. If the conflicting language registers in the opening stanzas of the poem enable the particularity of a subject to be presented through his speech (as a speaker), they also indicate the way that this same subject can be seen to come into being through structural changes within the poetic genre (as spoken).

As with *The Owl and the Nightingale,* I do not wish to get caught up in the critical debate as to which bird *wins* the dispute: for the purposes of this study, I am more concerned with the poem's exploration of ideology and textuality as implicated in the dreamer's subjectivity. So far this chapter has tended to concentrate on the class affiliations of cultural form, and specifically that of genre. It is a fruitful strategy when considering *The Cuckoo and the Nightingale* for, as I point out, the text draws consciously on these affiliations, and, as Lewis points out, it is written in a verse form unusual enough to draw attention to its own making. This literary self-consciousness—the dreaming poet-narrator emerging out of literary precedents and generic experimentation—mirrors the fractured loyalties and affiliations of the historical Clanvowe.[55] As a courtier he was an aristocrat who writes, a figure who therefore conflates the two oppositional identities explored in 'The Thrush and the Nightingale' in an attempt to negotiate the treacherous conditions of court life.[56]

In his essay on this very poem, Patterson points to the way that '[t]his expansion of literariness to include the court as a whole... helps to account for the pronounced generic shift in the literary system of fourteenth-century England,' going on to note that 'the literature of fashion produced within the court... was almost exclusively lyric'[57]—a genre that is intricately bound up, not with identity *per se*, but with the identity of a certain class.

The quotation from 'The Knight's Tale' consciously combines the identities of aristocrat and writer by the very fact that it summons up a narrative that investigates aristocratic ideology. That *The Cuckoo and the Nightingale* opens with a quotation from this text indicates that the poem emerges out of neither a 'natural' space that is a covert aristocratic code, nor those issues that the debate claims as its province—binary oppositions of a 'universal' application—but is engaged in critically considering the specific textual narratives and discourses that articulate those issues. The issue is debated on a large scale throughout *The Canterbury Tales* itself, where the noble ethos of 'The Knight's Tale' (which sees itself as a bulwark against incoherence/bestiality) is challenged by the very coherence and vitality of the narratives that follow it. As an introduction to a courtly poem, these lines thus gesture towards the literary, constructed quality of the ethical truths claimed by the aristocracy through the act of engaging with another text.

As in the earlier *querelles*, the issue is focused by discussion of the interpretation of the physical; but where the previous debates projected the disruption and reconstitution of a threatened aristocratic order onto the issue of women's chastity (and hence of the nature of their desire), because this text considers disruption within the narrator himself, the debate focuses on the *interpretation of desire itself*. The two coincide in the text's evocation of the idealized aesthetic world of the aristocratic lyric, and the simultaneous displacement of the old man within this setting. Incapable of either the heroic knightly gesture or the role of the virile courtly lover, at a stroke that which is repressed in narratives of chivalric ideology—'the individual subject in time and motion'[58]—becomes central.

Readings such as Lewis's actively repress this problematic subject by silencing his centrality within the debate. By concentrating on a nature perceived as non-ideological (i.e. accepting its presuppositions),and defining the bird-debate as a *divertimento*,[59] the hidden political aspects (never mind the sophistication and intelligence of at least part of its audience)[60] are silenced in the same moment. Yet Lewis's assessment of the poem-as-debate summons up the question of genre: categories and structures which are far from innocent of class implications. As I demonstrate above, in this poem the debate is complicated both structurally by its dream setting and by the self-reflection and self-questioning implied in the ideologically non-standard (Lollard) beliefs of its aristocratic author[61]—quite apart from the issue of the role of the courtier as a figure whose consciously constructed self-identity militated against the sense that an aristocratic identity should be 'naturally given'.[62] Though Patterson points to the passage attacking 'greete werryours... and of swyche folke me maken bookes and soonges and reeden and syngen of hem' in *The Two Ways* as an indication of Clanvowe's detachment from the 'more conventional chivalric attitudes associated with the anti-court party',[63] the very fact that Clanvowe chooses to refute chivalry indicates its significance. Confusion and self-questioning are inimical to an ideology that defines the private through an unremittingly public ideal, for chivalry 'stressed a collective or corporate self-definition and so ignored the merely personal or individual. It sought, as a code of behaviour, at every turn to foreclose self-reflection and critical distance.'[64]

'The Knight's Tale' is the perfect expression of the repressions involved in this 'corporate self-definition'. It is a curiously flat and quiet piece, obsessed with control, the natural world feared as the place of unregulated and therefore chaotic conflict; a deeply anxious text which lacks the melodious birdsong of lyric and romance. It thus provides a perfect external frame for the comic confusions of the old man and his subjective experience of desire as excessive, as fusing—not inverting—oppositions: 'Bothe hote and colde, an accesse euery day' (l. 39). Desire thus confuses established hierarchies by causing an oscillation between opposing positions, further demonstrated in the old man's awareness of both his desire and his lack of virility.

Examining the relation of chivalry to 'The Knight's Tale', Patterson investigates the public aspect of that ideology, the violent confrontations and battles through which desire is controlled lest it escape the ordering of the public lists and cause the chivalric subject to descend into fearful chaos as a 'cruel tygre' or 'wood leon'. Arcite is a solid chivalric subject, tossed about by impersonal forces that lead to his incomprehending extinction, tragic because purposeless. 'The Knight's Tale' thus reveals that honour and fame are arbitrary, that chivalry's ideological frame rests on incoherence which must not be questioned. But Patterson's comment that 'the economy of "The Knight's Tale", as of chivalry, is an oscillation between knowing and unknowing, between the simultaneous recognition and suppression of reality'[65] illuminates more than 'The Knight's Tale'. By evoking that text *The Cuckoo and the Nightingale* also engages in a debate with chivalry, but in this case the confusions emanate from within the dreamer, internalizing this same oscillation between 'the simultaneous recognition and suppression of reality'. It is a strategy that deflates the epic and tragic pretensions of the hero as mere textual strategies with little relation to the dreamer's experience. Without either an epic hero or the final closure of death, the confused protagonist may be comic, but his confusion also enables productive activity through self-reflection and self-parody: the narrator simultaneously dramatized as producer and product of the text, both poet and poem, just as he is both comic actor in, and substantial ground of, the debate.

Yet no class ideology merely constructs its own self-identity; part of its identity lies in its relation with its feminine other, part in its relationship with other orders. In this case the feminine is hidden within the class relationship between 'gentil' and 'churl', transformed into the symbolic disruption of desire—just as the issue of gender hid that of class in the economy of relationships within the thirteenth-century *querelle*. What is so interesting is that it is, yet again, the nightingale that provides the focus for the problem of subjective desire, allowing it to be investigated from an ideology that punitively represses it. In line with the subtle denigration involved in ascribing to subordinates those elements repressed within the dominant class-identity, her repressed aspects—the erotic associations of the oral tradition—are projected onto her opponent, the cuckoo. As I note above this playing out of stresses within aristocratic ideology appears in 'The Thrush and the Nightingale', in relation to the chastity of women; in this case, however, the focus lies on the interior of the class subject, rather than dramatizing a collective response to a group perceived as a threat. In both cases the more pressing problem (class/gender) is obscured by deflecting anxiety onto the less threatening element within the economy of relationships, but the issue here is further complicated with how those repressions are articulated through the (new) identity of the courtier. If chivalry represses the personal, individual desire, then this is what is projected onto the lower classes and confrontation with internal division avoided. Thus in the very moment that it introduces the desiring subject ('the subject in time and motion'), *The Cuckoo and the Nightingale* summons up the self-interest stigmatized as churlish and depicts internal conflict in class terms, both recognizing and denying it simultaneously.

The aristocratic nightingale provides the ideal against which deviation is measured, claiming the high moral ground by speaking of abstract 'honour and al gentilnesse' (l. 152), of 'worship' and 'ful ensured trust' (l. 153); similar terms to those employed by her thirteenth-century predecessor. Rigorously policing personal interest—if love may cause pain that is immaterial to its role in nurturing and civilizing human life—she thus rests entirely within the public arena. Where the nightingale is a chaste 'gentil' whose perception of love is a clear descendent of the non-physical physicality of thirteenth-century ideal femininity, the cuckoo is equally clearly wedded to the realist ethic associated with his clerkly forebear, rejecting the nightingale's ethos as an irrelevant abstraction. Yet though the arguments that the nightingale uses in support of love echo those of the thirteenth-century figure in relation to the place of women, those of the cuckoo—despite echoing the aggressive *mode* of his predecessor (the thrush)—do not repeat the same material. The cuckoo is interested only in the personal experience which he sees as 'truth', interpreting love as 'will' or lust. He sings of love in terms of individual experience, as leading to 'disese and heuynesse…and mony a grete seknesse' (l. 171)—words strikingly reminiscent of the opening stanzas of the poem where they describe unsatisfied desire. This nightingale's opponent is not a careerist clerk (a member of the aspiring literary class) but a restive churl; not merely a competing voice in the spring chorus but a bird associated on the one hand with the usurpation of another's birthplace, and, on the other, with cuckoldry and mockery, disrupting accepted pattern and law. The disparate identities of aristocrat and writer conflict within the narrator's self-perception—and in wider terms within the identity of the courtier—and yet again that desire is displaced onto a class opponent: the peasant.[66]

So far I have discussed the text in theoretical terms, without direct analysis of the poem, taking my material as given. I want now to look closely at the poem itself as part of an investigation of *how* these changes are effected within the text, a text which grows out of a reflection on the repression of the personal in chivalric ideology: that is, of the subjective human voice within that of the nightingale.

The opening lines of the poem do not merely summon up a fixed scheme by depicting the god of love as an absolute lord, they also repeat commonplaces about the effect of love in the courtly poetry associated with the nightingale. The poem thus opens, as does the *querelle*, by evoking the lyric. Literary conventions are followed in the expected disquisition on the effects of spring, and by the alignment of aristocrat with an emblematic reference to nature: for 'euery trewe, gentil herte fre' is stirred by love in May. An elegant recital of conventional spring restlessness follows, dramatically concluding: 'thus in May ben hertys set on fire, / And so they brenne forthe in grete distresse'.

These lines move from a rhetoric which rests on closure through its emphasis on the final rhyme word; one which climaxes in the near litany (ll. 31-35) of stanza seven in which every line opens with yet another addition to the might of love ('And of that... / And thereof... / And al for... / And thus... / And so...'). So far the poem speaks from within the abstract space of the aristocratic lyric and thus smoothly sets the scene for the introduction of a courtly lover. Yet the fact that the opening couplet is a quotation indicates the self-consciousness of this strategy. The text exists not in chivalric ideology but in the constructed narratives of that ideology and hence at one remove from its presuppositions. This is borne out by the comic shock—both to literary expectations and to the coherence of the ideology that they articulate—of the next few lines.

Control is suddenly lost and a sense of fluidity takes its place with verbs, spread out through the lines, taking over from the previously stressed nouns. Ornate mellifluous rhymes such as 'remembraunce'/'grevaunce', 'heuynesse'/'seknesse'/'distresse', or 'desyre'/'fire', are replaced by shorter, less exotic words: 'trewe-ly'/'vnlusty'/'I'; 'May'/'day'. As a change which marks a blurring of the boundary between the language of the courtly aesthetic and that of the everyday, it implicitly questions this separation and thus the values that such a separation enables to exist unquestioned.[67]

The shift in register is accompanied by bathos—the lordly narrator who deals in universal absolutes is replaced by a colloquial particular 'I', an 'olde and vnlusty' man lacking in dignity:

> I am so shaken with the feueres white,
> Of al this May yet slept I but a lyte;
> And also hit is vnlyke to me
> That eny herte shulde slepy be,
> In whom that love his firy dart wol smyte. (ll. 41-45)

The loose diction and odd bits of information recall Chaucer's dream narrators, non-aristocratic commentators, mock-innocently puzzled by events, caught up by powers beyond their control. The old man's cultural reference point is provided by a folk proverb— a sharp contrast to the rational knightly hero of a philosophic poem on the nature of love—and the pursuit of personal advantage:

> I thoght how louers had a tokenyng,
> And among hem hit was a comvne tale
> That hit were good to her the nyghtyngale
> Rather then the leude cuckkow syng… (ll. 49-50)

Yet immediately after displaying his superstition he chooses May the third (as Scattergood points out, a traditionally unlucky day) to try out his folk wisdom.[68] A pattern of 'oscillation between knowing and unknowing' is thus established, not just in terms of the representation of the subject but also through the invocation of contrasting genres and linguistic structures. As a strategy such juxtaposition works particularly well when the complex subject is inserted into an idealized aristocratic/lyric nature. The land he enters is harmonious and beautiful, and the description of the birds creeping out of 'her boures, / Ther as they had rested hem al nyght' (ll. 67-68) throws the narrator's restlessness into relief, their song reflecting an integrated society working together in leisured companionship:

> Somme songe loude, as they hadde playned,
> And somme in other maner voys yfeyned,
> And somme al out, with al the fulle throte. (ll. 73-75)

The emphasis on communal verbs indicates the social interplay of the birds' actions, and the courtly pursuits of dance and song: in sharp contrast with the isolation and passivity of the narrator, sitting alone by the river bank:

> They pruned hem, and made hem ryght gay,
> And davnseden, and lepten on the spray,
> And euermore two and two in fere... (ll. 76-78)

From an idealized external world, one in which realism is filtered through courtly decorum, the text turns to the inner world of the dream vision and its focus on the individual relation to desire. Thus the transgressive cuckoo of the dreamer's self-interest—that which drew him into the wood—speaks first, though it elicits a venomous denial from the dreamer himself:

> 'Now God,' quod I, 'that died vponn the croise,
> Yive sorrowe on the, and on thy foule voyse,
> For litel ioy haue I now of thy crie.' (ll. 93-95)

The dreamer instead wishes to associate himself with the lofty values of the nightingale yet he cannot speak her language. Trying to ingratiate himself with an over-familiar greeting, he is out of place in this abstract world, his words characterizing him as a clumsy intruder more like the mocking cuckoo:

> 'A! good nyghtyngale,' quod I then,
> 'A lytell hast thou be to longe hen.' (ll. 101-102)

The fact that neither bird replies when addressed increases the impression of his ineffectuality: he appears a powerless spectator at a debate taking place between emblematic aspects of his own self, a subject constituted by a conflictual class ideology. If his unwilling self-interest (qualified as lower class) speaking through the cuckoo, is defined by its unwelcome activity, the response of both the nightingale—of the fixed aristocratic ideal to which he aspires—and the dreamer is to try to eject the intruder from the lyric space which is her domain. Thus, as in both *Owl and the Nightingale* and 'The Thrush and the Nightingale', the nightingale 'bigon the speche' by attempting to make her opponent move to a different space:

'Now, good cukkow, go somme where thy wey' (*C&N*, l. 112)
'Vnwipt!' ho sede, 'awei thu flo!' (*O&N*, l. 33)
'Of londe ich wille the sende.' ('T&N', l. 84)

Like *his* predecessors the cuckoo answers with a blunt attack on the nightingale's person/self:

'What!' quoth he, 'what may the eyle now?' (l. 116)

The nightingale wishes to kill or burn anyone who opposes her (just as the narrator wishes to treat the cuckoo); the cuckoo responds abruptly and personally (as does the narrator): the birds' responses thus dramatize opposing impulses within the dreamer's mind, invoking the struggle between the classes as its explicatory paradigm. The cuckoo speaks of experience, echoing the realist concerns of the earlier thrush and accuses the nightingale of manipulating 'truth' through symbols (ll. 121-25); she omits personal experience to focus on the ideal, assessing those who refuse to 'serve' the god of love as unworthy to live (ll. 133-34). Yet the internalization of class conflict *within* the dreamer has the effect of blurring the division of groups of individuals into mutually exclusive classes: instead of revealing an abstract 'truth' about women (as 'The Thrush and the Nightingale' claims to do) the figure of the dreamer relates the 'truth' about desire to class position. Despite the impression of the dreamer's ineffectuality as a passive being constructed out of conflicting class discourses, his status as an active writer, creating the dream-text which *contains* these speaking figures and shaping the text out of the interplay of their representative voices, exceeds the individual discourses to assert a subjective complexity beyond either class position.

Like Lewis, many critics do not appear to address the complexity of the dreamer, but instead concentrate on attempts to decode the emblematic significance of the two birds. Yet this approach leads—through default—to an alignment with the ideology that the text as a whole implicitly questions by demonstrating their partial nature. Learned discussions which characterize the nightingale as a religious figure set against a secular opponent[69] accept the aristocratic equation of chivalry with virtue: the argument, in other words, of the nightingale. Those that seek to define the cuckoo as the voice of common-sense faced by fanatical idealism[70] subscribe to the same view, equating the cuckoo with

realism, the nightingale with the ideal. What varies is the value
assigned to the ideal, for these interpretations are two sides of the
same coin. For an ideological insistence on refined love and virtue, on public morality, has another side: the ferocious repression
of transgressors, whether from the outside—figuratively in the
churlish cuckoo, in actuality in the contemporary peasants' re-
volts—or from within—as in the old man's violent rejection of his
own desiring nature, espousing the chivalric insistence on the
ideal at the expense of the personal.

The power politics of the class structure underlying the ex-
changes are masked (again as in 'The Thrush and the Nightingale') by the femininity of the nightingale. Despite her violence
towards those who reject love (ll. 127-35), she assumes the role of
the innocent victim, breaking her heart in the face of a rough
misogynous world. Far from indicating the victory of the cuckoo[71]
who supposedly silences his opponent, it marks the figurative
nightingale's retreat into the cover of class and gender. It is a role
that prompts a protective response from the dreamer who sees
himself in her portrait of the aristocratic lover:

> 'For in this worlde is noon so good seruise
> To euery wight that gentil ys of kynde.' (ll. 149-50)

The debate turns on the interpretation of the word 'seruice'. For
the nightingale and the companionate birds of the lyrical wood, it
is semi-religious, both source and root ('rote' l. 71) of virtue, an
idealized form of feudal relations. In contrast, the churlish cuckoo sees it in realistic terms as a servitude imposed from without,
('an office of dispaire', l. 176); his rejection thus smacks of class
revolt. When he sings of personal betrayal and cuckoldry he
undermines the very basis of the aristocratic code of honour,
servitude and chastity. His speech reduces these terms to mere
words, stripping them of their status as indices of moral superiority, and thus questions any intrinsic difference between the two
birds:

> 'Yf thou be fer or longe fro thi make,
> Thou shalt be as other that be forsake,
> And then shalt thou hoten as do I.' (ll. 183-85)

When he attacks the irrational court of the god of love where 'ful selde trouthe avayleth, / So dyuerse and so wilful ys he' (ll. 204-205), the cuckoo's argument mirrors that of the thirteenth-century thrush. Yet again reason is associated with a restive lower class, with realism and with a despoiling masculinity: all set against a feminine figure of privilege and non-rationality, claiming religious virtues as her 'natural' province.

These then are the figures at the centre of the poem, crystallizations of the debate registered in the opening lines' concern with 'hie' and 'lowe hertys' and in the contrasting patterns of language allocated to the courtly opening and the confused old man whose subjectivity comes to dominate the whole poem. This fact disallows the possibility of considering 'hie' and 'lowe' as the unqualified and mutually exclusive terms they appear to be in earlier debates—aesthetically complicated by the literary frames and voices through which they reach the reader these figures shift into positions of relativity rather than functioning as abstract principles. The old man's complexity is mirrored in and further encourages the reader's complex response. The reader is caught subjectively by the sympathetic figure of the narrator, and delights in the contrasts and patterns of the text: the sophisticated construction of the natural world is delightful precisely because it is *recognizable* as a construction, as a literary text. In both cases the pleasure is rooted in excess, a subjective response which takes place beyond the confirmatory inversions of courtly love allowable within the aristocratic code, and shares in the old man's subjective desire ('Bothe hote and colde, an accesse euery day', l. 39).

What is constructed is a new economy of textual relationships, outside those controlled by a class ideology, constructed out of desire, not for a single other—for that desire is filtered and interpreted differently according to class or to the conflicts within the self—but for otherness itself. The literary space thus emerges out of this desire that spills over the margins of the class ideology. Like both the narrator's and the reader's subjectivities, this space is constructed out of conflict within an ideological system, reincorporating elements originally repressed within its class identity by being projected onto class enemies: a strategy that allows the initial frame to be exceeded. As both written in, and writer of, the dream-text, the dreamer thus functions as a figure for the literary itself, a place—as Patterson points out—of 'ideological opposition', one that grows out of and challenges the fixed scheme registered in the abstract summary of the nature and extent of power exercised by the abstract and absolute god of love:

> Shortely, al that euere he wol he may,
> Ayenst him ther dar no wight say nay;
> For he can glade and greve whom him lyketh,
> And who that he wol he laugheth or he siketh,
> And most his myght he sheweth euer in May. (ll. 16-20)

The fact that the dreamer enters the debate thus indicates the entry of the literary space into that of class ideology, one that takes place through a complex mixture of churlishness and chivalry, of the self-interest within the selfless—and that thus questions the relation between these elements. Though attempting to align himself with the nightingale, the entry into the debate of the old man does not—cannot—resolve the dispute in her favour. He brings the complexity of the human world with its changes and compromises into the abstract space of the emblematic debate, so his entry fundamentally changes the ground of the argument, bringing his will into collision with the individual figures debating within him. If by attempting to replace the invincible lord in response to the nightingale's plea for help, he becomes a comic substitute, betraying his cherle's nature by throwing stones instead of shooting arrows,[72] he shows himself to be not a mere spectator at the debate, one to be ignored, but one with an individual input which extends the poem—in terms of both its events and its scope—and thus creates a wholly different text to that of the earlier debate.

In this supplementary ground, that of the dreamer's subjectivity, the cuckoo's materialism reappears through the old man's words which unconsciously betray his own concern with self and gain. He considers himself 'euel apayed' on hearing the cuckoo's song; 'ryght wel apayed' by the nightingale's promise to sing for him. Effectively arguing against himself, against a faith in aristocratic ideals, he half-takes the cuckoo's part because his experience of the god of love, of desire, is that 'he doth me mekill wo' (l. 240). The nightingale's response is to defer to emblematic abstractions, the values of a closed ideological system which escape a rational analysis from outside their arbitrary boundaries. In an attempt to regain lost ground she directs the old man to the 'fresshe flour daysye', a reference to both the courtly cult of the daisy,[73] and the Virgin; thus towards public virtues and a concomitant denial of the self.

The act of writing cannot help but record the conflicts within the ideological system in the moment that it articulates those within the self. Though the nightingale is given the dominant voice in this debate she is undercut by the self-interest implied by the written text itself, become an object within the economy of the poem as a whole. Her gesture towards the daisy thus indicates a temptation offered to a vacillating and uncertain subject, pandering to his vanity in a promise to sing one of his songs. It is a promise that associates 'virtuous' behaviour with hidden egotism: a mixture of motives that undermines her solidity as an abstract principle *outside* the self as much as does the revelation that she is one aspect of a conflictual subjectivity—and, like the poet-dreamer, a singer.

The nightingale is far more than a transparent class signifier. In the academic *Owl and the Nightingale* debate, her status is intimately bound up with devotional lyrics, and though rejecting the self-assertion of the clerical writing subject in 'The Thrush and the Nightingale,' she remains strongly associated with the space of the lyric. She is therefore (and, as a figurative voice from the boundaries of the political, all my work so far has pointed in this direction) a *literary* figure who must inescapably summon up the literary even as it is denied. The ambiguity of the aristocracy's appropriation of the erotic nightingale from oral literature as a figure that denies desire is repeated in the ambiguity of an aristocratic literary figure employed to deny the literary. The double repression of self—through denied desire and denied writing—is caught in the same figure: that of the aristocratic nightingale, which both marks and polices her own double transgression.

Both Skeat and Spearing have the nightingale singing one of her own ('my') songs in honour of the narrator, while Scattergood's edition shows her singing one of his ('thy') songs (l. 250). But if the nightingale is an aspect of the dreamer, the distinction between the two possessives dissolves; the nightingale is no longer a figure in her own right. This is beautifully illustrated in the audacious contrast between the opening and closing lines of the text. Where the poem opens with a quotation from 'The Knight's

Tale', it closes with the nightingale singing a song which wakes the dreamer. Though it is not directly associated with the dreamer in the text, the implication is that the distinction between the aesthetic and the real has dissolved with this singing and therefore that the song may well be one of the dreamer's. The literary space marks a crack opening within the authority ascribed to the aristocratic speaker, for it is taken from another poet's text, one which itself gestures towards a questioning interplay of voices— and hence not to an impenetrable ideology. And out of that crack appears an individual voice, at once at the heart of the debate within the dream within the poem, *and* emanating from wholly outside its aesthetic frame(s) by referring to songs written by Clanvowe himself (1. 250; possibly 1. 289). Simultaneously what appears in this crack is the reader's delighted recognition of— and identification with—that individual voice and its traversal of ideological boundaries. In the earlier debates the reader's emotional identification is invoked by the feminine/aristocratic nightingale, who claims the abstract virtues embodied in the Virgin. Though the nightingale in this poem retains these associations with virtue, they remain *abstract* claims on the reader's emotions; the sympathetic human figure of the confused old man—a victim, like the reader, of conflicting forces both within and without his desiring heart—is far more seductive. As in no other debate it is thus the problematic voicing of the subject and of the subjective that provides the focus of this poem; the ground of both its construction and its readerly pleasure. Though this voicing is intimately bound up with the act of writing and its own relation to other literary texts, its literary quality allows for individual contributions to exceed those given texts, to create new ground. The poem's other title, *The Boke of Cupid,* by summoning up the act of writing thus becomes itself a reflection on the relation of personal experience to an impersonal courtly naming: between the stress on 'boke' and that on a courtly 'Cupid'.

Though this analysis could stop at this point, seeming to divorce the subject from the prohibitions of an ideology it exceeds through the act of writing, to do so would lead to a simplification of the issue. The fact that the debate takes place within the lyrical space defined by aristocratic ideology, and utilizes its pre-eminent singer, the nightingale, means that the relationship between the subject and the social is already determined under the dominant ideology; defining both the terms within which the conflict takes place and those of its resolution. Because of this the dream concludes with an alliance between the marginalized lover and the nightingale: the former accepting the latter's arguments—against self-interest and for the choice of symbol (the daisy) over reality— and sublimating his restless desire by composing the poetic text. Writing serves in part as a substitute for desire. Expressing a 'disunified self'[74] reaching towards an impossible unity, it is 'at once the means of communication and the barrier that impedes it, a gesture towards the intensity and singularity of feeling that generates it but which it can never finally encompass'.[75] The dreamer's acceptance of the substitute daisy has wider implications than the production of the particular text.

Primarily, the dreamer is enabled to speak within a social frame, illustrated in the depiction of the companionate birds of the lyric wood, and developed in the suggestion that they will come together in communal, rather than individual, judgment after the poem's conclusion. The reference to the Queen as ultimate arbiter of the debate may be a fitting compliment to a Queen who was known to support the Lollards,[76] but figuratively it serves a different function: confirming the aristocratic nightingale's victory by presenting her symbolic human counterpart. The two resolutions of the debate—on the one hand, the communal decision at court, and, on the other, the problematic decision of the individual dreamer, who inscribes the text of the debate—indicates an uneasy amalgam of positions.

Secondly, what the dreamer and the nightingale have in common—and which allows the uneasy resolution of their two positions—is their shared appropriation of the feminine in emblematic terms: the literary figure of the aristocratic nightingale.

The irrational violence with which chivalry polices transgressors of its mores can be explained by this last point. At root the aristocracy's class position and claims to a 'natural' superiority through birth are built on violence, and violence lies behind the mystifications of idealized virtues in an aggressive symbol such as the nightingale. Equally, when the lover of *The Cuckoo and the Nightingale* is led to sublimate a desire for his feminine other—the sexual love that awakens in spring—into the textual delight of writing, this feminine other is translated into the symbol, into the nightingale. As in 'The Thrush and the Nightingale', the emblem serves to deflect physical desire into the non-physical. Thus in both ideology and text the appropriation (and hence denial) of the feminine space is a strategy which enables power to remain—in ideological and in creative terms—the province of the masculine subject.

The fact that the writing subject and the chivalric subject jointly deny the feminine in this way is unsurprising: at the least a subjectivity conceived in terms of class conflict must replicate the repressions of its ideological paradigm.[77] What is more revealing is the function of the poetic nightingale in associating the two positions, not only in literature reaching back to the Greeks, but continuing in that produced by a culture rooted in the humanist subject.[78] Patterson's conclusion that court writing 'generates a mode of writing that comes to constitute, for much of English literary history, literature itself'[79] makes precisely this point—though he does not comment on the significance of the nightingale. In his concentration on the dreamer as a separate figure from the nightingale Patterson shows his concern with a solid subject—even if riven with opposing and incommensurable desires—with writing as an impossible attempt to communicate the intensity within. In this he too silences the feminine, both in this text and in the wider formation of the literary. I quote extensively from the summarizing comments of his otherwise splendid essay:

> Court poetry incorporates a set of irresolvable antimonies: interest and disinterest, work and play, the desire to transcend the social context and the unavoidable need to recuperate and refigure it... It...entails a mobile disunified self capable of assuming a variety of incommensurate subject positions. And it deploys a language not only laden with rhetorical tropes and topoi but capable of understanding its own rhetoricity—a language located, in Paul de Man's phrase, 'in the void of...difference'.[80]

Assuming the masculinity of the courtly writer,[81] he looks to the court as the site for 'the development of literary discourse *per se*'. This seems borne out by the figure of the nightingale. Repeatedly turning up in romantic and lyric poetry, the nightingale can be seen to trace the interaction of concepts of the natural with a sublimated femininity: one which denies the feminine as the very ground on which the aesthetic is simultaneously constructed and allowed a space of ideological opposition.

Though the difficulty of aligning conflicting group identities— here aristocrat, writer, courtier and Lollard—within the speaking or writing subject appears to be resolved in this text, the ground of its fragile resolution obviously creates additional and continuing problems for the *female* subject who writes. It is not just that writing is associated with desire (though it clearly is) but that the space of opposition, of textuality, shares the denial of the feminine that underlies the rigidity of the system it questions. In my final chapter I shall concentrate on the particular problems of a woman writing within the tradition built around this shared denial of the feminine by looking at the writings of the Victorian poet, Elizabeth Barrett Browning, and focusing on the significance of her powerful and claustrophobic rejection of nightingales.

Yet the figure of the nightingale suggests other possibilities, other ways of questioning the political paradigm. The example I wish to use is that of Shelley, to whom, and clearly based on ancient precedent, 'the poet is a nightingale'.[82] Shelley's textual practice avoids clear definitions, and is characterized by fluidity and slippage between inner and outer worlds, by an interest in relationships between elements rather than abrupt closure. Once disparagingly qualified as 'effeminate',[83] more recently as 'narcissistic',[84] such accusations have caused difficulty for those critics primarily interested in Shelley's politics, who consider them as tantamount to accusing him of insubstantiality, and much prefer to stress his radical rejection of inherited class and power structures.[85] Yet, as this chapter seeks to demonstrate, texts such as *The Cuckoo and the Nightingale* associate the politics of 'literature' with the denial of the feminine. In relation to Shelley it is counterproductive to divide attention between writing subject and political content, for the two aspects are interconnected: Shelley's radicalism is in part enabled by a conception of the writing subject which espouses elements repressed within the political paradigm and which thus leads towards what is usually conceptualized as 'feminine'. Yet again gender interacts with class but here its separation and ascendancy indicates a revolt against dominant power structures. Shelley's 'interfluous' nightingale is set against both materialism and violence.[86] But this is not a figure 'created' by Shelley but one with roots that are as traceable to the late medieval court as is the fractured and self-aware poet-dreamer of *The Cuckoo and the Nightingale,* though very differently conceived. The final part of this chapter thus discusses a poem in which this alternative reading of the nightingale and its alternative representation of the literary act appears. It is the early fifteenth-century *The Floure and the Leaf,* a text whose author combined the identities of aristocrat, writer and, significantly, woman. Her text expresses values in conflict with the aristocratic ideology she attempts to support, and is more concerned with the depiction of harmonious gesture and image—the role allocated to the feminine—than with contrasting discourse. Because of this the text risks dissolution (to rephrase de Man) 'in the void... of difference';[87] attempting to speak as a feminine chivalric subject, as a non-physical physical being, she risks the insubstantiality that haunts a lack of clear definition—and this insubstantiality serves as her courtly opponent. It is a text in which yet again the aristocratic nightingale, intricately associated with nature, femininity, desire and the literary, is unavoidably implicated.

Unlike *The Cuckoo and the Nightingale* with its old lover's disruptive and comic self-depreciation, *The Floure and the Leaf* is poised and well-bred, clearly located in the courtly circle. Its self-reflection is not a divisive experience rooted in an originally wholeness, but a healing one in which the narrator attempts to harmonize dissonance. *The Floure and the Leaf* is far more interested in the relationships between its contrasting elements than in the possibility of victory or truth of one of them. Its two elements are contrasting companies presented sequentially, rather than individual figures embroiled in interactive dispute. It refuses the earlier's text's division into fractured and unbalanced interior and exterior worlds, in conflict with each other and only resolved through a shared reduction of the feminine elements to the emblematic. Existing in an unchallenged aristocratic world, the class conflict of *The Cuckoo and the Nightingale,* which provided the paradigm of its construction of subjectivity, is absent: in *The Floure and the Leaf* there is no attempt to represent lower class figures either in their own right or as competitors (the servants are merely ancillary to the knights, part of the construction of *their* identity as leaders).

Structurally *The Floure and the Leaf* moves from the restless inner space of its aristocratic subject to the social space outside (the dream-vision that dominates the centre of the poem takes place outside the narrator), and juxtaposes contrasting companies of aristocrats rather than individual interacting figures. But since there is neither a clear image of the outer world as a political entity, nor, without that, one of the individual subject either, both facets are blurred and uncertain. In search of healing and harmony, the poem attempts to deny the conflict at the heart of the debate form itself. Where Clanvowe emphasized discontinuities, this text stresses integration; attempting to accept unquestioningly the characteristic aestheticization of the aristocratic life produces a new fear: that chivalric elegance may not only be a construction but no more than a glittering facade, that the elegant signifier may have no referent. The text's unspoken anxiety is thus of a lack of substance and place, replicating the displaced condition of the feminine in both chivalric ideology and writing. The narrator of *The Floure and the Leaf* is doubly displaced: there is no way that she can find any solid reference between social/ political 'reality' in which she is denied being and the aesthetic text which she is actively creating using values denied in the political arena. Her resolution of this problem—unlike that of Clanvowe—is thus to separate these two areas, these two identities, within the text. She rejects politics for an aesthetic self-reflection, thus unconsciously creating an arena in which the political world can be opposed, creating a text judged from a masculine perspective as feminine, narcissistic or insubstantial.

The Floure and the Leaf avoids not only conflict but the structure of argument that creates a rational/intellectual reader, assessing the arguments of the opposing sides to achieve 'truth' defined as reason. Its separation of the political from the aesthetic leads it towards the aristocratic emblem, emphasizing the surface at the expense of the interior, rejecting the intellectual as outside its province. In this poem, the subject does not fear fragmentation from within, but collapse into insubstantiality; so much so indeed that the Flower company, and the goldfinch are denied separate being and incorporated into the company of the Leaf (the nightingale) by the conclusion of the poem. Yet though the narrator verbally aligns herself with that company, she returns home alone to write. Thus if the former poem voices division and its attendant fear of divisiveness—the hidden desire for wholeness which is expressed in the alliance between the nightingale and the narrator—then the latter voices wholeness and its attendant fear of sameness—the hidden desire for meaningful division expressed in the final separation of the nightingale and the narrator.

Masculinity is defined through conflict in *The Floure and the Leaf*, while femininity is defined by gentleness and harmony. The text's 'feminine' qualities thus turn it—despite its attempts to align itself with a class ideology stabilized through its appropriation and repression of the feminine—into a text which cannot help but subvert that which it espouses. It is therefore significant that *The Floure and the Leaf*, popular for centuries, should fall from critical grace during a period in which violent conflict—that which the poem refuses—was the dominant mode of understanding both class relations and the natural world.[88] It is equally significant that Elizabeth Barrett Browning adapted the poem as a childhood dream of freedom in 'The Lost Bower' (*Poems*, 1844).[89]

Quiet and Feminine Transgressions: The Floure and the Leaf

So far I have avoided entering those critical disputes which appear irrelevant to the form of my interest in the nightingale. In the case of *The Floure and the Leaf*, however, the standards by which the poem was judged in the Victorian period clearly relate to an insistence on conflict, a need for self-determination; indirectly therefore to issues I consider central to the text and to the questions it raises about the implications of the literary/aristocratic figure of the nightingale. The sudden demise of the poem's critical fortunes illuminates the wider issue of the relation of the literary text to political ideology. Patterson has pointed out that the perception of medieval literature as the native 'classics' emerged with the extension of the electorate during the nineteenth century as part of an attempt to forge a national identity which accommodated the new voters. He sees this new interest in the 'medieval' as a fertile site of ideological conflict during the period; one drawn on by opposing camps to express or to question current values of nationalism and imperialism.[90]

In 1868 the popularity of *The Floure and the Leaf* was such that it furnished subjects for the Chaucer window in Westminster Abbey: the concrete expression of the ruling classes' transformation of great writers into national heritage. Yet within two years it was expelled from the canon and thirty years later relegated to mere 'prettiness' by the medievalists. From being considered as 'one of the finest parts of Chaucer'[91] to be dismissed as 'tinsel'[92]—the change is so striking that it raises unavoidable questions about what the Victorians looked for in medieval literature. As always, value judgments are self-revealing. If *The Floure and the Leaf* fears a lack of place and substance, through the fear of emptiness at the heart of its own beauty, an insubstantiality embodied in the company of the Flower, then that danger, that emptiness was current in the Victorian period:[93] it was one of the reasons that writers and artists—like Elizabeth Barrett Browning, the Pre-Raphaelites, John Ruskin—looked to the medieval past, seeking a world of definition and certainty. *The Floure and the Leaf* does the opposite, both in the conflict between the Leaf (nightingale) company and its weaker clone, the Flower (goldfinch) company, and in its refusal to espouse, in terms of textual strategy, the penetration and power that characterize what is seen as a solid and dependable: a 'realistic' world. Alert to the threat of collapsing national coherence, one rooted in extensive political changes but reconfigured as a moral crisis (the very problem articulated through *The Floure and the Leaf*), Victorian medievalists unconsciously rejected the poem's *implications*: wishing for transparency, they confuse its subject matter with its substance. Their condemnations have lasted into the violent modern world. Two examples suffice: Walter Skeat condescendingly allows it a 'flashy attractiveness'; C.S. Lewis genially pats an empty-headed 'authoress' on the head:

> If she cannot claim wisdom, she has a great deal of good sense and good humour, and is guided by them to write a poem more original than she herself, perhaps, suspected... She describes what interests her, selecting rather by temperament than by art; and she finds considerable difficulty in getting the right number of syllables into each line.[94]

What Lewis misses in *The Floure and the Leafe* is a sense of control, of virility, the penetrating vigour of *The Canterbury Tales*, the allegory of *Le Roman de la Rose*, or the questing of *Gawain and the Grene Knight.* His dismissal of *The Floure and the Leaf* rests on a rejection of what he sees to be its social milieu: 'comfortably circumstanced people of good breeding and goodwill'[95]—people rather too much like himself.[96] But this is exactly what the poem depicts: the domestic side of chivalry, where noble ferocity is an aesthetic game and no one gets killed—and where the whole chivalric enterprise risks meaninglessness through similitude. In love with a medieval world of noble conflict, Lewis, of course, *needs* it to have meaning. He decries the absence of the 'fierce monotony, the unreal black and white' of the medieval pulpit and its contemporary allegorical poetry, and dismisses the poem because it fails to differentiate Virtue and Vice sufficiently. His rejection of the poem thus rests on its emphasis on integration, an emphasis he sees as a moral failing.

Both *The Cuckoo and the Nightingale* and *The Floure and the Leaf* depict an individual's relation to the mores of an aristocratic court—conveyed in both cases by the figure of the nightingale—through texts which declare themselves as literary by evoking Chaucerian pretexts. In both the literary act is associated with the symbolic time of desire (the month of May), when an unspecified restlessness drives the narrator into the emblematic natural world. Yet from this starting point the two texts express increasingly divergent paths: in *The Cuckoo and the Nightingale* the narrator's restlessness is acknowledged as frustrated erotic desire; in *The Floure and the Leaf* the paradigm of erotic desire is supplanted by an equally powerful desire for incorporation into a harmonious whole: in neither text is the desire fulfilled. Where Clanvowe creates an assured comic dream vision, full of spontaneous actions and verbal quarrelling, *The Floure and the Leaf* conducts its arguments through a procession of images represented in spatial terms. The emphasis on images and visualized scenes is emblematic and appears at every level of the text. The individual significance of the goldfinch and nightingale, for example, is comprehensible allegorically through their imaged actions (eating the buds and flowers of the medlar tree; singing in the laurel)[97] and indirectly when they are depicted flying to the wrists of the ladies who lead the two companies: unlike the birds of earlier debates they are not given a thinking interior, they do not *speak*.

Despite the allegorical significance ascribed to the separate

figures within the text which presents them as opposing or alternative values, there are not striking differences between the nightingale and the goldfinch, the Flower company and that of the
Leaf. This is why Lewis scathingly remarks that in the poem 'the
Virtues ask the Vices to a picnic'.[98] Yet interrogated rather than
sneered at, the absence of a sharp difference between the two
aristocratic companies highlights both the difficulty and the significance of defining clear and separate identities. I want to discuss the poem in two ways: first in terms of the narrator's problematic relation to a chivalric identity which insistently 'stressed a
collective or corporate self-definition',[99] and then in relation to
the kind of writing that emerges out of a process emphasizing
coherence rather than conflict. This division follows the strategy
of the poem by separating the subjective (the writing) from its
political/class paradigm. Both approaches rest on a recognition
of the text's emphasis on harmony and coherence, equally
qualified as 'feminine' but according very different values to the
two arenas of the political and the subjective.

In discussing the dreamer's frustrated desire in *The Cuckoo and
the Nightingale* I have already considered the masculine subject's
difficulties—overcome through an alliance with the nightingale
and a joint repression of the feminine. For the female chivalric
writer, the problem is more acute. Her class identity, her gentility,
rests on the values of integration and harmony, on self-effacement: the denial of desire expressed emblematically in the chastity of the nightingale and the unobtrusive daisy. Her text thus
avoids the class divisions and conflict of the political world,
choosing instead the emblematic nightingale—feminine, natural,
an aristocratic figure of silenced desire and a literary trope—
declaring itself as 'natural', non-ideological. But the rejection of
any overt conflict turns the debate inwards and risks questions as
to what *constitutes* the difference between the two companies: the
fact that the Lady of the Leaf can effectively 'rescue' the troop of
the Flower indicates that there is no rigid or intrinsic difference
between the two. The aesthetic is sought as a refuge from the
ideological but the distinction cannot be maintained. Like *The
Cuckoo and the Nightingale, The Floure and the Leaf* opens with a
literary reference—declaring itself as a literary text engaging in
debate with other texts—and closes with a reference to writing:

this time unquestioningly the narrator's own. Unlike Clanvowe this activity is seen as a solitary pursuit and is not associated with the nightingale.

Though the opening passage of 'The General Prologue' provides *The Floure and the Leaf* with a specific *literary* paradigm—and hence figures an attempted flight from politics—the fact that its ideological subtext expresses desire creates supplementary difficulties which the later poem attempts to neutralize. The difference between the two openings indicates where the problems lie. Chaucer's stunning *Natureingang* overcomes the ideological problems of the aristocratic space for the clerk/writer at a stroke. The simple imposition of a deductive logical frame onto the lyric description contains the natural space within rational analysis, while its aristocratic abstractions are extended to include clerical concerns: astronomy (expressed in classical/literary terms) and religion. This 'natural' space is not a static one, not a statement which *places* the text within a particular class ideology which must be defended, but a complex world, a space, most interestingly, which is traversed by undifferentiated human figures ('folk'). It is a place defined by dispersed and reciprocated human (not natural) activity: pilgrimage, seeking and being healed; an economy of exchange. Though situated in the abstract space denoted by nature and the symbolic moment of May, it also operates in relation to named (real) places and individuals (Canterbury; the martyr, Thomas à Beckett) which draw it into a specific history of change and struggle. Chaucer's *Natureingang* then is far from being a traditional aristocratic opening: rather than adapting the trope—or omitting it altogether—he penetrates its heart, employing a vocabulary which displays an interest in interiors that characterizes his entire complex and interwoven text of voices. His figurative penetration is carried through into his treatment of the procession of types—a medieval trope which also appears in *The Floure and the Leaf*—who pass through that May landscape. Though qualified by profession rather than name, the types are penetrated and given voices[100] that allow them to enter into debate with both the bumbling narrator and the engaged reader. Though this is strongly reminiscent of Clanvowe, Chaucer goes one better by making his procession of speaking emblems enter after his narrator wakes up, *not* when he falls asleep.

In sharp contrast the opening passage of *The Floure and the Leaf* is striking in its total censorship of all expressions of desire and its avoidance of any individualized comment. Yet the avoidance of desire indicates an effacement of both self and the specific other by which self is defined. What is left is unfocused: an opening that slowly wells up out of the unchallenged linguistic register of courtly speech; an expression in which the narrator submerges her personal response in the indefinite pronouns of an undifferentiated community; a concern with spatial and visual imagery; an emphasis on wonder and softness rather than vigour and questioning. The transgressive act of writing is used here, almost against itself, to reinforce the qualities of chastity and stillness demanded of the courtly lady, expressed through its concentration on the pleasure of *image* in very beautiful, jewel-like pictures. Where Chaucer's text individualizes his characters through language, in this poem the only words heard within the two companies are parts of songs in a doggerel French, sung by the companies of ladies as they enact their group identity through the ritualized interweaving of the round dance.

Assessments of texts such as *The Floure and the Leaf* which omit politics and seek to connect its parts within an organic ('natural') whole seem to follow the poem's own model—accepting aesthetic closure in place of intellectual questioning. Derek Pearsall, for example, sees the text as adhering to the 'conventional pattern of spring setting followed by description of the garden'[101] without going into detail about the structure of such an opening, or considering its implications. More useful for my purposes is Rosamund Tuve's learned study of the influence of literary tradition on Middle English poetry,[102] which specifically compares these two spring openings, stressing Chaucer's direct links with the *Secreta Secretorum*, which meshed medieval humours with the elements and the seasons into a single formulation. She emphasizes the 'insatiable fecundity and generative power' of Chaucer's Nature as a semi-mythic force which seems to incorporate Venus (commenting that we should capitalize the 'Nature' that 'priketh ... in hir corages'). Yet she does not reflect on the value she ascribes to the penetration of Chaucer's writing, to his activity and expression of desire, elements absent in the later text.

Rapid and spontaneous movement is not a classless signifier: on the contrary it denotes a break (whether rash or decisive) in the pattern, and is thus a mark of individual volition. In medieval literature *all* movement is significant: after all a significant genre is the quest, where movement is translated directly into ethical terms. In relation to the aristocratic debates of this chapter alone, the nightingale is already in possession of her domain and her opponents are intruders to be expelled. The dissipation of energy in *The Floure and the Leaf*'s rewriting of 'The General Prologue' thus appears closely related to the text's rejection of both conflict and desire. Tuve's dismissal of *The Floure and the Leaf*—'merely a conventionalised list of the animals and plants renewed by Spring'[103]—is therefore very interesting. Not only does it appear to rest on an unquestioned preference for literary 'virility', but it also displays a clear antipathy to a text that denies conflict.

Tuve's discussion of the *Secreta Secretorum* provides a fascinating model for analysis. Illustrating her analysis with a wide range of examples, she divides the nature opening into rough but recognizable steps, moving from green meadows or woods and growing seeds, (step one), through to ripening summer corn (step seven). Birdsong comes second while the nightingale sings in the fifth section.[104] Though this is not by any means a conscious rule, as Tuve generously demonstrates, it remains overwhelmingly the pattern to which most of the poems adhere. Tuve's model enables radically different readings of the poem by making clear both what is *not* said and what *replaces* the not-said. In relation to *The Floure and the Leaf* the most important 'not-said' is the birdsong, for in the conventional *Natureingang* it is the inhuman voices of the birds calling to each other that express the desire projected onto the natural world and, by pointing up the unnatural isolation and silence of the poet, trigger his own entry, his own 'dark bird call',[105] into that liminal space.

Chaucer's *Prologue* transforms the conventional birdsong by linking it to human activity as a necessary stage in his logical argument ('Whan... Whan... Than...'):

> And smale fowles maken melodye,
> That slepen al the night with open yë,
> (So priketh hem nature in hir corages):
> Than longen folk to goon on pilgrimages. (ll. 9-12)[106]

'Melodye', disordered activity and desire come together in this text. In contrast *The Floure and the Leaf* poet, while retaining the deductive frame that introduces the desiring subject into the natural world ('When... When... So... That...so that...'), attempts to omit both inhuman melody and poetic desire. She leaves the birds outside the argument until the sixth stanza, and replaces the activity of Chaucer's sleepless (disordered) 'smale fowles' with the 'small flours' that spring 'here and there in field & in mede' (l. 9). The unnerving impression of the open-eyed desirous birds, intensely singing all night, is replaced by a unfocused image in which all energy is dispersed. This spring is neither disruptive nor traumatic; indeed it denies the closure of death itself—'So very good and wholsome be the shoures / That it renueth that was old and deede' (ll. 10-11)—a significant comment in that the two companies turn out to be ghosts.[107] Likewise, when the voices of the birds finally and briefly appear, distanced from these all-important first lines, they are described as healing rather than amorous, voicing connection rather than erotic disruption. Though their song does lead the narrator to listen for the nightingale, this hint of erotic desire is immediately controlled by being translated into a visual image: the overgrown path which leads to the bower—a natural space that echoes a human one ('a prety parlour'). Though the nightingale's expression of desire sets off motion away from the human, it only returns to the same space in a circular movement that effectively denies difference between the two.

Spring in *The Floure and the Leaf* takes place in a quiet and stable world of symbiotic sky and earth (with a comfortably seated and regal Phebus), whose rain does not erotically 'pierce' and 'engender' as in Chaucer but which

> ...discended [s]oft,
> Causing the ground, fele times and oft,
> Up for to give many an wholsome aire. (ll. 4-6)

Splitting, fragmenting, the piercing of desire: all these are notable in their absence. The scattered small flowers serve as emblems of continuity, opening out from seeds rather than from thrusting root and vein. What results is a peculiar stasis, a vacancy, a skating on an ornate beautiful surface. The narrator is peaceful: her world is still and quiet, her sleeplessness not that of the usual love-torn poet. She claims

> ... there nas earthly wight,
> As I suppose, had more hearts ease
> Then I, for I nad sicknesse nor disease. (ll. 19-21)

She passively registers the restlessness within her, without recognizing or questioning its cause. Though the significance and meaning of the two companies is 'explained' by the Leaf maiden at the end of the poem, this narrative restlessness is only explicable when she chooses to include herself in the company of the Leaf and the nightingale: an action which reveals an unspoken sense of dislocation and a need for stability and inclusion, a desire expressed throughout the poem through its emphasis on integration.[108]

Instead of seeing nature as separate, as other to herself, the narrator presents it as similar, not as a site of disorder but as one of order. Where 'every plaine was clothed faire', the narrator follows suit by pausing to 'put [on] my geare and mine array' before going out to walk among the oak trees. As I point out above, however, to harmonize the human and the natural in this way does not result in an unproblematic wholeness. If it did where would the disruption of the individual poetic voice fit in? It is significant that at the very point where the voices of desire traditionally sing, this text should place small flowers springing in emptiness. If desire marks the disruptive voice of the poem (and the poet's self-assertion) as a transgression of order, then its replacement by silence and dispersal marks not only repressed desire but an equivalent anxiety about an image and a voice which lack focus.

Earlier debates dramatize an academic desire for definition, their centres taken up with verbal disputes. But at the heart of this poem lies not words but an image of the open field outside the bower, an undifferentiated space which offers no shelter. Lacking the central focus of the laurel tree, there is no fixed place around which the company of the Flower can organize themselves and by which they can be protected, an *image* (rather than a dramatization) of the lack of differentiation within the company itself. The field of flowers thus in some sense represents a threat to the nightingale; not through the conflict of the debate (which helps define her aristocratic identity) but through a *lack* of conflict. The repression of desire throws up a new anxiety: the loss of meaning and difference. This is an alternative transgression, not that of the desiring subject which replicates the paradigm of class conflict and repression (as in *The Cuckoo and the Nightingale*), but one that refuses divisiveness—and hence risks dissolution. Though this is an anxiety that relates in particular to the female chivalric subject, it cannot be divorced from chivalry as a whole. Avoiding confrontation, it expresses the emptiness of a violent and irrational ideology when perceived from the peculiarly bodiless stance of its feminine subject.[109]

This bodilessness is recognizable in the narrator's description of the ordered grove of oaks she visits after dressing: each is 'streight as a line.../.../...and an eight foot or nine / Every tree well fro his fellow grew' (ll. 29-32). Yet again there is an emptiness, a lack of a central focus, an alignment between the narrator and the natural space. In line with its espousal of the emblematic, the text's unspoken desire (for the *fact* of the text registers a repressed desire) is expressed through spatial and visual imagery. Yet unfocused images can be read in contrasting ways: for the narrator (as a chivalric subject), they mark the danger of similarity, of a lack of definition and substance; on the level of the text (the literary), the emphasis on similarity between natural and the human becomes a textual strategy, integrating disparate elements into a harmonious whole.

In an unfocused world the reader—like the narrator drawn into understanding the world through visual images—unconsciously seeks visual stimulus. In this case it is provided by colour in the lovely description of the young oak leaves in sunlight:

> [They] sprongen out ayen the sonne shene,
> Some very red and some a glad light grene. (ll. 34-35)

There has been critical praise of these lines, centring on their 'naturalism'. Yet I think that this is very far from the point. Their beauty is a *literary* effect, rooted in textual relationships and reading practices rather than an objectively perceived nature: the red of real young oak leaves is insufficient to explain the enamel brightness these lines convey.

Again it is useful to go back to the structure and pattern of the *Natureingang*, and the aristocratic reduction of the natural to the emblematic. In the *Natureingang* colour itself is used emblematically: white and red paired to represent spring flowers, green for new leaves.[110] This spring opening is unusually subdued, with its empty fields and still meadows, colours being restricted to cool green and (implied) white. In visual terms, as well as in terms of the narrative complexity, the activity associated with Chaucer's text is missing. Thus the sudden starts of pure colour answer an unconscious need for difference, vibrating against the predominantly green background as complementary colours do. The use of colour thus both intensifies the reader's visual imagination and throws attention onto the visual, rather than the verbal, as the site of difference and meaning. And the association of visual pleasure with the narrative closure prefigured in the close of the stanza further links narrative signification to visual images rather than to events. It is a strategy perfectly in accord with an ideology that refuses rationality and questioning, that turns to the aesthetic as a category that excludes politics by reducing the natural to the surface of the emblem—the narrator herself functions in part as an emblematic wandering eye who records beautiful scenes without deciphering them.

This preference for the surface image rather than the interior, for the emblem rather than the actual, means that the allegorical figures of the flower and the leaf must be established before the potentially disruptive birdsong can be introduced. Yet if the reader is deflected by this strategy from an active search for rational/intellectual meaning, the problem of difference arises in another way. Depicted as parts of a harmonious pattern, there is very little to choose between the two emblems. There must be difference in order to stabilize meaning, and yet there must also be integration or differences will tear the text/company apart. Though there seems to be greater emphasis on the visual pleasure of the young leaves ('me thought was right a pleasaunt sight' l. 36), the overall impression of similarity blurs the distinction[111] and sets up another anxiety about the separation of the self. The slight suggestion of a *personal* opinion in relation to the leaves appears to prompt the narrator to listen to the birdsong: implicitly defining the self through the voicing of personal pleasure. But this suggestion is immediately dissipated through the use of an impersonal/indefinite pronoun:

And eke the briddes song for to here
Would have rejoised *any* earthly wight. (ll. 37-38, my italics)

As the narrator discovers a figure of her inner self in the small 'herber' the dissipation is translated into spatial terms. The individual subject is thus translated into a conventional literary trope, its momentary desire constrained in the figure of the healing (not amorous) rose tree, entwined with the sycamore around the private space of the bower:

> Wrethen in fere so wel and cunningly
> That every branch and leafe grew by mesure,
> Plain as a bord, of an height, by and by. (ll. 57-59)

By moving inside the hedge woven of flowers and leaves, the narrator enters the space behind the emblems which frame the poem: a space where two birds sing. But her movement within the emblematic does not reveal the complex conflictual interior of Clanvowe's dream world—in which abstract class positions are blurred in confusion—but an inner space which *mirrors* the outer world without difference, a doppelganger world which reflects the human, specifically aristocratic, directly: 'he that took the cure / It to make... did al his peine' (ll. 61-62) to shape the green space 'roofe and all, /... The hegge as thicke as a castel wall' (ll. 64, 66).

When *The Cuckoo and the Nightingale* moves inside the aristocratic version of nature it focuses on the confusions at its heart through the narrator's dream, and leaves the outer world to the margins of the poem. This text does the opposite, setting the aristocratic world at the very heart of the text, with the narrator's inner space providing its frame. Yet *The Floure and the Leaf* cannot be reduced to an inversion of *The Cuckoo and the Nightingale*, for where Clanvowe's debates disrupt the courtly harmonies of the companionate birds, these interior and exterior worlds are perfectly balanced. In this poem the narrator who sits within the arbour, gazing unseen at the companies without, is a single figure who does not interact with, nor have a counterpart in either space. Her significance is not related to her place (her class/gender position) but to her function as the voice which imposes shape and significance onto undifferentiated space; her closest counterpart within the poem is thus neither object nor competing subject, but a marker of difference: the hedge which is neither within nor without the arbour, which is associated with neither flower nor leaf but with the two growing together, a boundary that separates the two spaces and gives them meaning.

Neither pain nor disorder appears within the text, but the emphasis throughout on healing, and especially the fact that the private space of the bower is filled with the healing scent of the wild rose tree, indicates their unspoken presence:

> There is no heart, I deme, in such dispaire,
> Ne with thoughts froward and contraire
> So overlaid, but it should soone have bote,
> If it had ones felt this savour soote. (ll. 81-84)

The narrator's dislocation is indicated when she arrives alone, and when the two birds arrive before the two companies. What the narrator gazes at (with unexpressed desire) indicates that from which she is severed—the social world of the aristocracy—but it is troublingly divided in two aspects that reflect the two birds within the bower/within herself. Her awareness of choice marks out her difference from that which she wishes to embrace unquestioningly. Despite herself, therefore, she provides a different level to the two realms depicted emblematically in the text, a figurative marker registering the difference between the two spaces as she records the events outside her bower.

Like discussions of *The Cuckoo and the Nightingale* which omit Clanvowe's narrator and focus on the abstract significance of the bird-debate, assessments of *The Floure and the Leaf* which do not address the problem of the narrator similarly omit the significance of the subject within ideology, the necessary ground of both poem and critical act. Pearsall provides an example in his discussion of the choice of the goldfinch in the medlar tree as the emblem of the insubstantial troop of the Flower. Noting that the medlar's fruit is not ripe before it begins to decay[112] his interpretation fails to recognize that the goldfinch does not eat the fruit—only the buds and flowers—and works by imposing an authoritative 'truth' which cuts out variant readings. Rotten fruit falls in on itself, losing its shape and firmness; a perfect correlation of the lack of hierarchy and shape in the company of the Flower. Decay thus indicates a loss of solidity, no longer full and firm but limp and flaccid. The image unavoidably summons up the failure of the Flower knights to be 'proper' men, and the disastrous implications of a society dominated by 'feminine' qualities of integration and harmony. Attempting as a writer to express her 'femininity' and as a chivalric subject to deny it, the narrator's attempts to establish difference and meaning start to slide into each other, and to threaten her voice with a loss of substance and place. She is left hanging, drawn to the literary because it offers possibilities of resolution impossible elsewhere, yet attempting to contain the frighteningly plural and fluid possibilities it offers (through the rewriting of 'The General Prologue') because they undermine an ideology that tantalizingly offers a seductively harmonious, but illusory, resolution of the problems implicit within its own structures.

It is significant that it is the nightingale's song (literary and aristocratic) that brings the narrator's desire into focus, erupting into the poem to overcome the sense of displacement by removing her sense of self-consciousness. Erotic and literary desire coincide in the nightingale's voice which pierces her with the sudden violence of a rape-fantasy:

> So sodainly that, as it were a sote,
> I stood astonied; so was I with the song
> Thorow ravished, that, till late and long,
> I ne wist in what place I was, ne where. (ll. 101-104)

Desire can only be acknowledged when the self is disabled. The insistent paradigm, touched on in the last chapter, is that of the medieval romance, also described by the phrase 'listening to the nightingale': the love-affairs of Tristan and Isolde, Lancelot and Guinevere, and, of course, Tereus and Philomela. The status of this startling 'unique' moment as a trope in chivalric writing does not degrade it but points to a chivalric thought, one that links the debate about substantiality and morality of this small poem to the great medieval narratives that associate erotic passion with the tearing of the fabric of chivalry and the protagonists' ultimate destruction. Yet this link is only summoned up in order to be denied. *The Floure and the Leaf* avoids facing such destruction by turning the desire inwards, replacing a passion to be made whole through connection with another, with a narcissistic self-dissolution, expressed emblematically through translation into the space of religion:

> Whereof I had so inly great pleasure
> That as me thought I surely ravished was
> Into Paradise, where my desire
> Was for to be. (ll. 113-16)

Though highly significant here, this nightingale (unlike the birds of previous debates) is not given a voice throughout the poem. As part of the framing narrative consciousness, she appears only at this point and at the conclusion where she flies to the hand of the Lady of the Leaf, Diana, the goddess of chaste (aristocratic) love. Yet her association with Diana indicates that her value is as important as the nightingale in *The Cuckoo and the Nightingale*. She serves both as an emblem of chastity, the controlled desire of the ideal aristocratic (the Leaf company), and as a literary figure for the melodious, harmonious voice of the aristocratic lyric. To see how this figure is constituted and how she differs from the fixed aristocratic bird of *The Cuckoo and the Nightingale* it is necessary to consider both aspects, to look closely at the companies and the narrator herself.

The company of the Leaf is first characterized by the singing of its female figures: a 'world of ladies' (l. 137) who are introduced by the narrator in terms closely resembling those which describe the female nightingale:

> Me thought that I heard voices sodainly,
> The most sweetest and most delicious
> That ever any wight, I trow trewly,
> Heard in their life. (ll. 128-31)

These ladies are defined visually through their dress and the symbolic chaplets and crowns they wear. As the forerunners of a stately procession, they follow a recognized leader in their formal dance and song:

> But all they yede in maner of compace.
> But one there yede in mid the company
> Soole by her selfe, but all followed the pace
> That she kept. (ll. 163-66)

Social hierarchy supports the differentiation of gender, for the men ride separately from the women and their part of the procession is subdivided with class differences of servants and pages. Their actions too are ordered according to gender—the ladies dance and sing in unison; the knights engage in the ritualized combat of the jousting, dispersed about the field 'as evenly as they coud' (l. 278)—thus associating women with harmony and men with conflict. Like the birds and the young leaves, the ladies are

part of the natural world. The narrator does not distinguish between them—all are 'ful pleasant to behold' (l. 171). Where the
men are differentiated according to class, the ladies are defined
by 'womanliness':

> And, God wot, me thoght I was wel bigone,
> For than I might avise hem, one by one,
> Who fairest was, who best coud dance and sing,
> Or who most womanly was in all thing. (ll. 186-89)

That the category of 'womanliness' should reappear after the
knights have proved themselves in the jousts underlines its significance as an ordering principle that rewards the proper execution of the masculine role by instituting stability:

> ...every lady took ful womanly
> By the hond a knight, and forth they yede
> Unto a faire laurer that stood fast by... (ll. 302-304)

In the absence of pressure from competing class paradigms, the
difference of gender provides the operative frame *within* which
the company can operate securely; and the laurel tree to which
the company is drawn through this gendered difference serves as
a focal point *around* which the elaborate dance of society takes
place, reminiscent of the bower's rose tree in its protective and
healing scent:

> So that they should have felt no grevance
> Of raine ne haile, that hem hurt might.
> The savour eke rejoice would any wight
> That had be sicke or melancolius. (ll. 311-14)

Behind the image of the men and women circling hand in hand
around the tree lies the folk model of the fertility dances of May,
but as with the chivalric appropriation of the erotic nightingale of
oral literature, this tree is associated with chastity. It is therefore
unsurprising that the laurel should provide the nightingale's shelter, for both emblems reflect central ideological concerns of the
aristocracy. Yet though the company's health and stability are
crucially sustained by these emblems and by the policing of
gender difference that gives them significance, they are ultimately
arbitrary. Like the laurel tree and the nightingale, gendered
difference appears a constructed value, defined by surface activity,
by behaviour. The laurel tree may have a traditional emblematic

meaning, but in this text its value lies in what it does, its *function* in both creating a focal point within otherwise undifferentiated space, and in replacing the existing signifier of natural difference, the phallic Maypole.

Far from offering an alternative way of conducting the aristocratic way of life, the company 'that came roming out of the field wide' (l. 324), reveals the impossibility of productively questioning the fragile aristocratic ideal. If there is nothing below the emblematic surface then all that holds the company together is an adherence to arbitrary patterns of behaviour: the Flower company illustrates that *any* deviation leads to fragmentation and collapse. Not only do the knights of the Flower as a group lack servants, their individual lack of mastery is indicated by the fact that they walk hand in hand with the ladies (ll. 326, 334) rather than riding horses, and prefer to dance and sing with their partners. These two activities rest on interaction and harmonization, and thus illustrate the absorption of the knights into feminine roles, an effeminacy made even clearer by their failure to engage in jousting. In chivalric terms the company lacks the structure of class hierarchy and gender difference, and appears to have no leader. Without a guiding principle it is unsurprising that the Lady of the Flower should only appear after the company has been battered by the elements.[113] The company's undifferentiated adherence to the qualities of harmony, music and dance, of integration—here associated with the feminine—does not lead to a secure and ordered life. These qualities undermine it by laying the company open to the chaos, the lack of meaning below the mannered surface that emerges when the emblem is not differentiated from the real and the chivalric subject slips into the natural object. What they *do* express, however, are exactly those values that create the integrated, balanced artwork of the poem—a construction in which all elements are necessarily reduced to objects within an overarching pattern, placed and given value by the defining subjectivity of the poetic voice. Because of this the *text* displays a covert attraction to the company the *narrator* rejects.

The poem explores the psychological tensions between separation and incorporation, seen as contradictory impulses. This is very different to the class model of *The Cuckoo and the Nightingale* where the two come together, the dreamer stabilizing his individual (creative) identity by translating his errant desire into the emblematic terms of his aristocratic origin. As a text *The Floure and the Leaf* is interested in how figures or impulses relate to each other, not in the individual figure as the site of conflicting ideological formations. The single daisy—so important in *The Cuckoo and the Nightingale*—is insufficient as an emblem of the courtly life in *The Floure and the Leaf.* It may be suitable for the company's ladies who are as 'womanly' in their singing and dancing as those of the Leaf company (l. 347), but it is insufficient to express the necessary difference of the knights. The landscape of daisies lacks a focal point, a (phallic) signifier of difference, and because of this the Flower company suffers a disastrous collapse in the face of natural forces.

Where earlier debates raised issues through disputes between abstract figures of class ideology which presuppose a common ground—the repression of the feminine—in this text they are modulated by being channelled through a wondering, passive female narrator. Passing through a dream landscape of ghosts and flowers, of sudden tempests and goddesses and singing birds, this figure must attempt to shape it into a meaning that will allow her sense of dislocation to be assuaged and for her to be incorporated in an unambiguous company of the good—but though the Leaf maiden's unambiguous statement attempts to qualify and authorize the meanings assigned to the specific emblems, the text raises questions about value and significance which stretch beyond her answers. Lewis's assessment of the text as a 'moral allegory of love' rather than a 'courtly' one,[114] is shared by many critics, but it does not seem to engage seriously with the issues that the poem raises: that moral degeneracy is expressed through the failure of the men to differentiate themselves sufficiently from the women; that there is no *intrinsic* difference between the two groups, only behavioural patterns that the Flower knights can (and must) learn; that these two issues are caught up in the text's (feminine) refusal to acknowledge the violence necessary for a dominant social group to sustain its dominance; its flight from a political to an aesthetic realm, a flight which by seeing an alternative set of values unwittingly challenges the univocality of the political itself.

It is only through silencing the narrative figure—an act com-

plicit with her own (ideological) denial of volition and selfhood—
that it is possible to read *The Floure and the Leaf* as an allegory of
conflict between 'Virtue and Vice', Good and Bad. Such a judgment passively accepts the Leaf maiden's interpretation at the
close of the poem, one that roots itself *within* chivalric discourse
and questions nothing. A powerful ideological voice, it is yet
neither the voice of the poem within which it speaks, nor that of
the female narrator who stands at the difficult margins of that
ideology. Despite the emphasis on 'feminine' emblems (like the
nightingale) it is the force of the masculine figures that define
meanings in aristocratic society. But the need for violence is
proscribed to a feminine subject—violence is relegated to the
status of that which is repressed: the chaotic elements below the
surface of the emblematic image. When Lewis says that 'the
Virtues ask the Vices to a picnic', he implies that there is no common ground between them, no possibility of change. But this is
not, as Lewis himself remarks, a 'black and white world' but one
that addresses the real problem of the feminine subject attempting to write within the masculine chivalric frame, attempting to
speak when faced by the emblematic nightingale.

Speaking at the boundary of the ideology that it wishes to be
part of, *The Floure and the Leaf* struggles with the difficulties of
exclusion. The text espouses harmony and integration but it
recognizes the need to create structures which allow meanings to
come into being. The result is a radical split between the political
and the aesthetic; the ideological and the subjective. On a political level, the Flower company is rescued from chaos when the
Lady of the Leaf introduces order into its undifferentiated
interior. Sending for a horse to mount her counterpart she introduces a sense of hierarchy and class,

> And after that, to all her company
> She made to purvey horse and every thing
> That they needed. (ll. 428-30)

Then she separates the company according to gender and activity:
each of her ladies comforts a Flower counterpart while the knights
come together to hew down a hedge associated with the jousts[115]
for bonfires to dry their wet clothing. Finally nature is separated
from and made subservient to the human, becoming not a source
of disruption but one of provision: fuel for the comforting fire,

herbs for the healing ointments, 'pleasaunt salades' for nourish-
ment (ll. 405-13).

By assuming command and imposing a structure on the other
company, the Lady of the Leaf relates the companies' coherence
as social units, their divisions of gender and hierarchy, to their
feminine elements (as with the stress on the feminine nightingale
of *The Cuckoo and the Nightingale*), a way of deflecting attention
from the masculine conflict which in reality defines chivalric identity. Yet the strategy of putting a female figure in a position of
control and depicting the whole company equally engaged in
comforting and nurturing, unavoidably conjures up the possibility
of *un*differentiation: what characterized the disorder in the
Flower troop was the failure of its male members to perform their
masculine roles. The solution is as ambiguous as the feminine
space itself, for within this ideology the only unambiguous feminine figure is that of the nightingale—precisely because she is *not*
a woman. Her feminine marginality thus serves the project of
masculine self-definition, a figure of the repression of desire,
necessary for the proper knight.

As the birds curve to the ladies' hands the inner and outer
worlds are brought together and the narrator is released from the
seclusion of the bower. They are carried away in an idealized
image of the ordered aristocratic society which is clearly modelled
on the iconography of the hunt (associated of course with Diana
the huntress—here significantly dropping her rivalry with the
other deities of the pantheon) which so frequently illustrated May
in the Books of Hours.[116] This is clearly intended as a triumphal
progress, conveying a universal acceptance of the Leaf company's
values. But the reference to an iconic image raises unforeseen
problems. By changing the gender, number and function of the
figures the meaning of the icon subtly changes, and undercuts its
previous emblematic significance. The substitutions express consistent and significant changes: the proud single youth is replaced
by two ladies in graceful companionship; the hawk which preys on
nature by singing birds who associate the human with the natural;
the predatory hunt—condemned by the Leaf maiden as idle plea-
sure-seeking (ll. 536-39)—by the harmony of song. The image
thus signifies a society of integration and harmony in which all
the figures accept the security offered by gender difference and

social hierarchy. The image marks a return to the surface, a refusal to accept division from, or enmity to, the natural, and indicates the complicity of both the aesthetic image and the poem itself with the devaluation of 'masculine' values and preference for 'feminine' ones in the Flower company.

Where *The Cuckoo and the Nightingale* made the 'subject in time and motion' (an old man and a writer) the problematic centre and instigator of the debate, in *The Floure and the Leaf* the question of time is occluded in the static, emblematic patterning: the two companies are ghosts, only *images* of people moving through a brilliant landscape that lacks real differentiation, that hangs over a void that can only be shaped by patterning, by art. When the companies ride away both the narrator and the reader are left behind, facing the world of writing, of the text. This is strikingly different to the conclusion of *The Cuckoo and the Nightingale*, which links the text, despite itself, to the values of the political world outside its boundaries—even as it sets up a space of ideological opposition. *The Floure and the Leaf*, however, again despite itself, separates its aesthetic activity from the values which create meaning in a violent political world. Though the narrator aligns herself with the Leaf company (which has effectively absorbed its counterpart anyway) she goes home alone to 'put all that I have seen in writing' (l. 589). For all her desire for integration her voice thus indicates a fracture between her aristocratic and writing identities—not, as with Clanvowe, a final resolution. And where Clanvowe blurs the boundaries of his text by making the nightingale sing his/his dreamer's song—both moving inwards and out of the text on a single, class-orientated level—this figure has no direct relation to the nightingale but refers her writing to a different community, qualified not by the split between the gendered social activities of singing, dancing and jousting, but to the *un*gendered and private pleasures of 'them that lust it to rede' (l. 590).

If 'The Knight's Tale' interrogates 'chivalry's interior' it does so at the expense of its glittering surface of flowers, games and, crucially, love songs—those elements that define the aristocratic aesthetic, the movement to accept the emblematic in place of the 'real.' Patterson's phrase points to his interest in the interior to the exclusion of this surface, and, as he makes clear, there is little if anything below this exterior grace. I think that *The Flower and the Leaf* demonstrates why. It presents the other side of chivalry, focusing on grace and omitting the violence that dominates 'The Knight's Tale', translating warfare into the bloodless emblematic battle games of the tournaments.[117] Yet the very concentration on the aesthetics of the nobility shows the shadow of degeneration that haunts chivalry from within—without violence none of the games have significance. The textual emphasis on grace and harmony creates a writing subject implicitly in opposition to the arbitrary violence of the political world, a subject characterized by those feminine attributes seen as disruptive of the social identity the text itself attempts to espouse. The foregrounding of ambiguity thus becomes a form of opposition even though the ambiguous aesthetic text attempts to avoid the political altogether.

The 'narcissism' of Shelley's texts—poems such as *Alastor* or the unfinished *Triumph of Life*—are oppositional in this way despite Paul de Man's attempts to refuse them meaning outside the literary. De Man appears to be using an inverse reality testing—and hence, like traditional critics, equally represses the feminine. In texts characterized by this fluid and ambiguous voice, meaning lies in the *refusal* of solidity, of a single identity which would draw the textual and the political together in alliance. Meaning lies in the construction of the text on lines of gender which oppose the masculinity of the dominant subject position because that always serves to replicate the power structures of the dominant ideology. *The Floure and the Leaf*'s relegation to insubstantiality during a period characterized by a vision of both social relations and nature in terms of conflict and violence, terms which involve a repression of the values of nurturance and harmonization—and a transformation of woman to the chaste emblematic 'angel in the house' indicates just how significant these challenges are. These patterns are significant, not only in understanding the ideological basis for shifting assessments of texts, but also in considering the problems of the individual self-conscious *writer*. The silencing of the kind of writing typified within *The Floure and the Leaf* highlights both the difficulties and the resolutions of Victorian women poets faced with paralyzing constructions of femininity, which associated the act of writing with a transgressive desire for self-determination, traditionally resolved, as in Clanvowe, through the silencing of the feminine.[118] Yet the very pressure to constrain women in their separate spheres emphasized the relativity of certain values—including those of the governing class—and, at a time when the education of the élite was dominated by the classics, medieval traditions could provide a site of resistance to those denied access to the education of the rulers.

Chapter 4

Fragmentation and Alienation: Victorian Nightingales

Placing the Nightingale: Literary and Critical Debates

> Miss M's a nightingale. 'Tis well
>   Your simile I keep.
> It is the way with Philomel
>   To sing while others sleep.
>
> —Gerard Manley Hopkins, 'On a Poetess'[1]

> I have no doubt the Darwinian theory on the subject is that the feathers of birds once stuck up all erect, like the bristles of a brush, and have only been blown flat by continual flying... If you fasten a hair-brush to a mill wheel, with the handle forward, so as to develop itself into a neck by moving always in the same direction, and within continual hearing of a steam whistle, after a certain number of revolutions the hair-brush will fall in love with the whistle; they will marry, lay an egg, and the produce will be a nightingale.
>
> —John Ruskin[2]

> —Oh owl-like birds! They sing for spite,
> They sing for hate, they sing for doom!
> They'll sing through death who sing through night,
> They'll sing and stun me in the tomb—
> The nightingales, the nightingales!
>
> —Elizabeth Barrett Browning, 'Bianca among the Nightingales', xvi, 5-9[3]

These small snatches from the work of Gerard Manley Hopkins, John Ruskin and Elizabeth Barrett Browning exemplify the way the nightingale could summon up issues of both class and gender for Victorian writers. All express—and deflect—anxiety about current issues through oblique allusions to the classical Philomela, but the differences between the three are even more significant than this broad similarity. Where the passages of Hopkins and Ruskin rest comfortably on the classical myth and its victimized protagonist, that of Barrett Browning transforms the passive individual nightingale into multiple aggressors, undercutting the classical paradigm with medieval patterns, invoking in particular the medieval debate through the fractured title and opposed voices of her text.

Invoking a familiar classical myth, Hopkins assumes the lazy authority of the classically educated élite to ridicule the presumption of a female poet. His rather snide epigram implies that the foolish 'poetess' is not only predictable but irrelevant to the masculine coterie his poetic voice seeks to represent. Yet the use of ridicule is more revealing than Hopkins intends, for it suggests a response to a threat, just as the pointed urbanity gestures towards a fear of insubordination. I would suggest that a more topical reference, one which Hopkins avoids acknowledging, lies hidden within the classical topos, for the nightingale also evokes the sentimental poetry that filled the popular journals from the mid-eighteenth century, and well into the nineteenth. In those poems the nightingale functions as a shorthand signifier of 'poetic' melancholy: a self-reflective cipher for the preoccupation with sentiment and surface.[4] Many of the writers of this formulaic poetry were women, but this was not necessarily the case: by ridiculing an insubordinate nightingale-poet *as* a woman, Hopkins displaces a class-based anxiety onto the difference of gender. In a striking development of the kind of resolution seen in *The Cuckoo and the Nightingale*, the learned put-down displaces the disruption of sentimental verse and the challenge it implies to the social order onto not the category of the feminine (as in the medieval debate) but the individual female writer herself. By equating sentiment with a 'feminine' self-indulgence the female artist is neatly disqualified as a poet by what is perceived as her 'femininity:' poets who write similar 'sensitive' verse must be equally self-indulgent and, by sleight of hand, effeminate.

Despite its apparent differences, the second passage rests on similar premises. This time, however, the emotion and art associated with the nightingale are evoked in a positive way: to expose

the desiccated poverty of modern theory. Though the first part of
this passage is concerned with a robin it is notable that when he
wants to develop his argument, Ruskin calls up and represses the
victimized protagonist of the Philomela myth in a mechanistic
parody of metamorphosis. In this version sensuality and music/
poetry are reduced to ciphers—the hair-brush and the steam-
whistle respectively—and further violated by being strapped to the
wheel of necessity. The 'birth' of the nightingale is denuded of
meaningful struggle and demeaned to the mechanical 'produce'
of a prosaic Victorian romance. The sentiment and unearthly
melody of the 'poetic' nightingale are evoked by their *absence* to
illustrate those elements of the marvellous lacking in a crudely
materialist world.

Both Hopkins and Ruskin draw on the classical topos of the
nightingale to advance their particular ideological positions. In
the first text she is qualified primarily by the 'natural' superiority
of the sophisticated male poet (the nightingale as emotional
female); in the latter she suggests sensuality, passion and art—
attributes conspicuously absent in a clockwork universe (the nightingale as figure of both nature and desire). For both Hopkins and
Ruskin, therefore, the nightingale usefully functions as a victim-
figure, effective because she can be subjected to the urbane control that they employ to demonstrate their masculine (and educated) security. Both passages repeat the violation the myth
inscribes by reducing the figure to a cipher, silencing its individual voice as a figure for poetry. The emphatic assertions of
superiority do not convey supreme confidence, however, but seem
to demonstrate anxiety in the face of change: in class relations
and in conceptions of nature respectively; in the construction of
gendered difference in both.

It is unsurprising therefore that Barrett Browning's poem
should differ in its use of the Philomela myth. Hopkins and
Ruskin present the nightingale as an object, a static figure to be
manipulated for their satiric purposes. The third passage, however, takes on and modifies such easy objectification. Here the
victim herself struggles to speak, her voice lacking clarity and
almost overwhelmed by the inhuman (nightingale) voices that
press around her. To the female speaker of 'Bianca among the
Nightingales', a strategy of objectification and manipulation of

the 'feminine' nightingale (as practised by the previous poets) proves impossible. The Philomelic figure is too close to the bone. In this passage the nightingales are overtly repressive, their sinister role being to draw the female into a sphere of mingled desire, pain and silence. But though Bianca seeks to disentangle herself from the nightingale-chorus, her voice is hopelessly entwined in their calls. Despite pursuing her lover to another country—and thus apparently breaking the pattern of passivity imposed upon her by Giulio's desertion—she remains defined by her suffering, by the desire and loss that initiated her speech and to which her speech obsessively returns. The chorus of nightingales functions like that of a Greek tragedy, voicing the constraints of accepted meanings as a counterpoint to the speaker's desperate utterance. Unable to escape this economy of victimization, Bianca's final words are not aimed at the lover who has abandoned her but at the nightingales that 'sing through [her] head'.

The chorus of nightingales may appear to invoke the classical victim I suggest lies within the passages by Hopkins and Ruskin but the simplicity of that pattern is compromised by allusions to a different (medieval) precedent. The most striking example occurs in the final stanza (above) which simultaneously summons up and refutes *The Owl and the Nightingale*. Bianca associates the modern nightingales with spite and death, seeing them as no different to their medieval enemy. These 'owl-like birds' are active aggressors, figures that 'mock and deride' the female victim who struggles to speak through and against their cries. Both as a nightingale and victimized by nightingales, voice defined against and yet with the bird linked with poetry that silences the feminine, Barrett Browning's sprawling monologue foregrounds the very conflicts that the tight, controlled satires of Hopkins and Ruskin seek to contain. The text is self-reflectively aware of the relationship of power to voice, of words to a sensed 'reality': something that Hopkins and Ruskin smooth over in their easy assumption of a particular literary norm. Barrett Browning's passionate agonized Bianca broods over the words her lover has forgotten, seeking stability and finding none. The text is a perfect example of the kind of movements Isobel Armstrong discerns in a poetry she sees

to be 'obsessed with a series of displacements... [and] unparal-
leled in its preoccupation with sexuality and what it is to love'[5]—
the latter aspects tellingly frozen to cipher in Hopkins and Ruskin.

Because Barrett Browning's poem engages directly with the
figure of the nightingale, I will discuss the entire poem in detail in
the final chapter. What I wish to emphasize here is the uneasy
recourse in all three passages to the past, a strategy which seeks to
avoid an increasingly unstable present. Yet the very use of an
unfixed figure such as the nightingale betrays the difficult self-
conscious dependence of these Victorian writers on their literary
forebears. In 'Bianca among the Nightingales' these elements
come together in the confrontation of the female speaker with
the 'feminine' nightingales, of the voice of eventful moment with
that of familiar repetition, of motion with stasis, and of the ongoing narrative with the voice of the chorus. One way of reading
this encounter is to see it as dramatizing the difficulties of the
female writer wrestling with an art in which the feminine is silenced—either construed as sentimental and irrelevant or sublimated out of existence. But I think that this is an approach which
hives 'Bianca' off into a special enclave of 'women's poetry'.
Accepting Armstrong's claim that gender functions as 'a primary
focus of anxiety and investigation' within Victorian poetry[6] allows
the significance of the poem's overt engagement with gender to
be extended. Most fruitfully, it allows me to use it as a paradigmatic Victorian text in order to 'read' Victorian critics.

The conflicting subtexts[7] of 'Bianca among the Nightingales'
illustrate many of the perspectives available to Victorian scholars.
Critics like Shires and Armstrong, for example, may choose to
emphasize fragmentation and alienation (Bianca's conflict with
the nightingales); like Gayatri Chakravorty Spivak, they may focus
on the forces of containment which fix the individual in a set
position within (imperialist) ideology (the nightingales without
Bianca);[8] or, like Sandra Gilbert and Susan Gubar, they may
detach the female speaker from the surrounding ideology and
consider her as an essentially separate being: 'woman' (Bianca,
wholly detached from the repressive nightingales).[9] Critical denigration of the poem serves equally to focus those other, more
traditional approaches that appear to align themselves with the
perspectives of Hopkins or Ruskin. The poem may be dismissed

by critics such as William Irvine and Park Honan, as an example
of emotional self-indulgence, in the mode of *Casa Guidi Windows*
which they accuse of emotional excess: '...a signal instance of the
way in which verse pumps Elizabeth up beyond any possibility of
coherent and rational discussion.'[10] Alternatively it may be reduced to a spontaneous biological outpouring, qualified by Peter
Dally as the 'result of an unusually large dose of opium'.[11] I would
like to align myself with those critics who examine ideological
fragmentation exposed through conflict but, by considering the
nightingale-topos itself, to re-appraise the nature of that conflict.
My study of the nightingale has emphasized its value as an index
of changing ideological boundaries and, through this status as an
index, has sought to expose complex relations between the categories of gender, class, nature and art. One of the most striking
aspects of the nineteenth century is its self-conscious obsession
with the past: through the figure of the nightingale, related to
poetry in two very different literary traditions, I want to suggest
that these literary traditions can be seen to have been gendered.

The literary space was increasingly contested in this period,
reflecting, as many studies demonstrate, a fractured educational
provision that allocated classical literature to upper-class men,
and 'English' (including medieval) literature to those excluded
from the élite—as Brian Doyle points out, 'English was considered
a "woman's subject" unsuited to the masculine intelligence.'[12]
Rather than attempting to control the dissemination of the ambiguous text, the literary market-place sought to raise the individual writer's consciousness of accepted norms, of class and, most
importantly, of gender. In relation to the figure of the nightingale, the double standards applied to male and female writers
neatly apportion out its ambiguous qualities to the sexes: creative,
positive meanings (sensitive, sensual, exotic) being assigned to
the male poet and disparagingly negative ones (predictable sentimentality, weakness) to the female one. But subordinating the
textual to the sexual in an attempt to control the ambiguity of
writing itself merely shifts ambivalence from text to the double
heritage of the literary 'space'. Both the figure of the nightingale
in general and its particular reflection in the work of Barrett
Browning demonstrate that the literary inheritance of the nineteenth century was not a single 'tradition' centred around the

writings of the classical 'fathers' but involved an ongoing debate between the writings of different pasts, a debate which equally had differing significance to the various gendered/class-defined groups.

A Fractured Inheritance

> Begin, and cease, and then again begin,
> With tremulous cadence slow, and bring
> The eternal note of sadness in.
> Sophocles long ago
> Heard it on the Aegean, and it brought
> Into his mind the turbid ebb and flow
> Of human misery.

—Matthew Arnold, 'Dover Beach', ll. 12-18

'Dover Beach' expresses the sense of belatedness and loss felt by many nineteenth-century writers. Deferring to what they saw as the melancholy grandeur of the Greeks and the secure faith of the Middle Ages, they sketch a world defined through privation, with 'neither joy, nor love, nor light, / Nor certitude, nor peace, nor help for pain' (ll. 33-34). Marginalized in its own time, a lesser descendant of powerful precursors, Victorian poetry is intensely aware of the instability of identity—the common thread to its interest in historical, social and subjective identities being this sense of loss. As Arnold points out, the note of sadness reaches back to Greek tragedy and it is no surprise that the tragic nightingale should repeatedly turn up in Victorian poetry—though the Victorian nightingale cannot be directly identified with its classical precursor without risking oversimplification. To do so would be to fall in line with the Victorian model of history as a series of well-defined and distinct categories in a linear progression—and Arnold's vision challenges this model in its very inception: his 'progress' is haunted by the multiple shadows of the past, shadows that cannot be constrained into clear and distinct categories but move confusedly towards a moral chaos only redeemable through personal love.

But 'Dover Beach' does not only dramatize the fractured, doubting Victorian self. That self is created through an awareness of the loss of a double inheritance—an awareness that undercuts the linear model of history promoted during the nineteenth century. Armstrong considers that this historical model—of chronological development through clearly defined historical periods or phases—has been so thoroughly absorbed into modern common-sense perception that the unique quality of the second half of the nineteenth century has tended to be lost: a sign that Victorian ideas have been normalized to the extent that they are no longer questioned. One result is that only comparatively modern history is seen as relevant to contemporary understanding—with medieval history and its writing suffering in particular. Armstrong's own interest lies in the effect of this historical model on the study of Victorian poetry which begins to be 'seen in terms of transition...either on the way from Romanticism, or on the way to modernism'.[13] I would like to stress a different approach and, instead of relating the poetry to its immediate predecessors (the Romantics) or to its immediate followers (the modernists), I want to explore the relations with its *medieval* precursors. This approach associates the breakdown of the enlightenment subject (as illustrated in the doubting self of 'Dover Beach') with the fragmentation of enlightenment values, and suggests that comparisons can fruitfully be made with the pre-enlightenment poetry discussed in the previous chapter. What emerges is not a simple repetition of medieval patterns but an uneasiness over the same boundaries expressed in shared fascinations: with the body, with the place of the feminine; with female chastity; with a desire to subjugate a fearful chaotic nature. Once again the nightingale provides a useful literary index in a poetry that self-consciously explores both its relation with its pasts and its place within a present culture which seeks to marginalize and silence its oppositional voice.

The procedure employed in previous chapters—of concentrating on patterns within the texts, examining the relations of abstracted elements through the figure of the nightingale as the variously defined voice of poetry—proves inadequate to a time in which Armstrong suggests 'literature' and 'the literary' were increasingly conceptualized as 'a distinct category with a particularly important part to play in the education of a mass culture'.[14] It was a role which Shires qualifies in terms of disruption: 'Victorian representations are noted for simultaneously venting various ideological positions, airing multiple points of view... The airing of multiple points of view fosters intervention in the status quo and thus challenges hegemony.'[15]

Though the question of a fractured subjectivity is *informed* by a breakdown in the dominant ideology, the Victorian subject cannot be discussed only as a *product* of that ideology: in part because of a self-consciousness about its own making and its own predecessor texts. The brooding concern with the self that straddles both poetry and the wider culture makes it imperative that the individual gendered subject be discussed as well as its context. Like Linda Shires, I consider that it is necessary to find a way of accounting for 'motivation and political will';[16] like Lee Patterson, I feel that the self-conscious subject cannot and should not be reduced to a nexus of conflicting ideologies, that 'the self may be made, but it is also self-made'.[17]

Decentring Writing and Reading: Medieval Comparisons

Current interest in the decentred quality of Victorian poetry may seem to be governed by a contemporary interest in fragmenta- tion—expressed more directly in feminist, deconstructive and postmodernist theories—but it has a critical lineage which reflects historical circumstance. The end of the Second World War led to a massive social readjustment, especially of gender roles, a change which sensitized critics to those elements of self-doubt and self- consciousness in Victorian poetry that are so burningly present to our own uncertain time.[18] This pattern reveals the impact of historical change on the areas of critical interest, responding to and repeating the patterns of disintegration appearing within the literature, choosing literature which reflects our current anxieties and position.

Correspondences between late medieval debates and Victorian poetry imply a similar choice, an attraction rooted in shared ideological instability. The Victorian artist's attraction, on the one hand, to the graceful ideals of self-sacrificing honour and femi- nine chastity and, on the other, to the comic physicality associated with the lower classes (associations promoted within the medieval genres of the romance and the fabliau), are yet more significant. The attraction suggests that, despite their evident differences, Victorian artists and medieval courtier-poets had in common a shared anxiety about their positions within their respectively changing worlds. From this perspective the structural similarities between medieval court writing and Victorian poetry are far more significant than a simple 'escapist' desire for an unsullied world[19] or a passive element that mediates more complex political affiliations [20] but demonstrate nineteenth-century affinities with the ideological uncertainties of an earlier period of crisis.[21]

Changes in the respective relations of writing to power structures sharpen the value of comparing two such different periods. Fourteenth- and fifteenth-century court writing emerged from within the centre of power; in the nineteenth century literature was institutionalized at the margins. This shift is accompanied by an equivalent shift in the 'site of ideological opposition' Patterson locates in medieval court writing: in this new de-centred context it is the *writer* rather than the writing that is oppositional. Similarly Armstrong points out that 'the displacement of the aesthetic into secondariness forces the poet to conceptualise him- or herself as external to and over against what comes to be seen as life.'[22]

In *The Cuckoo and the Nightingale* gender operates as a category through which direct conflicts between individual desire and repressive class ideology can be mediated by a joint repression of the feminine/class other. In the alienated, self-conscious context of nineteenth-century writing, however, a simple confrontation between individual desire and an ideology which represses that desire but offers something in place is no longer possible. The repression of the other no longer provides the resolution but the starting point: nineteenth-century literature courts instability, actively investigating its relation to its others.[23] One response to this active courting of instability which foregrounds the conflicts repressed in the wider culture is the growth of a corrective in the various frames supplied by publishers, critics and journals. These frames collectively intervene in the transmission and *reception* of the text, to subordinate the textual to the sexual. The individual (usually male) reviewer 'placed' the ambiguous text for its readers by applying and affirming prescribed sexual roles.[24] Both writing and reading become gendered processes as a result, for the fluid text is created and read through grids which select different patterns according to gendered paradigms.

The significance of the past is not, of course, to be restricted to the relation of Victorian poetry to medieval debates. The boundaries between past(s) and present were a source of obsessive and anxious investigation at every level and new fields of knowledge—geology, palaeontology, archaeology, philology—sprang up in response to the desire to categorize and classify, to subordinate difference to the pattern of overarching schemae that progressively traced development from points of origin. In the process however still more boundaries were disrupted, most significantly that between the human and the natural. The nightingale's associations with the feminine and the natural, with literary models of two very different pasts and with the voice of desire itself point to the further complication of the meanings assigned to it in the poetry of this time.

Evolution and the Victorian Nightingale

> Evolutionary theory implied a new myth of the past: instead of the garden at the beginning, there was the sea and the swamp... There was no way back to a previous paradise; the primordial was comfortless. Instead of fixed and perfect species, it showed forms in flux, and the earth in constant motion, drawing continents apart... Nostalgia was disallowed, since no unrecapturable perfection preceded man's history.

—Gillian Beer, *Darwin's Plots*[25]

> The poet is a nightingale, who sits in darkness and sings to cheer its own solitude with sweet sounds.

—Shelley, *Defence of Poetry*[26]

The mass of nineteenth-century scientific explorations of the past grew out of a desire for secure and stable knowledge, yet failed to produce either object. The massive scale of geological time revealed by Charles Lyell's *Principles of Geology* (1830–33) appeared to dwarf human values, while the theory of natural selection published in Darwin's *Origin of the Species* (1859) was popularly interpreted (despite Darwin[27]) as justifying a rapacious human society based on the 'survival of the fittest'. This bleak vision not only, as Gillian Beer points out, destabilized the past as a source of 'unrecapturable perfection',[28] it also degraded the romantic dream of an unspoilt and natural Eden. Under the influence of Darwinian theory nature came increasingly to be seen as a place of flux, inhabited by vicious predators and their terrified prey, a world driven by appetite that mirrored or even outstripped the violent competition of an industrial and materialistic society.[29] A mixture of fear and fascination explains the Victorian taste for animal paintings, schizophrenically split between the beribboned lapdogs that decorate suffocating domestic interiors, and the stricken stags, standing at bay or torn to pieces by hunting dogs, in a vicious natural world.[30]

In 1798, Coleridge's conversation poem could insist on the joyousness of real nightingales ('in nature there is nothing melancholy') while still using the figure to conduct a conversation about poetry and poets.[31] Twenty-three years later Shelley's famous *Defence* might move away from such realism, but his claim that 'the poet is a nightingale'[32] still rests on the Romantic vision of the natural world as a purer space in order to dramatize the poet's role as a prophet speaking from the edges of a benighted society. By the mid-nineteenth century, however, neither the purity of nature nor the prophetic role of the poet seemed tenable. As Beer points out, Darwin effectively linked the civilized with the bestial in a way never seen before: '…ascent was also flight—a flight from the primitive and the barbaric which could never quite be left behind.'[33] Haunted by the nightmare possibility that man might 'reel back into the beast'[34] the Victorians were faced with 'a choice of nightmares'. The world of Conrad's *Heart of Darkness* is a product of that bleak vision: a work which directly links the civilized with the barbaric, and sees a journey into the 'primitive' world of insatiable appetites *as* a journey both into the past and into the self. Nothing is sacred or pure: western idealism is inextricably linked with exploitation; western society 'a whited sepulchre' that provides the only refuge from the horror of bestiality. As in the brittle thirteenth century, the self generated through the destabilizing of major categories in the dominant ideology sought to focus itself by retreating to the definition provided by gender—much of Conrad's ambivalent fascination with the natural world is displaced onto the role of women. *Heart of Darkness* explicitly links the necessity of keeping women ignorant and separate from male adventures with a masculine search for origins,[35] one that takes place within a fearful and predatory nature which is penetrated and despoiled, even as it sucks men into its lustful shadows.

Such a complex, self-conscious and uncertain world provided fertile ground for the Philomelic nightingale, specifically evoked in the 'eternal passion [and] eternal pain' of Arnold's *Philomela* and Swinburne's *Itylus*, or hanging like a ghostly echo behind the final aching lines of Browning's 'Two in the Campagna' which speak of 'Infinite passion and the pain / Of finite hearts that yearn'. Despite Coleridge's (disingenuous) protestation, the figure has never evoked a 'real' nature. As both he and Shelley realized, it has always been associated with poetry and passion, an association which became far more evident as the nineteenth century progressed. The nightingale song that accompanies Rochester's first proposal to Jane in Brontë's *Jane Eyre* is not only shorthand for romance but is prophetic, suggesting impending loss from the alien natural world through which Jane has to struggle to achieve her strange happiness in an unhealthy damp house. I do not want to make direct, conscious links between this brief nightingale and the bestial figure of Rochester's first, Jamaican, wife, but there is a sense in which the nightingale partakes of the ambivalence associated with the natural world at this time. The nightingales that turn up everywhere in Victorian writing seem to articulate on a minor scale the desire for a less mechanized, less materialistic world projected elsewhere onto other, subordinated cultures. The intimate correspondence between the 'increasing embourgeoisement' of the West and the contemporary passion for 'orientalism'[36] is inscribed in appropriate miniature in the direct association of the Victorian literary nightingale with the sensual bulbul: the nightingale of Persian poetry. Yet the greatest testimony to the complex evocative power of the nightingale lies in a poem that does not even mention her: Arnold's 'Dover Beach', the poem that provides one of the epigraphs to this chapter. Arnold boldly transfers the mingled passion and pain of the nightingale, associated through the distinctive word 'darkling' with the individual poets, Milton and Keats—and hence with their brilliant poetry[37]—to a vision of a belated, benighted and *in*articulate mass society:

> And we are here as on a darkling plain
> Swept with confused alarms of struggle and flight,
> Where ignorant armies clash by night.

It is a bizarre testimony to the inescapable allusiveness of the nightingale that, on the eve of the new century Hardy should choose to rewrite Arnold's magnificent hopelessness in 'The Darkling Thrush' by replacing the unspoken figure of the nightingale with an old and battered bird which stands doggedly outside the human world and cannot—unlike its poetic forerunner—be twisted into its reflection.

Indexing Displacement: Victorian Poetry and its Nightingales

> Teleology is displaced by epistemology and politics [in Victorian poetry] because *relationships* and their representation become the contested area: between self and society, self and labour, self and nature, self and language and above all between self and the lover.

—Isobel Armstrong[38]

> I shall not see the shadows,
> I shall not feel the rain;
> I shall not hear the nightingale
> Sing on, as if in pain;
> And dreaming through the twilight
> That does not rise nor set,
> Haply I may remember,
> And haply may forget.

—Christina Rossetti, 'Song'

As a index of difference, the literary nightingale simultaneously evokes each of the five categories into which Armstrong divides Victorian poetry's central concern with relationships: in medieval debate and love poetry it is associated with the poetry of a particular class in conflict with other classes ('self and society'); in both classical and medieval writing its association with nature can be extended to include a refusal of human labour ('self and nature'; 'self and labour');[39] in both contexts it signifies the literary voice and erotic desire ('self and language... self and the lover'). Above all it is linked with the primary signifier of otherness, the feminine, to the gendered difference that Armstrong suggests mediates all five categories.

This rich allusiveness underlies the delicate otherworldly quality of Rossetti's beautiful 'Song' with its ambiguous nightingale. The poem quietly summons up the relationships that make up the material world at the heart of Victorian poetry, only to reflect on its own—and their—dissolution. It places its own voice at the very edge of that world by dissolving first the loving responsibilities of the lover to the beloved that make sense of a world of human relationships (the gifts of 'song', 'roses', 'cypress tree'), and then, unnervingly, the self's relation to an elemental world of change that finds its focus in the painful nightingale song. As one of those 'sad songs' rejected as pointless in its opening lines, the 'Song' thus negates its own being, incorporating the love and death separately signified by the rose and the cypress, but entwined in the song of the nightingale. The poetic 'I' comprehensively distances itself from both difference (light and dark) and the relationships that create meaning out of difference, resting in a twilight without change. The poetic voice echoes in the void beyond death where human memory—that which confers meaning onto the passing of time—has no meaning. The terrible lightness that characterizes the allusions to memory turn the richness of ambiguity into the repetitive poverty of mere chance ('if thou wilt... / and if thou wilt' / 'haply... / and haply...'). At its very heart lies the lyric voice of the nightingale that sings 'as if in pain', the specific literary memory evoked being the meditation on death and poetry in the 'Ode to the Nightingale.' Hauntingly anticipating its own silence, the poem thus simultaneously enacts and undoes the fragile lyric voice, effortlessly evoking a languid sense of being 'half in love with easeful death'. But even this literary memory seems empty and inconsequential—the insouciance of the Keatsian echo undercuts the vivid sensuality of its original. This small spare song manages to suggest both the insecurity that powered the nineteenth-century desire to structure and contain the present through an obsessive concern with the past, and the ultimate pointlessness of these projects when faced by the individual dissolution of death.

Memory and forgetfulness determine the construction of an ongoing identity, while mutually defining relationships with the other cannot be conducted without the continuity provided by memory. That both stanzas of this quiet poem should conclude by undercutting memory thus indicates Rossetti's engagement with a central nineteenth-century concern. The Victorian obsession with the past has already been linked to an anxiety about the present: from this perspective, a concern with the medieval past acquires special significance for an unstable Europe. For the Victorians,

Britain prior to the fifteenth century could be seen as a younger and simpler self, untroubled by the social unrest and crises of faith that plagued their own age, a time seen famously as *before* individualism.[40] Medieval churches, castles and cathedrals provided visible remains of a past which could be romanticized into a shared heritage to consolidate the nation-state.[41] The Poets' Corner in Westminster Abbey is a perfect example of the transformation of literature into heritage. Medieval literature was stripped of its sophistication and questioning and presented as the literature of the 'age of faith' whose passing Arnold mourns in 'Dover Beach'.

Always made to serve a purpose, the past is used here to police present identity by distancing and placing inadmissable elements into a safe closed arena, and thus to shore up a gap in the self. Yet to give these elements place is to recognize them and give them substance, opening up the dangerous possibility that they may be interpreted differently, may acquire active rather than passive characteristics. The function of the medieval in this sense is remarkably similar to that of orientalism: to locate the self by presenting a mirrored other and to create places for resistance that depend on the centre for their being and which therefore lead back to that centre. The mirrors reflected different ambiguities: orientalism presents the sensual and the lascivious, the unfamiliar and exotic; medievalism, both idealized aristocratic romance and the 'earthy' pleasure of a communal society. This project explains how the elegant and sophisticated poet Chaucer became popularly reduced to a figure of jovial bawdy humour—and in schools and cinema that is how he often remains.

In this context a figure like the nightingale becomes doubly complex. Because its allusiveness emerges out of an accumulated residue of past meanings—which include *both* classical *and* medieval traditions—it not only wonderfully expresses the various relationships Armstrong lists as central to Victorian poetry but highlights the significant relationship she misses: the relation of self and past (different) selves. Not even the rose has such rich and varied associations for the Victorian writer; no other has been so clearly associated with the elements that trace the boundaries of dominant ideologies.[42] Associations with the literary voice in both classical and medieval literatures echo behind its seemingly decorative appearances in the self-reflective literature of the day. Accompanying the romanticized, gently grieving, stylized subjectivity Rossetti's poem appears, on the surface, to invoke is a more substantial concern with the relation of the literary space to the speaking—and changing—self. A study of the nightingale in Victorian poetry therefore provides a marvellous focus for its wider ideological concerns.

The frequency with which the classical nightingale appears in Victorian poetry shows the attraction of the victimized Philomela to the artist marginalized in an aggressively mechanistic age. Yet, as I point out in Chapter 1, the voice of this nightingale does not merely provide a dramatic correlative of the sensitive suffering soul but impersonally traces and records the violation inflicted on the marginalized elements of a political society. By reiterating the traditional association of women with an inarticulate and picturesque suffering rooted in pain and loss (the classical nightingale), the male artist may attain a displaced mastery of his feminine other and, through this, of his 'feminized' self. But what provides the *male* poet with mastery debilitates his *female* colleague. As in chivalric writing, the masculine colonization of the 'feminine' space generates additional insecurity about the place of the feminine itself and leads to a desire to freeze or silence its disruptive potential. Yet again the nightingale serves as an effective index of these changing boundaries. Tracing the voice of the nightingale in Victorian poetry may well reflect on the self-enclosed 'expressive' tradition Armstrong ascribes to the female poet, but it also radically illuminates wider problems concerning the relation of art to contemporary ideologies of gender and power.

Problems of Gender and Literary Tradition

From the abused Procne to the reclusive Lady of Shalott...women have been told that their art...is an art of silence. Procne must record her sufferings with...the voice of the shuttle' because when she was raped her tongue was cut out...the Lady of Shalott weaves a story in a tower like a coffin (and) escapes only through the self-annihilation of romantic love-madness.[43]

The complexity revealed through the figure of the nightingale creates problems for critics, especially those concerned primarily with the category of women. Sandra Gilbert and Susan Gubar, for example, draw attention to the cultural links between Tennyson's romantic heroines, the classical story and the swooning romantic poetry they associate with the myth (though, unfortunately, they name the wrong Greek girl). Their analysis is, however, frozen by a policy of reading both poetry and myth as representation. Gilbert and Gubar do not consider the story of Philomela as anything other than a story of violation, a violation which they can lay bare. By reading it as a myth about 'women' which faithfully replicates the patterns of an equally fixed patriarchy, they fail to recognize its ability to trace and *articulate* violation: its self-reflective function as a myth about voice as well as about silence. Tennyson thus becomes only one more repressive male: his Lady of Shalott a cipher of masculine violation; his poem reduced to an act of silencing. Yet this is clearly a reductive reading—as a comparison with Armstrong's discussion demonstrates. In line with her focus on gender as a 'primary focus of anxiety and investigation' within a specific historical moment, Armstrong associates the repressed feminine with the repressed social by suggesting that 'the starving handloom weavers who were being displaced by new industrial processes... hover just outside the poem and become strangely aligned with the imprisoned Lady'.[44] This is a very different approach to that of Gilbert and Gubar who appear to see a continuous and continuing trans-historical narrative of oppression in which women are (the) only victims. The undeniable power of their analysis lies in their role as saviours of the distressed, but in the process they lose the ambiguity of the poetic text, their lack of self-reflection effectively denying what it is that they attempt to practise: the possibility of opposition to oppressive gendered norms.

Delores Rosenblum's vigorous analysis similarly draws energy from its desire to speak for the silenced. Because of this, despite its sophistication, her discussion of the nineteenth-century obsession with the 'visionary female face' and the difficulties it created for the female poet (specifically Barrett Browning)[45] makes me uneasy. If there is no way out for the victimized woman whose problems are conceived as unmovable, from where does the female critic speak? The problems of Joplin's analysis of the myth of Philomela (discussed in Chapter 1) erupt repeatedly and insistently.

Like Joplin, Rosenblum roots her discussion in the 'fact' of a single literary tradition which 'silenced' women: '...inheriting a literary tradition in which the seeing self is usually male, the seen other, female, what stance can EBB [*sic*] take towards the face that above all means *in silence?*'[46] Starting from this assumption of a single 'literary tradition', Rosenblum then moves to a meticulous discussion of the bewildering ambiguity caught in the portrait of the dead mother in Barrett Browning's *Aurora Leigh*. But ambiguity need not silence or stifle: it can as easily stimulate.[47] As with Gilbert and Gubar, problems lie in the unquestioned assumptions on which Rosenblum builds, the history of victimization she decides to see in the past. But the ambiguity of the feminine means that—as I argue above—reading itself can become a gendered process and different 'pasts' become associated with different values. Rosenblum's concern with *silence* omits any grey shades— and there were plenty in an imperialist empire in which it was not merely a question of speech or silence but of *which* language was spoken and by *whom*. There is no room for either colour or class in her analysis. Gayatry Chakravorty Spivak's analysis of feminine complicity in the imperialist project is highly pertinent.[48] Speaking or being silent within a vast empire in which the primary marker of national identity lay in the English language cannot be reduced to the simplification of a gendered difference in which *men* could speak and *women* could not. Middle-class women who spoke standard English took precedence over those who did not, and even those who spoke with non-standard accents or dialects. Though there may have been a growth of interest in dialect poetry in the nineteenth century its main interest (as today) lay in its curiosity value, while literature written in non-European languages had very little, if any, influence on the mainstream. Writers writing in English from those cultures are equally faced by 'silence'.

Spivak's analysis of the various critical approaches assigned to texts from different parts of the world is particularly fruitful in relation to the presuppositions that underlie the analyses of critics such as Gilbert and Gubar, and Rosenblum. She outlines a double standard of critical thinking: 'an isolationist admiration for the literature of the female subject in Europe and America...supported and operated by an information-retrieval approach to 'Third World' literature which often employs a deliberately 'non-theoretical' methodology with self-conscious rectitude.'[49]

This outline fascinatingly suggests the mapping of the mind/body, intellectual/physical split, conventionally gendered masculine/feminine, onto whole bodies of literature, in a way that emphasizes the role of perception: of the *reader* who explores according to predetermined value systems. The pattern recalls my own suggestion that the double standards Victorian critics applied to male and female writers gendered the process of reading. Spivak's outline is flexible enough to be applied to any literature that destabilizes the unexamined assumptions supporting the western individual.[50] In relation to a *historical* study such as this it seems strikingly relevant to the treatment of medieval literature by contemporary critics who, as Patterson seems never to tire of pointing out, employ the medieval period as a lesser, simplistic other against which they can define their own projects.[51] If the imperialist state seeks to deny its cultural others as part of its insistence on the universality of its own cultural project, then this project cannot be restricted to relationships within the present. The shadows of past selves cannot be allowed to disturb present patterns: the past must seem lesser, or simpler, or unreal. The failure to recognize medieval elements within Victorian (and other) literature that seems pervasive among modern critics suggests a complicity in the 'isolationist admiration' Spivak perceives unconsciously at work in much contemporary feminist criticism.[52]

Modifying Spivak's outline in order to accommodate the past—seeing it as 'mythologized' (or 'feminized') in the pursuit of present homogeneity—allows the possibility of variant interpretations of that past, especially from the perspective of groups disadvantaged within the dominant ideology. Just as Spivak questions the methodology of feminist critics who isolate the study of the female-authored novel from its ideological context, so I wish to question the failure to consider the ideological ambiguity of a pervasive Victorian medievalism. Gilbert and Gubar do not examine the medieval heritage; Rosenblum looks back to 'Petrarchan amatory patterns' as if these patterns are no different from those of classical literature. When Dorothy Mermin, a prominent and sensitive critic of Barrett Browning, discusses medievalism—which she does only twice in her otherwise admirable book on the poet[53]—she sees it in terms of an 'escapism' that the poet left behind. Mermin's discussion of Barrett Browning concentrates on the Romantics and the classics for her notion of the 'literary tradition', stressing, as do many other critics, the masculine accomplishment signified by learning classical languages. She relates it to Walter Ong's description of the implications of learning Latin for boys in the Renaissance: '[It was] a puberty rite designed not only to exclude girls and women but to separate boys from female society and in particular from female language, the mother tongue.'[54]

Yet if learning the classics provided entry into a separate world of authority which left the mother-tongue behind, then medieval writing represented continuity, part of an unbroken line of '*mother*-tongue' literature leading to the present. The two literary traditions with their respective 'ancients' attained wholly different connotations. Where, for example, classical literature was unfamiliar and exclusive, medieval writing was *inclusive*, familiar not only in its language but also in its Christianity. The very absence of elements of Latin—the language of the fathers, of law and administration, of classical learning—within medieval English was supposed to render it 'purer', to prove it closer to 'nature', an argument I came across in the early 1980s when I first studied Chaucer. Yet if this approach in its more naive form is no longer current, the failure of many modern critics to recognize the complexities of medieval literature demonstrates its subtle continuity. Mermin, for example, does not notice that Barrett Browning's poem 'The Lost Bower' rewrites *The Floure and the Leaf* to the extent of paraphrasing passages of its forebear. More seriously her analysis is distorted by misreading medieval elements as representations of an unmediated nature: as the 'feminine' alternative to a creativity defined only in terms of 'masculine' classical paradigms.[55] Despite the sensitivity of her readings Mermin's failure to examine a home-grown tradition of English-language, mother-tongue alternative to the classics leads to a single, gendered conclusion: by silencing the medieval she reiterates the insistence on the single and the masculine by which a patriarchal system silences its others—including its women.

Gendering Literary Traditions

> Never nightingale so singeth:
> Oh, she leans on thorny tree,
> And her poet-song she flingeth
> Over pain to victory!
> Yet she never sings such music—or she sings it not to me.
> —Elizabeth Barrett Browning, 'The Lost Bower', xxxix

It is therefore fitting that I should start this final section with the passage from 'The Lost Bower' which rejects the nightingale song, the song that in *The Floure and the Leaf* was associated with the true aristocratic company, with the clear differentiation of sexes and the fixed and unchanging laurel tree. 'The Lost Bower' can be read as more than a psychological self-portrait (Mermin's approach) or as engaging with a single medieval text: it can be seen to engage with literary tradition *per se*, in terms not only of the classical 'fathers' but of the patterns of medieval literature. That Barrett Browning elects to rewrite *The Floure and the Leaf* itself points to her ability to draw consciously on patterns outside the 'Petrarchan amatory tradition' noted by Rosenblum. She rejects the universal significance of the nightingale song as a figure of poetry ('never nightingale so singeth') and emphasizes the relation between text and receptor ('or / She sings it not to me') in the production of meaning. The policing of gender roles by the literary establishment thus allows a space from which they can be questioned: Barrett Browning's emphasis on the reader's role is perfectly in accord with the Victorian emphasis on double standards but it allows her to suggest that there is no 'given' tradition, that meaning is relative. If the voice of the nightingale is not addressed to her, other choices are available. As I shall demonstrate in the more detailed discussion of Barrett Browning's poems in the next chapter, this poem chooses the figure of the daisy (that which *The Floure and the Leaf* opposed to the nightingale) for the qualities in which I consider the medieval text has a covert investment: harmony and integration, openness rather than hierarchy. The fact that the flower reappears with a similar function in other poems suggests that it is a conscious choice.

The suggestion that there is no 'given' tradition is not a radical move: literary tradition has always been a contested arena with different factions associated with a different range of material. The eighteenth century 'battle of the books', in which the 'moderns' were set against the 'ancients', is a pertinent example of partisan conflict about what constitutes 'the' literary tradition. As Beer points out, the different educations received by different social groups meant that class relations were inevitably implicated in the argument. Quoting from a discussion of the issue in Richardson's *Sir Charles Grandison* she notes that:

> Richardson's social and literary circumstances made it inescapable that he should defend the position of the 'moderns'. He was not a man of classical learning and, as his acutely sensitive social consciousness forever reminded him, he was not a member of the 'world'.[56]

Though Beer does not mention gender here her argument can be extended to include it. The very fact that Richardson gives the voice supporting the 'moderns' to a woman, Harriet Byron, indicates the relevance of this debate to women[57] while Beer's suggestion that 'the debate had…particular force for the novelists, since the forms they were evolving found no sanction among the ancient literary kinds'[58] extends the likelihood still further.

Richardson's eighteenth-century support for Milton demonstrates the jockeying for position of the rising bourgeoisie within an accepted status quo. Social instability in the early nineteenth century, however, took more extreme forms with savage repressive measures being taken against public disorder.[59] The spread of education at this time was part of a conscious strategy of discipline, an attempt, above all, to control the restive working classes.[60] Yet this education still maintained privilege in the crucial differences between the 'cultured' education available to the élite and that offered to those outside: the former group were saturated in the classics, learning Greek and Latin literature, philosophy, etc.; the latter group, which included women as well as the less well-heeled middle classes, learnt modern languages and English-language literature as well as more technical skills. The dispute between 'moderns' and 'ancients'—each with its covert claim for social status—is sidestepped in an education rooted wholly in English-language literature, a literature that instilled nationalist pride and claimed its own 'ancients',[61] but 'literature' continued to be differentiated according to education and the languages in which the different groups were educated.

I want to argue that these separate traditions should not be seen as transparent carriers of identical patriarchal values. Beer's comment on the eighteenth-century novelist's preference for 'modern' literature can be modified, for example, in the light of medieval genres—in a way that highlights gender. The major forms of *classical* literature were drama (especially tragedy for the Victorians) and the epic: both genres in which 'masculine' values of war, violence and death were uppermost. Popular forms of *medieval* writing, on the other hand, include the romance and the lyric: genres in which the 'feminine' concern with relationships and love is central—concerns at the heart of the novel, the form most frequently written by women. Other medieval genres provide models of a literature understood not as representation (cf. Rosenblum) but as an arena of contested meaning: centrally of course, the debate, particularly in the direct discussion of the *querelle* which foregrounds rather than silences the issue of gender.[62]

Beer's comment on the role of class in directing eighteenth-century preferences for either 'modern' or 'ancient' authors thus politicizes the activity of reading. Discussing the 'revived and conscious classicism' of the 'so-called "younger Romantics"', Marilyn Butler takes a similar line: '…the battle for the defence of the classical and Mediterranean South was stoutly fought for a decade from 1812 by a generation of liberal English writers who believed they were fighting for their political principles.'[63]

Butler's argument extends to the political implications of Coleridge's religious medievalism which she sees as 'professedly exclusive' and deeply conservative.[64] The value of this argument is not that it establishes clearly defined and unchanging meanings[65] but that it suggests that the arts of particular nations can be read *in relation to* particular ideological positions: positions that are then—as in both *The Floure and the Leaf* and Barrett Browning's conscious rewritings—open to subversion.[66] The nostalgic medievalism pervasive among Victorian artists, architects and thinkers must be theorized, not only in terms of its role in the imagination of the nation-state, but also in its reflection back onto the problem of gender that dominates the period. It is clearly in the interests of feminist critics to destabilize notions of a single 'literary tradition' and to replace it with a recognition of the class and gender implications of its contestation.

The double associations with 'masculine' authority and political radicalism help to explain why so many Victorian women passionately wanted to learn the language and cipher-like script of Greek and why their attempts to do so might still be marked by exclusion from the educated privilege it signified.[67] In *Aurora Leigh* Romney's comment on Aurora's Greek verse marks this exclusion. It is not 'real' Greek but 'lady's Greek / Without the accents' (II, ll. 76–77). I want to suggest that this hunger for a masculine language and the literature associated with it is accompanied by an additional attraction to a medieval writing feminized in contrast. The distinction between the two is sharply evident in Barrett Browning's work. Generally recognized as the most intellectual woman of her day, she 'undertook intense study of English and Greek prosody'[68] and chose to write on two very different literary traditions: the Christian writings of the Byzantine Greek Fathers (the most obscure of classical literatures) and English poetry from medieval verse to the writings of her contemporary world (a literature shared with everyone she knew). The distinct values associated with a scholarly father-tongue literature and the 'tender' 'sweet' singing of a mother-tongue poetry are clear. Rosenblum's pity for the woman faced with a literary tradition which silenced women seems both misplaced and condescending: Barrett Browning had several traditions[69] and they meant different things.

Seeing language and literature in these terms—as mother- and father-tongue traditions—allows a model of gendered difference to be read into the alien sublimity of Greek pagan literature and that associated with the home, with a cohesive and domestic life.[70] As a strategy of thinking about intertextuality, it has particular relevance to Barrett Browning's work, which is fundamentally interested in language and communication, while suggesting a different approach to the difficulties faced by intellectual women to that adopted by Deirdre David in her exemplary study of *Intellectual Women and Victorian Patriarchy*.[71] David accepts the premise that literary models are unreservedly masculine when she asserts that Barrett Browning's 'entanglement in the ideological matrix of sex, gender, and intelligence that produced the Victorian

woman intellectual seems to have determined a firm identification with male modes of political thought and aesthetic practice.'[72]

David's sophisticated reading of Barrett Browning's place as an
intellectual draws on Gramsci's concept of the 'traditional intellectual' who claims to stand for transcendent values and harks
back to a (mythical) point of cultural homogeneity. She sees
Barrett Browning's writing as registering no anxiety, as leaning
back to a feudal state in scorn of a materialist age, and rejecting
the modern realism of the novel.[73] But David needs to reconsider
the significance she ascribes to the medieval ideal she sees as
being so attractive to Barrett Browning. Its significance cannot be
reduced to the cardboard univocality of 'a "mythical" point of
cultural homogenity'. For many an educated Victorian the Middle
Ages were far from being 'masculine'. Kevin Morris draws attention to Charles Kingsley's assessment of St Francis as 'unmanly,
superstitious', and to his reliance on gendered paradigms:

> ... even his nationalism and racism, which also stimulated his anti-
> Catholicism, were sexually inspired: since the Anglo-Saxons, 'a
> female race', had been impregnated by 'the great male race—the
> Norse' (*LM*, I, 201), the English had the correct proportions of
> male and female, and could not, therefore, tolerate the intrusion
> of an effeminate Latin Church. Medieval monasticism typified this
> effeminacy, for it was 'essentially a feminine life', wherein men
> resorted to 'the weapons of crafty, ambitious, and unprincipled
> women' (*LM*, II, 212-13).[74]

The vehemence of this attack and its clear equation of medievalism and femininity suggests that there may well be different
reasons for Barrett Browning's attraction to the medieval than
political conservatism. It also raises interesting questions about
the silencing of the medieval in many feminist readings of Victorian writers.

If, as David suggests, Barrett Browning's work grows primarily
out of other texts, then her anxieties are unlikely to emerge in
her representations or her fluency. It is more likely that they will
be found within the *textual*—in the constant seeking for generic
change (especially in *Aurora Leigh*) which indicates a desire to
shift, to change the accepted norms;[75] in the strange juxtaposition
and confrontation of (masculine) classical and (feminine) medieval traditions. To suggest that literature always figures repression

is to deny its ability to express multiple and conflicting things—to refer back to the myth of Philomela, it denies its ability to articulate the violations of a violating society. If David rests on an analysis of 'literary tradition' that has no place for the feminine then it is unsurprising that she sees confidence rather than uneasiness in Barrett Browning's constant innovation and generic manipulation, her insistence on peculiar rhymes and archaicisms. From my own interest in the poetic nightingale as the literary voice of both classical and medieval cultures, I would argue differently, for I see that this figure provides an index of Barrett Browning's own anxieties about art and gender as much as it provides an index of shifting boundaries of ideological change.

Chapter 5

Bitter Confusions: Barrett Browning among the Nightingales

> Children have been menaced (before now)
> by nightingales, so why should not
> the bride be made uneasy by a web
> of lace and artificial roses?
> —Brenda Chamberlain's epigraph to her etching,
>   'The Bride Enmeshed', Black Bride series, no. 4

> The poet went out weeping—the nightingale ceased chanting,
> 'Now, wherefore, O thou nightingale, is all thy sweetness done?'
> —'I cannot sing my earthly things, the heavenly poet wanting,
> Whose highest harmony includes the lowest under the sun.'
>
> The poet went out weeping—and died abroad, bereft there;
> The bird flew to his grave and died amid a thousand wails.
> And, when I last came by the place, I swear the music left there
> Was only of the poet's song, and not the nightingale's.
> —Elizabeth Barrett Browning, 'The Poet and the Bird'[1]

Barrett Browning was undeniably acquainted with the long association of bird and poetry: she closely annotated her volumes of Shelley's prose, paying particular attention to the *Defence* where he identifies the poet with the nightingale,[2] and if she dared to be *slightly* critical of Milton[3]—the poet who most closely associated himself with the nightingale—her verse displays a fascination with his work.[4] Weaving her texts from others to an unprecedented degree, one would expect the nightingale to be prominent in her poetry even if it presented her with difficulties, and in her prose she employed the nightingale as a synonym for the poet.[5] Yet this is not the case. She did not object to the lamenting nature of the nightingale—she considered that 'the *ai ai* of Apollo's flower is vocally sad in the prevailing majority of poetical compositions',[6] while her favourite passage from her favourite playwright was Cassandra's agonized interview with Clytemnestra in Aeschylus's *Agamemnon*[7] (the passage I singled out as playing particularly on the Philomela figure)—but she distinguishes the 'weeping' poet from the 'wailing' nightingale in her own verse. As in the early poem quoted above, the ninth *Sonnet from the Portuguese*) sets the melancholy music of the poet against the 'valley nightingale', while as I note in the previous chapter, the poet-song of the nightingale is not addressed to the female auditor in 'The Lost Bower'.

Aurora Leigh (1857) attempts a new poetry rooted in the female voice. Aurora's very name suggests her renewal of the darkened political world associated with Romney. Yet the bird with which she is associated is not the nightingale but the lark. This may seem to be purely decorative, an individual choice with far less signifi-cance for feminist readings than the female body-imagery which pervades the poem, but, on closer examination, the refusal of the nightingale seems very deliberate. In writing the story of the female poet, Aurora, Barrett Browning confronts aspects of the classical tradition in which the poet grows out of a victim figure— a raped and silenced girl—and one way of reading *Aurora Leigh* is to see it as recasting the myth of Philomela. In this version the roles of the two 'sisters' are merged and rearranged: the raped girl becomes a loving mother, while after initially writing success-ful but insubstantial ballads, her 'sister' becomes a true poet. Like Procne and Philomela both women are linked to a single man, but rather than being a deceiving rapist, Romney himself is a victim of the materialist society that Barrett Browning sets against art. In order to allow Aurora a voice as a female poet, Barrett Browning also rewrites the conclusion of the myth. Where Procne and Philomela invert their role as nurturers by dismembering Procne's child—and are then expelled from the human commu-nity as birds—Aurora and Marian are able to move away from a treacherous fatherland,[8] to find a motherland in Italy and to-gether to care for Marian's son. As mother and erotic object, the mythical sisters can be seen as alternative, complementary selves;

by refusing either to be reduced to Romney's object or to compete with Marian for his attentions, Aurora (unlike Philomela) keeps her tongue. This marks a fundamental change in the myth, one that does not reject the authority of the classical pre-text but opens it up to allow the female poet to continue to speak in the 'human' world.

One way of attempting to rewrite the classical myth in order to make place for the female poetic voice is to introduce elements of medieval poetry. *Aurora Leigh* is often seen as an epic poem with the content of a nineteenth-century novel, an approach which sets up a binary opposition between past and present, poetry and prose, in which poetry is inevitably cast as classical, ancient and masculine and prose is seen as modern and feminine. This rigid distinction serves the purposes of neither the feminist critic nor Barrett Browning, restricting options by disallowing the possibility of a third category, of an 'ancient' poetry which is neither classical nor concerned with the battles and defeats of the 'masculine' epic, a medieval poetry in which the female nightingale speaks for the winning (aristocratic) side. The emergence of the female poet in *Aurora Leigh* is intimately caught up in a debate about the relative merits of art and politics: the very choices that mark the abstract resolutions of *The Cuckoo and the Nightingale* and *The Floure and the Leaf* respectively. It is an uncompromising stance: the alternative to Aurora's inclusive world of art is a world of political expediency in which the repression of the *feminine* figured in *The Cuckoo and the Nightingale* is shockingly literalized as the prostitution of *women*.

Language, Literature and Relations with the Past

> I do not ask, I would not obtain, that our age should be servilely imitative of any former age. Surely it may think its own thoughts and speak its own words, yet not turn away from those who *have* thought and spoken well. The contemplation of excellence produces excellence, if not similar, yet parallel.[9]

This passage from the preface to Elizabeth Barrett Browning's 1833 translation of *Prometheus Bound* expresses her commitment to both a 'modern' voice and the 'excellence' of past literature. Her poems grow from other poems, her voice from a mixture of other voices 'if not similar' yet parallel. This interest in the relation of present to past voices is foregrounded throughout her work as demonstrated in the two extensive essays on literary tradition: 'The Greek Christian Poets' and 'The Book of the Poets', that she published in *The Athenaeum* in 1842. The second is the more interesting for my purposes, for, in a review of an anthology of English poetry, she links the 'originator' of that poetry—Chaucer—with the nightingale, drawing on its medieval associations with spring love and poetry rather than the classical ones of pain and lamentation. It is a quiet comment but in view of the repeated references to poets as nightingales in the rest of the piece, it is significant.

> He was made for an early poet, and the metaphors of dawn and spring doubly become him...He is the good omen of our poetry, the 'good bird', according to the Romans, 'the best good bird of the spring', the nightingale, according to his own creed of good luck, heard before the cuckoo.[10]

The poem to which she refers here is, of course, *The Cuckoo and the Nightingale*, and, possibly drawn by the nightingale reference, the very next poem to which she alludes is *The Floure and the Leaf*—as revealed by the sustained allusions: the daisy and the fragment of French song in its praise (*si douce est la marguerite*), the references to the young oak leaves, and the 'visions of ladies in white and green [glimpsed] between the branches'. Both of these poems were thought to have been written by Chaucer at this time. Her article is keen both to establish a clear line of inheritance from the 'child-like' Chaucer to the 'adult' world in which she and her readers live, and to set him beside the great poets, Homer and Goethe, the classical Greek and the modern Romantic. This reference to the nightingale is thus part of a wider project of establishing Chaucer's poetry in a fresher, more delicate world, his voice the 'dawn' of a new literature, a project with implications for her own desire for a new poetry in *Aurora Leigh*. Though there are few nightingales in *Aurora Leigh*, her name and the vocabulary of renewal demonstrate links between her voice and that of Chaucer and the promise of a new world, in Aurora's case built on a mixture of love, poetry and women: the classical paradigm rewritten without its pain.

How the past was to be related to the present (the concern voiced in the passage from the *Prometheus Bound* preface) was a concern that Barrett Browning shared with many of her contemporaries (especially, and significantly, Browning). Her first published poem, *The Battle of Marathon*, is an epic based in classical Greece. It works with a very simple idea of the heroic past as quite distinct from the writer: a lost age of masculine battle. In this text the poet *commemorates* lost virtues: she neither investigates the historical event nor questions its dislocation from the present. As she grew older, however, this model no longer satisfied and she increasingly questioned the nature of history itself as something separable from the present. Her poetry thus tends to draw the past into her present. In the modern epic of *Aurora Leigh*, for example, dramatic interest moves into the psyche and the heroic struggle takes place against received patterns of behaviour, that inheritance of the past, rather than against other nations (as in the classical model)—or the corruptions of a materialist society which can be left behind (as in Wordsworth's *Prelude*). This same questioning of the past provides another way of understanding the restless negative energy of the poem briefly discussed in the previous chapter, 'Bianca among the Nightingales'. This lyric marks a further shift inward from the vast cultural scope of the epic, focusing on the individual at its centre. In 'Bianca' the very identity of the abandoned woman falls apart under the pressure of vivid memories which erupt uncontrollably into a vague, lost present. History, in the poetic voices of the nightingale thus confronts and interpenetrates the desperate speaker: 'the nightingales sing through [her] head'. The poem's nightingales evoke both Greek tragedy and medieval erotic love, and the shifting significance that the speaker sees in their cries destabilizes any certitude as to their meaning: much as Giulio's defection has undermined her ability to believe in the solidity and referentiality of language itself (v, 8). If Armstrong's analysis of the role of gender as a mediator of wider issues is accepted 'Bianca' appears as a paradigmatic Victorian text from yet another perspective: her anguish is more than an individual anguish, the poem articulates more than the problem of the female poet. The tremendous sense of constriction, the immense anxiety about voice, the determination of the present through the past, the natural turned threatening, the concern with the relation of nationality and identity: the extraordinary intensity of this small poem dramatizes the problems of the alienated individual in the unstable Victorian world.

'Bianca among the Nightingales' is such a strange passionate poem that it forms the obvious focus for this chapter. It draws together patterns from both medieval and classical literature in its quest for a new voice that allows space to the feminine. But in the self-conscious arena of Victorian poetry it is insufficient to detach the poem from its context and to see it only in terms of an abstract negotiation of past literatures. The immediate context of 'Bianca' is provided by Barrett Browning's abiding interest in the relation of female figures to linguistic and literary patterns. The quest for a new poetry invokes two paradigms—the medieval literary tradition seen as originating with Chaucer and the paradigm of the individual voice that is caught within the Philomela myth. Both of these elements seem important to Barrett Browning though both of them are modified in her practice. I want to argue, for instance, that the development of the female poet in *Aurora Leigh* rewrites the Philomela myth—as does the minor poem 'The Runaway Slave at Pilgrim's Point'. The use of medieval tropes, on the other hand—particularly the gardens, birds and daisies found in the romance and lyric—provide a gentle counterweight to the strenuous classical heroics to which she is ambivalently attracted. Both of these points create a significant difference to the way the poetry is read. This is why I want to discuss various short lyrics and consider *Aurora Leigh* before focusing on the most important poem for this study: 'Bianca among the Nightingales'.

The model of feminine poetry as a radical revision of earlier patterns, rather than an acceptance of a subordinate place in the decorous 'expressive' poetry Armstrong identifies as the female tradition,[11] can be seen within various individual poems from 'Caterina to Camoëns' to 'Bianca among the Nightingales.' I will discuss both in detail later but 'Caterina to Camoëns' serves as an example of this point here. In this dramatic monologue the dying beloved creates a personal voice out of the words of her absent lover, the Portuguese poet, Camoëns, who had written that her eyes were 'the sweetest ever seen'; just as the poet herself takes over and reinterprets those same words to create her poem. Though often seen as a mawkish love poem, I believe that the twisted and uncomfortable syntax of the text makes it deeply self-reflective, its muscularity drawing the reader's attention to language as a *material* which can be—and is being—manipulated. The dying woman who grasps her lover's throwaway words and builds an intricate claustrophobic world around them establishes an eerie dominance over that material. She destabilizes the platitudes of the amatory convention employed by Camoëns by confronting them with what they seek to escape: decay and, finally, death.

'Caterina' transforms an impersonal lyric fragment into the refrain of a monologue through which the personal story (the repressed element) speaks. The play with genre continues in *Sonnets from the Portuguese* which uses 'Caterina' as its (unspoken) starting point, transforming the monologue into the sonnet—and then transforming the sonnet into narrative by placing it in a series.[12] It thus provides a highly complex example of a text written out of other texts: a voice refracting—and challenging—other voices, other patterns. Because of this it highlights language as a material capable of being twisted into new shapes. Armstrong also stresses a struggle with authority, considering that the text meditates on dependency and 'the temptation to disappear before the object of adulation'. For her too the problem turns out to be one of language: '…it attempts to discover a language to represent and go beyond a master–slave relationship.'[13] Mermin's subtle analysis also looks at the problems of communication and the desire to *say* new things in her reading of *Sonnets from the Portuguese*, seeing the text as encapsulating the peculiar difficulties of the female poet.[14] In speaking her love the female poet struggles with the roles poetry traditionally allocates to the sexes—the active poet-lover and the passive beloved: such prescriptive roles exclude both female lover and female poet. She goes beyond Armstrong, however, by centring her analysis on the problem of *reading*. According to Mermin the widely felt embarrassment of readers encountering the text is a response to its daring transgression of these roles—not to any intrinsic sentimentality. That this embarrassment is not felt by the text's popular readers suggests that Mermin is correct: these readers are not embarrassed because they have not internalized the rules which Barrett Browning transgresses.

Despite the subtlety of both their readings, neither Armstrong nor Mermin sufficiently considers the role of the past: the fact that the complex voice of the poem takes and transforms the voice of a younger self which itself takes on and transforms that of the sixteenth-century Camoëns. Armstrong sees the poem in terms of its consideration of a paradigmatic *relationship*, Mermin feels that it deals with prescriptive roles. And though Mermin notes the Homeric echo (Achilles pulled back by Athena and the links with Renaissance love poems),[15] she does not examine Barrett Browning's reconsideration of her *own* earlier text, signalled by the reference to 'the Portuguese'. It is a striking recovery: 'Caterina to Camoëns' meditates on death by dwelling on past words that attempted to fix the moment ('sweetest eyes were ever seen') and insistently confronting them with a decaying woman; the first of the *Sonnets from the Portuguese* reconsiders this very topic to see poetry emerging out of love not death:

> ...a mystic Shape did move
> Behind me, and drew me backward by the hair,
> And a voice said in mastery while I strove, ...
> 'Guess now who holds thee?'—'Death,' I said. But there,
> The silver answer rang... 'Not Death, but Love.'

Though Mermin cogently discusses the exclusion of women from classical education as an important factor in disabling them from participating in high culture (and is very aware of Barrett Browning's nuanced classicism) she sees no role for the medieval literature to which they *did* have access except as escapist fantasy (see her discussion of 'The Swan's Nest' in *Origins*). She sees Barrett Browning's restless innovation in terms of 'potential voices' that look forward not as reconfigurations or hybrids of past literatures: 'it is as if she held in suspension all the elements of Victorian poetry, all its potential voices, with now one, now another, precipitating into verse.'[16]

Yet Barrett Browning's experimentation is deeply rooted in past patterns: her most popular poems (and those she wrote with the greatest fluency) were ballads. It is surely significant that she chose the ballad as the vehicle for the transgression of literary gender roles she examines in 'Lady Geraldine's Courtship'. The contemporary world that she insistently addresses being fascinated with origins and time, the modern voice she sought to establish was equally interested in the past. These 'innovations' had to look backwards before they could change the patterns of the present.

Gardens, Birds and Daisies: Barrett Browning's Medievalism

Like 'literary tradition', 'nature' has become a key category in much feminist criticism: the former being related to an educated masculine élite, the latter to the unlettered inspiration provided by the 'feminine' muse. Yet each category has a long and complex history and, as this study amply demonstrates, the standing of one in relation to the other not only varies in response to contemporary ideological change but interacts with residual meanings from earlier literature and its traces of past changes. The concept of 'nature' has no fixed meaning, but is caught within a mesh of relationships. As the chapter on English debate poetry demonstrates, medieval chivalry associated itself with an emblematic, controlled nature, rather than with the rationality which is conventionally attributed to the 'masculine'. For the nineteenth century the term is still further complicated by its standing in an English-language literature—rooted in medieval writing—itself 'feminized' as marginal to the education of the élite. Any division between masculine 'literature' and feminine 'nature' is thus doubly confused: by the patterns within the medieval texts themselves and by the interpretative context within which they were consumed. Medieval images of nature are as literary as images in classical writing and they challenge simplistic associations of nature with the feminine. Critics such as Mermin who interpret the enclosed spaces of gardens and bowers within Barrett Browning's poetry as negative 'feminine' images expressing restriction[17] fail to see the positive medieval patterns that haunt those images; the bower as an emblem of nature; the walled and secluded garden of medieval literature with its rich religious and erotic overtones. Assuming that these spaces are prisons, they fail to see that they may *also* be magical spaces. The open and enclosed spaces of Barrett Browning's poems represent a complex debate on different forms of poetry: they are *not* a simple representation of feminine repression. 'The Lost Bower' (1844) provides a perfect example: it rewrites *The Floure and the Leaf* itself, while a general 'medieval' context is established through references to *Piers Plowman* and Chaucer. The poem's explicit rejection of the open view

from Malvern hills for the tangled growth and hidden pleasures
of the wood implies a rejection, not of a masculine 'literature' for
a feminine 'nature', but of one kind of writing for another. And
Barrett Browning's facility was such that she modified that kind of
writing by summoning up the medieval garden without its nightingale. She shows instead a marked preference for the daisy: like
the nightingale associated with the feminine in both *The Cuckoo
and the Nightingale* and *The Floure and the Leaf.*

A consideration of medieval literary patterns radically changes
the way the enclosed spaces of Barrett Browning's poetry are
interpreted. Yet when Mermin discusses the restricted topography
of *Sonnets from the Portuguese*—

> ... the space [the poem] occupies is symbolical and highly schematic.
> It is sharply constricted on the horizontal plane but open to
> heaven above and the grave below... In her childhood [Barrett
> Browning] ran from one place to the other... but the movements
> she imagines for the future are almost always vertical...[18]

—she relates it to contemporary convention:

> ... the space, which becomes at the end a garden of art, belongs like
> the story enacted within it as much to Victorian artistic convention
> as to the setting of Elizabeth Barrett's life.[19]

Despite the fact that the examples she cites (including Tennyson's 'Lady of Shalott' and D.G. Rossetti's *Ecce Ancilla Domine*) are
clearly influenced by medieval art and legend[20] she makes no
suggestion that this convention might be influenced by older
traditions. But where Tennyson and Rossetti present the enclosed
female as erotically attractive in her helplessness and in the mixed
pleasure and pain that such a situation implies for the masculine
spectator, Barrett Browning replaces the passivity of the central
figure with the vertical *movement* associated with spiritual development.[21] The claustrophobic emotion dramatized in 'Bianca
among the Nightingales' builds on the creative ambivalence of a
restricted and constricting world, a world rooted in medieval patterns which appears in a more positive light even in her earliest
texts. The discussion of individual poems which follows focuses on
the significance of medieval literary patterns and the absence or
complication of the medieval nightingale as Barrett Browning
struggles to construct a modern voice which speaks outside the
conventional patterns of gender.

'Hector in the Garden'

Elizabeth Barrett Browning's childhood passion for Greek literature was focused in a warrior-shaped flowerbed at the centre of
her garden. In 'Hector in the Garden' (published 1850; probably
written 1844)[22] she sets the mixed reverence and fear with which
she viewed this figure in a wider context, struggling with her
longing for the simplicity, freedom and intensity of the lost self of
her past, seeking to find a new and personal voice as an adult.

Mermin associates the Homeric 'Hector' with the thunder of
paternal power and considers that the poem concerns 'an imaginative impasse that actually occurred…during the poet's childhood'.[23] She claims that

> …sound or movement from the floral figure aroused in the young
> poet the kind of 'terror' that is associated with the animation of the
> inanimate or revivification of the dead and could be allayed only by
> the example of birds singing in a pear tree, their song untainted by
> ambition or will.[24]

In this reading, fear pursues the child into the adult poet, making
the act of recreating the lost garden and its flowerbed equally
terrifying. She fears to revive

> …the Greek heroes of [her] childhood fantasies, nature, and the
> childhood that Homer and nature represent. She is afraid that they
> will drag her back into dreamy oblivion—into death—as things
> returned from the dead traditionally do.[25]

But the poem does not set an unmediated 'nature' against the
Homeric figure: *both* are literary. Far from being concerned with
the poet's anxiety or fear of creation (which reduces and 'explains' the poem in terms of autobiographical representation),
'Hector in the Garden' seems to be centrally concerned with language and ways of speaking. The child's perception is informed
throughout by *poetry* —even in the passages on 'nature'. If 'the
sun the pleasure taught [her] / Which he teacheth everything'
(ll. 11-12), the little girl qualifies such pleasure immediately in
terms of language: the thrush sings in Lydian (Elizabeth Barrett
had just begun to learn Greek); she has an effective 'charm'
against the rain (again magical language); and the companionship with the sun and associated emanation of light—

> We our tender spirits drew
> Over hill and dale in view,
> Glimmering hither, glimmering thither
> In the footsteps of the showers... (stanza viii)

—echoes the myth of Eos or Aurora, the goddess of the dawn who, in early versions, accompanied her brother Helios throughout his daily journey.[26]

Mermin sees these three relationships only in 'Homeric terms' and does not pursue their wider implications. Though 'Hector' lies at the heart of the child's garden, 'he' lies in the 'green shade' of two trees: the laurel, the tree of poetry, and the pear, associated in medieval literature with fertility—and the child looks to the birds in the pear tree for song, not to the passive giant. Even the description of the girl's loving service is related to the art of poetry:

> With my rake I smoothed his brow,
> Both his cheeks I weeded through,
> But a rhymer such as I am,
> Scarce can sing his dignity. (stanza viii)

If 'Hector' seems to capture all the light of the garden with his peculiar mixture of violence and delicacy—

> Brazen helm of daffodillies,
> With a glitter toward the light,
> Purple violets for the mouth,
> Breathing perfumes west and south;
> And a sword of flashing lilies,
> Holden ready for the fight (stanza x)

—the figure does not produce an 'imaginative impasse' (Mermin) in the girl: she has herself already been associated with light and her 'terror' is a stimulating mixture of hope and fear with which the child plays, not once but 'sometimes...often'.

Though the influence of the lost spirit and military might of the Greeks (figured in 'Hector') is counterbalanced by the setting of a real garden, the fertile tree, singing birds and small flowers of medieval poetry are clearly important. The daisy's tender roots penetrate 'Hector's heart through his breast plate'; the key adjective is 'tender', earlier applied to the 'spirits' of the girl and the sun; the key noun, 'daisy'. As I note in Chapter 3, the daisy represented 'feminine' delicacy and purity in the courtly love lyric, in the dream poem and in relation to the Virgin,[27] while the daisy also responds to the nightingale's song in Milton's first sonnet. When the child wonders

> If the disembodied soul
> Of old Hector, once of Troy,
> Might not take a dreary joy
> Here to enter—if it thundered,
> Rolling up, the thunder-roll? (stanza xii)

it is significant that she sees the daisies as providing his resting place and spiritual renewal:

> In this body rude and rife
> Just to enter and take rest
> 'Neath the daisies of the breast—
> They, with tender roots renewing
> His heroic heart to life. (stanza xiii)

Here the daisy is set against the hero and linked to the wider context of the birds and pear tree in an image strengthened by repetition and an insistence on both its age and its vitality:

> Did the pulse of the Strong-hearted
> Make the daisies tremble round?
> [it] ... was hard to answer, often:

> But the birds sang in the tree.
> But the little birds sang bold
> In the pear-tree green and old,
> And my terror seemed to soften
> Through the courage of their glee. (stanza xv)

But the poem counterbalances the young girl's limited perception with the more comprehensive vision of the adult. Where the child tends the left-overs of the great Greek poets and hopes that her creation will be animated by their spirit, the adult poet sees the gentle spirit of medieval literature hovering in the background. The difference in spirit between the two literatures is expressed by the 'dreary joy' of the Greeks (in line with current thinking about paganism), and by the hopeful (Christian) 'courage of [the birds'] glee.'[28]

To the adult poet not just 'Hector' but the *whole* garden, 'rich with pansies' and 'romances,' revives like a waking dream—an impression reinforced by the glowing colours and textures of the medieval dream poem or the literary genre of the romance:

> Oh, the birds, the tree, the ruddy
>> And white blossoms sleek with rain!
>> Oh, my garden rich with pansies!
>> Oh, my childhood's bright romances! (stanza xvi)

By setting 'Literature' (the figure of Hector) against 'Nature' (the garden) Mermin establishes two poles which she thinks equally exclude the female writer and thus contends that the poem concerns a woman's fear of creativity. But medieval literary patterns completely undercut this reading while, as I point out above, anxiety about creativity was not restricted to the Victorian woman writer. Recognizing that she alludes to two literatures within the poem both enables the problem to be focused more clearly and clarifies the conclusion. The poet's half-pagan childhood shared the symbolic perspectives of the Greek and the medieval worlds; as an adult she has 'put [those] childish things away' as superseded in a modern Protestant age.[29]

Though the shift from a delicate balance between charm and oddity to a tone of overt didacticism in the final three stanzas appears clumsy to the modern reader, this is in part due to a failure to recognize the poem's double recuperation of literary and personal pasts as part of a quest for a modern voice which incorporates past patterns rather than submitting passively to them. The adult poet determinedly writes for the present. The renewal once symbolized in the daisy and the birdsong is now directly associated with death and 'courage' through appeals to angels and to God—an active creativity and a new heroism constructed on Carlylean grounds of self-defining work:

> And despite life's changes, chances,
>> And despite the deathbell's toll.
>> They press on me in full seeming
>> Help some angel! stay this dreaming!
> As the birds sang in the branches,
>> Sing God's patience through my soul!
>
> That no dreamer, no neglecter
>> Of the present's work unsped,
>> I may wake up and be doing,
>> Life's heroic ends pursuing,
> Though my past is dead as Hector,
>> And though Hector is twice dead. (stanzas xvii–xviii)

As in the poems mentioned previously, Barrett Browning does not reject established patterns but subtly plays off one against the other, modifying the outcome to fit the modern world. The main modification is the omission of the nightingale: the chief singer of the medieval bird-chorus as well as the bird of poetry. The poem wrestles with problems of poetry, tradition and gender which summon up the figure of the nightingale, but the medieval topos which sustains the child's imagination is that of the daisy. If the child learns her craft in the shadow of two literatures, the poet selects the aspects which she needs for her adult voice.

'The Lost Bower'

'The Lost Bower' (published 1844), concentrates on the enclosed bower as a creative, as well as a safe, space. The poem alludes to several specific poems, but overriding all of these is the rewriting of *The Floure and the Leaf* with its bower and singing birds. Barrett Browning's version, however, differs radically from its forebear. The medieval text divorces the aesthetic from the political in an (impossible) attempt to integrate itself within the company of the Leaf; here the subject seeks, not for integration within an ideology which denies the self, but for a personal voice, a poetry which foregrounds the (feminine) subject. Both texts open by relating themselves to other literary texts: *The Floure and the Leaf* rewrites the opening lines of Chaucer's *Canterbury Tales*; 'The Lost Bower' refers to Langland's 'visions'. Yet where the medieval poem's literary reference is a near-contemporary work, in deferring to literature from the same period, Barrett Browning looks back to a recognized origin, to the emergence of a new (English-language) poetry. As in 'Hector in the Garden', struggles with language involve struggles with literary precedent related directly to present identity: Barrett Browning foregrounds the individual poetic 'I' denied in the earlier texts.

The greater length and complexity of 'The Lost Bower' allow for a more sustained examination of issues raised in the shorter text. The enclosed space is still there, but it is no longer associated with home and has become a private space hidden within a gendered literary landscape. The open spaces are masculine, the hills standing as a silent Greek chorus:

> Close as brother leans to brother
> 　When they press beneath the eyes
> Of some father praying blessings from the gifts of paradise.
> (stanza viii)

The enclosed space of 'the wood, all close and clenching' (l. 51), on the other hand, is associated with women and medieval poetry. Here 'the poets wander' and

> Bold Rinaldo's lovely lady
> 　Sat to meet him in a wood:
> Rosalinda, like a fountain, laughed out pure with solitude.

> And if Chaucer had not travelled
> 　Through a forest by a well,
> He had never dreamt nor marvelled
> 　At those ladies fair and fell
> Who live smiling without loving in their island-citadel.
> (stanza xiv–xv)

The woman's restlessness in *The Floure and the Leaf* seems 'unnatural' in a world that denies disorder, where the inner world of the bower reflects the patterns of the world outside its boundary. In Barrett's rewriting, however, those spaces are defined according to paradigms of 'masculine' and 'feminine' writing and her modern poem seeks out the *difference* which the earlier poet feared. The original poem sought fixity and moved outside time by presenting companies of ghosts; Barrett introduces temporality into the very foundation of the poem: firstly, by the fact of rewriting which summons up a past voice and modifies it with her own, particular voice, and secondly, by making this same poetic voice refer back to a different childhood self. This text is deeply aware of its reliance on the past. Just as in 'Hector', where the laurel-tree and the pear-tree with singing birds provide the nurturing background for the childish cultivation of the classical heritage, here the association of the distant Malvern Hills with 'Piers Plowman's visions' establishes the medieval backcloth to the heroic quest. Because space is made to signify—pointing to literary traditions, to childhood memories, to different genders—movement from one space to the other expresses choices about language and meaning. The rejection of (masculine) open spaces as a facile acceptance of the established order covertly expresses a desire for new (feminine) things which involves a reaching back to a dif-

ferent past. The heroic poet's quest to establish her personal voice
is imaged through the heroic child's attempts to find her own way
through tangled undergrowth. Yet the quest for a new voice
requires a reassessment of the past: the preface to the translation
of *Prometheus Bound* springs to mind. By being related to the
aesthetic (compare 'Hector') Barrett Browning's heroism is not
locked in the past, cut off from the present as is that of Tennyson
in the bleak *Idylls*. Where his heroes are long-dead knights, hers
are the long-dead poets, the 'old singers': knights have long since
disappeared but there are always new poets—including the writer
of this poem.

The debate between open and closed spaces, masculine and
feminine/classical and medieval literatures, is focused in the figure of the nightingale. Where the medieval lady listens for the
nightingale and then loses herself in the sudden beauty of its
song, Barrett Browning's echo of the earlier poet's words is divorced from its original object and related to the discovery of the
bower itself: 'I stood astonied—I was gladdened unaware' (stanza
xvii). At a stroke the figure of the nightingale—and the kind of
poetry with which it is associated—is displaced. The inner space of
the bower becomes the space of poetry rather than the nightingale's song which links the inner world to that outside. Mermin's
failure to recognize that there is a specific medieval text behind
'The Lost Bower' means that she misses its quality as a debate.
Though she does consider that the child's adventure is 'conceived
in specifically literary terms', she relates those terms only to a
child's fairy-tale: the story of Sleeping Beauty. She sees Barrett's
child protagonist taking on both the prince's role, by battling
through 'the briars that entrapped [her], and the barrier branches strong' (stanza xvi), and that of the princess who lies suspended within the magical space. From this perspective she reads the
girl's active/passive ambivalence as an index of the prepubescent
child's freedom from restricting gender roles. It is a problematic
reading, for Mermin assumes that the poem is about the *story*, not
about the poetry—and this text (like all Barrett Browning's other
texts) is deeply concerned with language and pattern rather than
representation. The child's activity and passivity is defined in
relation to the enclosed space which stands as a figure for both
original text and poetry itself. The poem enters and reorders its

medieval predecessor in order to make itself, and the child enters the physical space of the bower from which she was initially excluded and internalizes that space within her adult self as poet.

The most significant element of this poem about poetry and poets must be its insistence on the necessary relation between past and present, a relationship that takes place on two levels: of the present poem with its literary inheritance and of the adult poet with her girlhood self. In a deliberate shift from prescribed patterns both cases are relationships mediated by the space of the bower—not by the poetic nightingale. Fairy-tales and medieval poetry bring these two levels together: the first as the literature of childhood; the second as the childhood of (English) literature. I do not want to deny the validity of Mermin's concentration on the fairy-tale—but to highlight what is omitted, the significance of the discussion of literature itself. The physical 'passivity' Mermin associates with the trapped princess is not a fixed negative quality; as in 'Hector in the Garden' and the *Sonnets from the Portuguese,* it is an activity of a different kind,[30] one that allows for the intense activity of imagination and reverie. The stillness of the child within the bower is that of the female artist, a stillness like that of the child of 'Hector' who gently tends her flowerbed and expends her energy in imagination.

The bulk of the poem is taken up by seventeen stanzas of stillness as the child wonders about the garden-bower, its creator and its possible inhabitants. Where *The Floure and the Leaf* placed the companies physically outside the bower, glimpsed by a restless girl through its tightly woven branches, here the ladies—a medieval lady hooded like her hawk, waiting for a lover (stanza xxii); a Dryad, 'feeding in the woodland on the last true poet's song' (stanza xxxiii); fairies, escaped from a female church ('Ave Marys'; 'the chiming of St Catherine's' [stanza xxxiv])—*enter* the bower through the child's imagination, ghosts not of people but of medieval romance, classical myth and Christian folk tale. These figures belie their seeming passivity by being defined by verbs (i.e. by activity) and are significant because of their relation with poetry, story, music—not, as in *The Floure and the Leaf,* because they investigate masculinity. The child is thus as intensely creative as the 'old singers' that throng into her mind and the music emanates as much from her imagination as from any external force

> On a sudden, through the glistening
> Leaves around, a little stirred.
> Came a sound, a sense of music which was rather felt than heard.
> (stanza xxxv)

The references to the variety of different writings create a sense of the richness and variety of poetry: the music is not a fairy-tale (or 'natural') counterweight to a male-dominated literary tradition. By restricting the literary elements of the text to the fairy-tale, Mermin's reading unconsciously sustains the gendered division interrogated by such richness. Choosing to drop the references to the medieval lady, she perceives the bower only in 'pagan' terms—

> [it] seems to combine nature and art like a palace made by dryads and fairies, figures from a pre-Christian mythic nature[31]

—and sees the stillness within the bower as a recoil from 'pagan' creative energy, a return to a patriarchal Christianity:

> ...she is... 'lifted' back to the open hilltop, which is now heaped with affirmation and praise; 'the true mountains', testimony to the 'the truth of things' and 'the beauty of the truth', 'Nature's real'... [In] a thwarted attempt to hide in the heart of nature, to a God beyond nature, she has come back to the world ruled by God.[32]

But the reading falls down when the role of medieval writing in constructing what Mermin sees as 'the heart of nature' is taken into account. *All* representations within the poem are 'literary': the open space is itself enclosed by other spaces. The classical hills of the opening were shadowed by the greater hills—'for mountains counted'—of 'Piers Plowman's visions'; the wood is not the preserve of women and pagan nature-spirits but of *Chaucer's* women and the stories belonging to childhood. The integration of inner and outer worlds that takes place within the bower does not indicate a recoil from 'pagan' creative energy but the crystallization of the moment that occurs in the poetic act and which allows the child to become poet herself and, having internalized the poetic space, to externalize it with such grace in this text.

Though the bower is central, the music retains the links with birds and women of its 'Chaucerian' forebear:

If it *were* a bird, it seemèd
Most like Chaucer's, which, in sooth,
He of green and azure dreamèd,
    While it sat in spirit-ruth
On the bier of that crowned lady, singing nigh her silent mouth.
(stanza xli)

As Mermin suggests, the image of the music as a 'garment rustling downwards' (stanza xliii) is 'quasi-sexual': but it is the voice of adulthood only 'felt' by the child. It does no service to the complexity of Barrett Browning's poetry to simplify it to an analysis of the loss of freedom that accompanies a girl's puberty. Seen as the voice of poetry, the music of the bower incorporates its dual traditions even as it casts them off. In a familiar way it summons up both classical ('Pan or Faunus', stanza xxxvii), and English, poetry (the lark; the nightingale)—only to deny them. The music is neither that of the (male) lark, given cosmic significance by Milton and Shelley, nor the more earthbound (female) Philomela:

Never lark the sun can waken
With such sweetness! when the lark,
The high planets overtaking
    In the half-evanished Dark,
Casts his singing to their singing, like an arrow to the mark

Never nightingale so singeth:
Oh, she leans on thorny tree
And her poet-song she flingeth
    Over pain to victory!
Yet she never sings such music,—or she sings it not to me! (stanza xxxix)

The nightingale is essential to the text's desire to connect its 'lost bower', not only to the medieval rose-bower, but to the classical tragic secrecy of 'Oedipus's grave-place 'mid Colonus' olives swart'[33] (the ugly convolution indicates difficulties of integrating classical tragedy into a smaller personal world), but it remains only a voice within the bower, the use of the present tense denying its relevance to the narrator's present, as well as past, self.

The reference to the nightingale's 'poet-song' and the writer's exclusion from that song were discussed in the previous chapter but I want to dwell on the significance of the last line by referring to a very similar line in an earlier poem. In the Chaucerian

'Vision of Fame' (1838), an angel taught that fame and poetry must be paid for with youth and beauty. But the speaker claimed that the lesson was not for her: there being no place for her voice, 'she did not sing this chant to me' (l. 73). The singing, the gender of the singer and the object of the denied song are all repeated in 'The Lost Bower', but the ambivalence of the second version is significant. It suggests that by 1844 Barrett Browning sees her exclusion as relative rather than absolute. By referring to the Chaucerian/medieval tradition, she is able to accommodate it to her own voice by choosing to foreground its forgotten or marginalized elements.

Locked into her reading of the text as autobiography, Mermin sees the child's loss of the bower as resulting from fear of a creativity which she associates with the masculine: the grown woman cannot be prince as well as princess. But the poem is far more ambitious and there are compensations, accommodations. The bower's significance lies in its reconciliation of oppositions—activity and passivity; 'masculinity' and 'femininity'; medieval and classical; past and present; inner and outer—all focused in the still but intense act of creation, internalized when the child internalizes the bower. And it is in this internalization that the figure which *opposes* the nightingale in *The Floure and the Leaf* reappears. In *The Floure and the Leaf* the restless woman attempts to find a place in the patterns of aristocratic life by listening to and associating herself with the idealized nightingale and the company of constancy, of the leaf. Rereading her medieval forebear, however, Barrett Browning chooses the principle of integration—not of hierarchy and difference—and demonstrates her poetic debt to the medieval tradition:

> Oh, the golden-hearted daisies
> Witnessed there, before my youth,
> To the truth of things, with praises
> Of the beauty of the truth;
> And I woke to Nature's real, laughing joyfully for both. (stanza
> xlvii)

The daisy is stunningly translated from the principle of the effeminate company (whose failure to differentiate itself sufficiently makes it vulnerable to the chaotic elements), to that of the individual female writer (whose vulnerability is to be applauded as a mark of sensitivity). The 'golden-hearted daisies' recall the daisies whose roots tenderly renewed Hector's 'heroic heart'; here, however, they mark the new hero, the new singer, for Barrett Browning figures *herself* as the daisy enduring the sun and buffeted by the storms:

> For God placed me like a dial
> In the open ground with power,
> And my heart had for its trial
> All the sun and all the shower !
> And I suffered many losses,—and my first was of the bower.
> (stanza lxvi)

The lost bower is the lost Eden, the lost paradise of childhood, the pattern of desire itself and, as such, becomes a focus for the child's imagination, blossoming into multiple further literary associations—fairy-tale, tragedy, Persian tale.[34] Translated into a symbolic space within the self,[35] the bower becomes the site of a creative stillness that replaces physical activity:

> Through the fingers which, still sighing,
> I press closely on my eyes,—
> Clear as once beneath the sunshine, I behold the bower arise.
> (stanza lxix)

The internalized bower reawakens elements from medieval and classical writing which are tentatively attached to the music. Yet the varied references are held together by unanswered questions which leave the status of the nightingale hanging:

> Thrush or nightingale—who knoweth?
> Fay or Faunus—who believes? (stanza lxxii)

Similar questions concerning the nature of poetry pervade Barrett Browning's verse. Yet though the few references to the nightingale are often accompanied by allusions to her 'poet-song', these references appear perfunctory rather than significant and nothing is made of them.[36] The astonishing violence of 'Bianca among the Nightingales' thus seems to erupt out of nowhere—or to be related only to a story of foiled passion.

The struggle for a female voice appears in lyrics as disparate as 'Bertha in the Lane' or 'The Romaunt of the Page', which depict women expressing their love through self-sacrifice rather than language; poems like the monologue of 'The Runaway Slave at

Pilgrim's Point' or 'The Cry of the Children' find powerful voices in speaking *for* victims; the poem 'The Virgin Mary to the Child Jesus' and the play *A Drama of Exile* supply the voices of Eve and Mary which Milton omitted from *On the Morning of Christ's Nativity* and *Paradise Lost* respectively. 'Bianca among the Nightingales' takes on all these elements. In an unholy application of the principle that operates benignly in 'The Lost Bower', the various integrations—subject and object, past and present, received patterns and personal voice—produce a feminine poetry that finds its voice within the poetic economy through the paradoxical grounds of pain and exclusion.

I believe that the association of poetry with violation, pain and femininity, familiar from the myth of Philomela (which, from her reading, Barrett Browning clearly knew), haunts her work and appears to be reworked in the structural pattern of at least two of her poems ('The Runaway Slave' and *Aurora Leigh*).

Barrett Browning's quest for a new feminine poetry is, however, not to be seen only in terms of representative figures like Bianca: she wrote verse not novels. Struggling with conventions included struggling with the limits imposed on the woman's voice which decreed that it strive for softness and grace—*The Edinburgh Review* reproved Barrett Browning for *Poems before Congress* (1860) by commenting that 'to bless and not to curse is a woman's function'.[37] Her knowledge of languages (she commented particularly on Greek) attuned her to the *sound* of poetry and she could produce wonderfully modulated verse. That she chose instead to produce angular and choppy lines marked with uncomfortable if striking images is a choice that reflects her desire to write outside the affective and harmonious simplicity associated with the 'poetesses' of her time. She may make her poet praise Lady Geraldine's 'woodland singing', but her own verse is deliberately harsh—considered 'muscular'.[38] It is *not* the voice of the nightingale. These experiments with genre and rhyme seem part of a desire not just to *represent* women differently but to *speak* in a markedly different way. Her double traditions are drawn together in this search for a new voice which is unlike that of the nightingale. The earlier poems tend to draw on them separately—'The Lay of the Brown Rosary' invokes Gothic mysticism, medievalism, women; 'The Rime of the Duchess May', medieval ballad, a simpler world; 'The Dead Pan' summons up past glories of the classical world; while 'Wine of Cyprus' is filled with praise for the ancient past. In later poems the two traditions are more closely worked together—most obviously in *Aurora Leigh* and (stunningly) in 'Bianca'. The complex relations between the literary nightingale and the feminine, between the melodious voice and that of the woman, the violence and confusion of both Bianca and the nightingales can be seen in relation to the textual voices and female figures of the earlier poetry to which I now turn.

Bird, Angel and Murderer: Geraldine, Caterina and the Runaway Slave

Barrett Browning criticized women poets like LEL and Felicia Hemans for their single-minded concentration on love,[39] and when her own lyrics discuss love, the material provides the focus for examinations of other issues. Poems which appear to be about love—such as 'Lady Geraldine's Courtship' (1844) and 'Caterina to Camoëns'—are as interested in the problem of writing a new poetry with space for the female voice as are 'Hector in the Garden' and 'The Lost Bower.' That this female voice is not to be detached from social relations is evident in 'The Runaway Slave', where the female speaker flees the most oppressive of social relations: that of slavery.[40] In the first poem the Lady Geraldine takes on the active (conventionally masculine) role by wooing Bertram, a poet rendered passive (effectively 'feminized') by his lack of social status and the intensity of his emotions; in the second Caterina ventriloquizes words once spoken by her poet-lover and changes their meaning in the process. Both texts relate the speaking voice to wider contexts: social (the power relations between the aristocratic Geraldine and the peasant Bertram) and topographic (the relations between absent poet and his present beloved). The obsessive insistence on sugary heroines implies something more: it hints that there might be a negative image of the pure angel, that, as Nina Auerbach suggests, the angel may become demon.[41] The unnamed slave of 'The Runaway Slave' shows this figure in revolt; cast out of the blissful space she becomes both anguished and destructive. There may be no nightingales in this poem but a classical paradigm insistently comes to mind that points to the text's pertinence to this study: the depiction of Procne's thoughts as she murders Itys in Ovid's chilling version of the tale of Philomela.

'Lady Geraldine's Courtship'

> ... I could not choose but love her: I was born to poet-uses,
> To love all things set above me, all of good and all of fair.
> Nymphs of mountain, not of valley, we are wont to call the Muses;
> And in nympholeptic climbing, poets pass from mount to star.
> (ll. 29-32)

Bertram's praise of Geraldine in 'Lady Geraldine's Courtship' seems to establish his status as the Petrarchan lover and hers as the symbolic beloved. It also appears to support the Petrarchan expectations raised by the title—that the beautiful aristocrat is courted by her fine lover. As has been noted many times, however, Barrett Browning sets this pattern up in order to subvert it by the simple ploy of separating the lover from the poet. In *this* poem Lady Geraldine courts the silent Bertram. But the modification is not restricted to a simple separation and reallocation of roles; in the process of change the terms themselves and the values associated with them have to be renegotiated. The most significant of these changes lie in the association of poetry with a 'feminine' passivity and the ability of the idealized Geraldine to *speak*.

The text is informed by a mixture of literary models—Petrarchan lyric, medieval ballad, epistolary novel—with structures and patterns repeated and modified in relation to their original status. As well as being the idealized beloved Geraldine is coloured by an association with the medieval lyric—specifically with the enclosed space of her park and the small birds singing within it. As the stimulator of others' songs, the 'warden / Of the song-birds' (ll. 107-108), Geraldine evokes the fertile garden and magical bower of 'Hector' and 'The Lost Bower'; in his still, instinctive response, Bertram is aligned with the creative girl within it. As in those poems, the social world is unimportant, summoned up, like the Petrarchan patterns, only to be set aside. The aristocratic Geraldine elevates art above 'dry' politics, by aligning herself with a statue representing a female Silence:

> '...when all is run to symbol in the Social, I will... throw you
> The world's book which now reads dryly, and sit down... with
> Silence here.' (ll. 135-36)

In line with the Petrarchan convention itself her lovers see no difference between the two: 'A fair woman flushed with feeling... / Near the statue's white reposing—and both bathed in sunny air' (ll. 139-40). The two figures are strangely linked: where the sculpture is made of stone, Geraldine seems almost bodiless; where the sculpture is silent, she is overwhelmingly represented as either a transcendent or a bird-like voice. As befits an angel she speaks with 'holy sweetness, turning common words to grace' (l. 308); as an instinctive being she is likened to a bird—'she would break out on a sudden in a gush of woodland singing' (l. 171). Both metaphors unite in the description of the spiritual voice: 'so cadenced in the talking, / [it] Made another singing—of the soul! a music without bars' (l. 178). Art, nature, femininity and spirituality seem to coincide with a familiar pattern in the figure of Geraldine. Yet there are subtle modifications to that pattern, notably the fact that Barrett provides the voice with *subjects* for conversation:

> And she talked on—*we* talked rather! upon all things, substance,
>   shadow,
> Of the sheep that browsed the grasses, of the reapers in the corn,
> Of the little children from the schools, seen winding through the
>   meadow,
> Of the poor rich world beyond them, still kept poorer by its scorn.
>   (ll. 189-92)

The idealized figure of the silent beloved is altered even as it is evoked: the lovers come together over poetry (compare Dante's) but their love is cemented through *talk*. The disruption of the ideal is made even clearer in the 'Conclusion' where the interplay between poetry and the enclosed space, between Bertram and Geraldine, comes to the fore. The poem shifts its focus by moving *into* the enclosed space—here the bedchamber—while simultaneously moving *outside* the poet whose voice has dominated the poem so far. Just as the unearthly music drifts to the girl sitting in the bower, so Geraldine drifts into the weeping Bertram's room, repeatedly described as unreal, as a 'vision', an 'apparition', 'a dream'. Her ghostliness displayed in her pale face and white hands, Geraldine glides in from the window as a 'dream of

mercies', 'a vision...of mercies'. Her wraith-like figure simultaneously evokes and negates the vampiric 'belle dame', and the
desolate hillside on which Keats's doomed and deserted lover is
condemned to loiter is translated into the 'desolate sand-desert'
of Bertram's heart. Keats echoes through the sensuous sound of
the poem as well, through rich murmurous vowels, multiple half-
rhymes and numerous internal rhymes. The passage constructs an
aetherialized world in which Bertram demands stasis:

> Said he, 'Wake me by no gesture—sound of breath, or stir of
> vesture!
> Let the blessèd apparition melt not yet to its divine!
> No approaching—hush, no breathing! or my heart must swoon to
> death in
> The too utter life thou bringest, O thou dream of Geraldine!'
> (ll. 393-96)

Though the destructive 'belle dame' hovers in the background,
Keats is evoked in order to be refuted: the poet-lover receives his
heart's desire and this 'vision...speaks'.

As 'Lady Geraldine' was written to pad out the 1844 volume
of poems, it was probably written after 'Caterina to Camoëns':
Bertram's outburst of passion in 'Lady Geraldine' is fuelled in
part by reading Camoëns: 'that poem you remember, / Which his
lady's eyes are praised in as the sweetest ever seen' (ll. 227-28).
The cross-reference demonstrates Barrett's own fascination with
the phrase she had twisted into the refrain of 'Caterina'. Both
poems are interested in the relation between the ennervated
woman and the art object: the dying Caterina seems a more extreme version of the bodiless Geraldine. But where Geraldine is
proud, beautiful and pure, the object of Bertram's song, in
'Caterina' the pattern is more complex: the object of the male
poet in his absence reflects on herself as object and the poem
emerges out of the gap between the real—and fading—Caterina
and the fetishized depersonalized figure she became in her lover's
poem. The process is complicated still further by the fact that
Caterina obsessively identifies herself with that fetish, displaying
the alienated narcissism that results from seeing the self as another's object. As the voice of a woman caught within restricting
conventions, the poem conceals a brittle violence in its circular

denial of life—under its self-sacrifice lies the possibility of poison, of curses rather than blessings.

'Caterina to Camoëns'

Nothing I have read about this poem seems to me to do justice to its queasy fascination, its sickliness lying in the thrall of hidden violence. I would cite this poem against David's assertion that Barrett Browning displays no uneasiness with her role as a traditional intellectual. This text presents a deeply alienated monologue disguised as self-sacrifice, an 'I' speaking within an enclosed space into a void, a self that grasps words and makes new things out of them, creating a narcissistic universe with herself as both subject and object, fractured into speaking self and seen other, into an 'I' and her 'eyes'—though the latter are the blind objects of another gaze and do not seem to belong to her at all.

Though there are no nightingales, the association of the classical trope with the feminine victim gaining a voice, with poetry emerging out of pain, is central to a dramatic monologue in which a dying woman thinks over the poem in which her poet-lover referred to her eyes as the 'sweetest ever seen'. The classical paradigm focuses attention on the question of power: the woman could not be *more* passive, her words more self-effacing—yet she is all powerful, effectively transfiguring her lover's words, conferring new meanings in his absence. Befitting the concern with image (the eyes) and speech (Camoëns's poem and the new poem built on its foundation), the poem is dominated by the relation between vision and voice. Caterina's opening lines transform her to a gaze that sees across distance and into both past and future:

> On the door you will not enter,
> I have gazed too long: adieu!

Sibylline, selfless, almost dead already, she seems a male vision of the all-seeing feminine, with her short, panting lines:

> Come, O lover,
> Close and cover
> These poor eyes, you called, I ween,
> 'Sweetest eyes were ever seen!' (stanza i)

Obsessed with her image, Caterina bases her self-evaluation on *his* reported praise, achieving a tortuous distance from ordinary life and its concerns which at the same time dislocates her connection with her own self:

> 'Blessed eyes mine eyes have been,
> If the sweetest HIS have seen!' (stanza ii)

Rosenblum notes that the self-effacing 'eyes' and 'gaze' of Caterina point to the Victorian male's preoccupation with the rapt female face, commenting on the difficulties this reification causes the female artist who 'attempts to gaze at the visionary face'.[42] Mermin seems to suggest that Barrett Browning colludes with the dominant tradition in 'Caterina' by accepting the male point of view:

> ...being absent, [the poet] sees her only in memory, not as she actually is, and when she speaks to him he does not reply...[the poem] defines women in the amatory tradition as derivative, secondary, powerless, and doomed.[43]

But there is no indication that Camoëns *does* see Caterina 'in memory' nor does that matter—what she echoes are his words, his poem. Caterina does gaze at the rapt face—but she exposes it as a literary construct by placing it in quotation marks and making clear the distinction between her present self and the image by which he saw her. The poem thus simultaneously addresses the construction of poetry and the construction of woman as masculine other—and makes links between the two processes. Mermin's emphasis on the lover is not shared by this self-reflective poem: he is not even mentioned by name and if she 'speaks to him' she expects no reply. Though Caterina is 'doomed' she uses her future death to her own advantage: she is far from 'powerless' and her extreme self-effacement leads in a strange way to dominance. Caterina's words have a hypnotic strength which forces the reader to assess and re-evaluate her lover's lines. It is a disturbing poem: Caterina's self-abnegation is almost masochistic, appealing to a murky desire for dominance, and hence carrying a hidden aggression. It has affinities with contemporary studies of obsession, most strikingly with Browning's fascination with disturbed mental and sexual obsession, particularly in 'Porphyria's Lover' and 'Johannes Agricola' from his *Madhouse Cells*. It is interesting that Browning liked 'Caterina' so much.

As a still figure in the centre of an enclosed space, Caterina is recognizable as an artist. But where the music of Barrett Browning's other artist figures is stimulated by an external source—singing birds ('Hector'), music ('The Lost Bower') a melodious voice (Geraldine)—her voice turns incestuously in on itself, encompassing another's words. Hemming in speaker and reader, the claustrophobic refrain dominates the poem, even confusing the two categories by making its speaker a reader who speaks what she reads. In Camoëns's absence there can be no challenge to Caterina's interpretation. Interest is thus squarely on her, not on the lover who exists merely as a reflection of words spoken in the past. She speaks directly, her words gaining power in inverse relation to her ability to move, confidently drawing on literary tropes (e.g. the association of the cypress with mourning) to express sorrow and lost love. In control of the future, she issues (gentle) commands:

> Cry, O lover,
> Love is over!
> Cry, beneath the cypress green… (stanza x)

As in the previous poems creativity is associated with physical passivity, spirituality and a female figure within an enclosed space. The female figure is again characterized by singing—though angels, rather than birds, are summoned up, and churches, rather than parkland. Caterina is implicitly identified with an angel throughout the poem, but this angel is *not* passive. The stanza in which the identification surfaces openly turns on a single verb: Caterina's *action* in looking at 'Heaven':

> [will you] recall the choral singing
>   Which brought angels down our talk?
>   Spirit-shriven
>   I viewed Heaven,
> Till you smiled—'Is earth unclean,
> Sweetest eyes were ever seen?' (stanza xii)

The poem concludes with Caterina turning into a real angel 'with saintly / Watch unfaintly' looking down on her lover. Yet though the lines exemplify the Victorian fascination with deathbed scenes, with cloying sentiment, memories, tears and heartbreak, unlike other Victorian deathbed scenes (that of Little Nell provides the

standard reference), Caterina's projected death gives her increased power and vigour. At the moment of dissolution, she is
creepily dominant, her language permeated by verbs of which she
is the agent:

> I will look out to his future;
>   I will bless it till it shine.
> Shall he ever be a suitor
>   Unto sweeter eyes than mine… (stanza xix)

But is the blessing contingent on the greater 'sweetness' of the
imagined other woman? is there a hidden threat should Camoëns
be 'a suitor' to a woman with *less* sweet eyes? Barrett Browning
clearly does not intend such a reading, but her text certainly
allows it, and highlights the dangerous instability of such self-
abnegation. Humility can switch to vengeance, the creative artist
in different circumstances may twist to destructiveness. As in fairy-
stories the gift of blessing is accompanied by that of cursing:
Barrett Browning points out in 'A Curse for a Nation' that 'a curse
from the depths of womanhood / Is very salt, and bitter, and
good' (ll. 47-48).

In 'Bianca', a poem which bears a strong structural resemblance
to 'Caterina', the speaker *has* been abandoned for 'a worthless
woman' and she broods over his words, her belief in any truth
tarnished by betrayal. Caterina's words are haunted by the violent
shadow of the woman's curse; in 'Bianca' this violence twists back
on itself to burn the disorientated speaker. Both look back to the
past and to past relationships with absent lovers in order to find
meaning in the present. Each text is interesting in itself yet sheds
light on the other. The same is true for the next two poems: 'The
Runaway Slave at Pilgrim's Point' and *Aurora Leigh,* whose female
speakers do not refer to relationships with the past lovers in order
to define their voices. The female figures in each poem emerge
from the enclosed space (even if the images remain within the
text) and interact in a more complex materialistic world. Both in
the end reject that world for a new female voice linked to spirituality and love. I see both poems as grappling with the problem
of a feminine poetic voice which exposes the violence implicit in
the repression of the feminine shared by art and politics. Obviously 'The Runaway Slave' offers itself to a study of its content—
slavery and racism—or suggests readings that interpret the slave as

a figure of the repressions faced by women. I want instead to link it to the myth of Philomela/Procne: the myth of the poetic voice that emerges out of violation and pain.

'The Runaway Slave at Pilgrim's Point'

The links between blessing and cursing are clear in the opening stanzas of 'The Runaway Slave' where the hounded and exhausted slave drops to her knees to curse the land which the pilgrims 'blessed in freedom' (l. 21). 'The Runaway Slave' traces the emergence of a voice out of loss and pain, a voice which reflects back on the creativity that blossomed with love:

> I sang his name instead of a song,
>   Over and over I sang his name,
> Upward and downward I drew it along
>   My various notes,—the same, the same!
> I sang it low, that the slave-girls near
> Might never guess, from aught they could hear,
>   It was only a name—a name. (ll. 78-84)

Like Marian in *Aurora Leigh*, however, the singer is betrayed, raped and bears an illegitimate child—and her song stops. When her newborn child cried she could have 'made him mild' but she cannot sing 'the only song I knew' to a child whose whiteness and glance remind her of his violent father, the master who dragged her lover away from her. She suffocates him instead, buries the body in the forest and runs away, first cursing and then dissociating herself from the fractured society ('White men, I leave you all curse-free / In my broken heart's disdain' [ll. 252-53]). The poem ends as she throws herself into the sea: a place where differences are dissolved and the white child awaits her 'in the death-dark' (l. 251).

What interests me about this poem is the familiar convergence of betrayal, violation, child murder and transformation: all elements which recall the Philomela myth, the myth of poetry and violation. The Ovidian version in the *Metamorphoses* in particular comes to mind with its chilling depiction of Procne gazing into her son's face and assessing his likeness to his father before she kills him. As in the myth the poetic voice is gained by moving to the periphery of the polis, here defined as a land in which the binary oppositions of black and white dominate all relationships and reduce them to abstract commodities. The slave-woman blurs the physical and ideological boundaries that define this state. Her love for another slave ('Could a slave look *so* at another slave?' [l. 63]) and the song that emerges from that love together refute those who deny the slaves humanity[44]—as does her final refusal to curse her oppressors and to be defined as their victim within an economy of 'whips and curses'. Vertical and horizontal movements puncture the physical boundaries of the racist state: she digs below the surface of the earth and throws herself off its edge. In each case traversing the boundary enables a transformation to take place: the white child becomes dark in the dark earth; dissolved in the sea the black woman will meet and love her white child. And once the surface differences of white and black have been destabilized, all other boundaries blur. The dead child sings his mother's song of love and the drowning woman leaves the opposition of black and white behind as she gains her freedom, including free speech, by entering the world of flux.

The familiar patterns generate new ways of thinking about the poem. The slave-woman appears to merge the figures of Procne and Philomela: she is the singer, the raped girl, the mother who murders her child; her poetic voice reveals the violations which she has suffered but in the end it leaves all bitterness behind. Finally she herself is transformed when she leaves the divided human world behind:

> The clouds are breaking on my brain;
> I am floated along, as if I should die
> Of liberty's exquisite pain. (ll. 247-49)

It is an act that marks her freedom from the cycle of violation–revenge–violation that dominates the oppressive society. Barrett Browning rejects political resistance (the curses of the slave community), believing that change can only be effected through the love which connects and respects woman and man, mother and child, Christ and the world, black and white. The reciprocal relationship between the slave and her lover provides the example. They are not passive victims but actively creative—he carves her a bowl; she sings his name as a song—and hence marked out from a slave community defined as a mass shrinking from the whips of the drivers. But, as in the myth, love and creativity are impossible within the confines of the state and, because there is nowhere else to go, the unnamed slave kills herself rather than remain there.

The form that the Philomela/Procne myth takes in 'The Runaway Slave' reflects the rigidity of the materialist society within which the slave finds herself. Its boundaries are mapped so closely onto life and death that they can allow no change, yet the slave-woman is more 'alive' when she drowns in 'liberty's exquisite pain' than when she was a commodity on the racist/patriarchal market. Christ is the only figure able to heal the divisions and loathing that the poetic voice records. By identifying the bleeding slave-woman with the wounded Christ, Barrett Browning thus associates poetry with religion, the passionate individual voice with transcendent truth. The feminine voice thus becomes the true voice of poetry. Both elements—the Philomela/Procne myth and the figure of wounding and sacrifice—recur in *Aurora Leigh*: Barrett Browning's attempt to create a place for the epic feminine voice in a new poetry that incorporates and goes beyond gendered difference.

Birds and Women: Aurora Leigh *and the Later Poems*

> Barrett Browning's poetry, with the exception of some lyrics and the *Sonnets from the Portuguese*, urgently addresses questions of the place of poetry in a changing culture and the function of the poet in a materialist society.[45]

There is no place for mutual respect, or for the art that accompanies love, in the racist patriarchy of 'The Runaway Slave'. In *Aurora Leigh*, however, Barrett Browning creates a positive alternative to the materialist society in an art which provides a model of living which rests on *relationships* rather than commodities. Not only therefore does the poem trace the growth of a female poet but—as in the transposition of roles in 'Lady Geraldine's Courtship'—it also depicts the way a complex system of binary oppositions begins to unravel with a single change. The construction of a matriarchal community rooted in mutual respect, in art and in the nurturing care of the next generation depicts how the development of the feminine poetic voice alters the hierarchies of dominance, of class and gender, that underpin the existing patriarchal system. The old system is built on repression: the alternative to Aurora's world of love and art is one in which the abstract

repression of the feminine is literalized in the repression of wom-
en—most shockingly through rape and prostitution. The myth of
Danaë, the girl raped by a shower of gold, is as pertinent to masculine art (such as that of Vincent Carrington) as it is to materialist patriarchy.[46]

Because the poem is centrally concerned with the birth of the
poetic voice, the myth of Philomela and Procne proves useful
once more. In 'The Runaway Slave' the isolated figure of the slave
takes on the roles of both Philomela and Procne. *Aurora Leigh*
however expands upon the ambiguities of the myth by breaking
up and redistributing the various roles of Philomela and Procne
between Aurora and Marian. The violator in this poem is not a
single Tereus figure but a materialist (patriarchal) system. Aurora
challenges the values of that system by stressing the central importance of love: Romney can be detached from his 'misguided'
materialist beliefs. Where Tereus married one sister and raped
the other, silencing her in the process, Romney was to have
married Marian but marries her 'sister', Aurora, instead. In that
Marian and her child had made their home with Aurora, this
marriage associates all four in a new community based on love,
respect and art.

As I point out above, Barrett Browning not only rearranges
elements of the classical paradigm, she refuses to be restrained by
old forms and constructs new ones by weaving a disparate range
of literary genres and individual texts together. *Aurora Leigh* is
commonly described as a hybrid of two forms—the novel and the
epic poem—and hence as an attempt to integrate 'masculine' and
'feminine' forms of writing. Cora Kaplan looks to specific texts,
seeing it as 'a collage of Romantic and Victorian texts reworked
from a woman's perspective'.[47] Both approaches see such hybrid-
ization as actively disrupting masculine authority: Kaplan describes *Aurora Leigh* as 'the fullest and most violent exposition of
the "woman question" in mid-Victorian literature'. Yet once again
considerations of literary inheritances omit *medieval* patterns, in
particular, aspects of the medieval vernacular debate. As demonstrated in Chapter 3, debates like 'The Thrush and the Nightingale', *The Cuckoo and the Nightingale* and *The Floure and the Leaf*
mediate their ideological arguments through discussions about
women, chastity and/or desire. The emblematic 'nature' of the

first two of these aristocratic debates is set against the intrusive materialism assigned to the clerical and churlish figures respectively; that of the third attempts to defend the substantiality of the aristocratic ideal itself. In refusing the patriarchal materialism of contemporary bourgeois society, *Aurora Leigh* draws on the debate for a beautiful jewel-like alternative associated with women, poetry and love (identified specifically with the nightingale), literalized in the motherland of Italy where Aurora, Marian and the child live together in peace.

Discussing *Aurora Leigh* David focuses not only on its female body imagery—the breasts and milk celebrated by many feminist critics—but on the equally important figures of wounding and healing. Yet 'woman' is not the same as 'body': prioritizing the body need not imply that the primary focus lies on 'female sexuality'. The twelfth- and thirteenth-century identifications with the body and blood (and breasts) of the wounded Christ spring to mind, suggesting that the body is a shifting signifier: at times associated with the natural, at times with the spiritual, at others with the feminine—and sometimes with all three.[48] Barrett Browning encourages the association of body imagery with the spiritual through the images of the wounded Christ that appear in both *Aurora Leigh* and 'The Runaway Slave'. Reflecting her own interest in *The Floure and the Leaf*, the language of wounding and healing recalls the hidden violence and the stressed feminine healing of the medieval text. At the same time Barrett Browning's deliberate staging of a debate between art and politics echoes that poem's inability to align the aesthetic with the political. Despite refusing the nightingale as the bird of poetry, the text itself appears to invoke, rework and—incredibly—realign both the classical myth and the medieval aristocratic bird in the construction of the text itself and in the values it espouses.

Though both Mermin and Angela Leighton consider Barrett Browning to have left medieval 'escapism' behind after her marriage and move to Italy, I think that her habit of thinking through literary texts and traditions remains embedded in her work. The romance landscape and allegory of medieval literature colours the backcloth to the events of the poems as much in *Aurora Leigh* as in earlier texts such as 'Hector in the Garden' or 'The Lost Bower'. As in those texts, indices of this influence lie in the pervasive use

of both bird imagery and the enclosed space within *Aurora Leigh*:
elements which continue to be associated with women and art.
The rich imagery of breasts and milk so celebrated in recent
criticism should not obscure the 'great image of the bird, the
spread wings and open beak, [which reaches] from end to end of
the nine books of *Aurora Leigh*' noted by Alethea Hayter in 1962.[49]

Hayter sees the bird imagery in *Aurora Leigh* as a unifying and
uniform textual device rather than as a topos which signifies in its
own right.[50] Yet the imagery does not provide a mesh of connections that is fixed and coherent from start to finish. The poem
opens with unspecific references to birds but as it progresses
those birds are differentiated and associated with particular individuals. Some examples prove useful. In Book I the motherless
Aurora is

> …as restless as a nest-deserted bird
> Grown chill through something being away, though what
> It knows not. (I. 43-45)

Her aunt 'had lived / A sort of cage-bird life' (I. 303-304) and

> I, alas,
> A wild bird scarcely fledged, was brought to her cage,
> And she was there to meet me. Very kind.
> Bring the clean water; give out the fresh seed. (I. 309-12)

The figure of the girl in 'Hector in the Garden' who listens to the
singing-birds and wanders over the hills in the early morning,
here reappears as a *real* Aurora. As she grows into a poet she is
increasingly associated with the lark:

> …Alas, near all the birds
> Will sing at dawn,—and yet we do not take
> The chaffering swallow for the holy lark. (I. 951-53)

> …Now I might cry loud;
> The little lark reached higher with his song
> Than I with crying. (II. 743-45)

> The music soars within the little lark,
> And the lark soars… (III. 151-152)

> I took a chamber up three flights of stairs
> Not far from being as steep as some larks climb (III. 158-58)

'The June was in [Aurora], with all its multitudes / Of nightingales singing in the dark' (II. 10-11) when she first declares herself 'woman and artist'. Yet the overtly sexual image that follows—
of 'rosebuds reddening where the calyx split'—indicates which
part of the description is uppermost. The nightingale seems so
rich and sensuous as to be almost a temptation. When prostitution and rape are the alternatives to art the body becomes a site of
ambiguity. Though Barrett Browning fearlessly discusses sexual
attraction in the magnificent passage in book nine (ll. 820-23),
she avoids identifying poetry—and the poet—with erotic desire.
Aurora wishes to write a new poetry, purified of the past with
which the nightingale is so clearly caught up. Yet it attracts her
too:

> I must not linger here from Italy
> Till the last nightingale is tired of song,
> And the last fire-fly dies off in the maize. (VI. 301-303)

The Italian night is filled with remembered birds and insects
expressing movement, light and sound: moths, fireflies, 'melodious owls' and 'the silent swirl / Of bats'. Significantly left till the
last, the nightingales appear in a passage reminiscent of both
'The Lost Bower' and her own *A Drama of Exile* (where the night-
ingale-song both reminds Adam and Eve of Eden and marks their
exclusion):

> … and then, the nightingales,
> Which pluck our heart across a garden-wall,
> (When walking in the town) and carry it
> So high into the bowery almond trees,
> We tremble and are afraid, and feel as if
> The golden flood of moonlight unaware
> Dissolved the pillars of the steady earth
> And made it less substantial. (VII. 1069-76)

But the nightingale's links with desire can be sexual and material
as easily they can be chaste and spiritual. The song's beauty is
ambivalent, the 'golden flood' uncomfortably recalling the images
of Danaë which permeate the poem. These two passages occur at
points in the text where Aurora is longing for something seemingly irretrievable: in the first she thinks of Romney; in the
second, of her lost childhood. Though the nightingale may call
Aurora to Italy she cannot continue to be defined by its voice. It is

vital that Barrett Browning frees Marian from being qualified as a sexual object; likewise Aurora must be chaste: defined by her vocation as a poet not by her association with a man.

> I am a woman of repute;
> No fly-blown gossip ever specked my life;
> My name is clean and open as this hand. (IX. 264-66)

Barrett Browning seeks to separate poetry from erotic desire (the nightingale) and to associate it with spiritual desire (the lark) instead. The task is as difficult as that of *The Floure and the Leaf* in which the individual desire of the speaker draws her towards that from which she is excluded: an ideology which denies individual desire. *Aurora Leigh* sets art against a materialist politics and the nightingale, like that of 'The Poet and the Bird' sings of 'earthly things', not 'of divine'. Where Aurora is associated with the lark, the bird most frequently linked with Marian is the Christian dove:[51] as befits her name (Mary) and her semi-religious motherhood.

Though bird references occur throughout the poem, they are applied neither to Romney nor to Lady Waldemar, for they mark female creativity: either of poetry or of motherhood. When Romney uses a bird image it strikingly recalls the bird most closely linked to demand and appetite—the cuckoo:

> I beheld the world
> As one great famishing carnivorous mouth,—
> A huge, deserted, callow, blind bird Thing,
> With piteous open beak that hurt my heart... (VIII. 595-98)

As in Clanvowe's poem, however,[52] the image pertinently suggests the greedy intruder that ejects the rightful occupants of the nest, and that figure is associated with the lower classes. The connection leads back to the medieval underpinnings of the poem, for the enclosed spaces into which the 'cuckoo' figure attempts to move are, as in the earlier texts, associated with women—and poets. The references range from the 'cage-bird life' of the dissatisfied aunt (I. 304), to Aurora's green bedroom (so like the bower of *The Floure and the Leaf*) from which she wanders into the garden to crown herself with ivy (I. 28), to her attic room in London, or to the many enclosed spaces linked with Marian. The privacy of these spaces highlights the violence of the *dis*locations

of the text: the vagrancy of Marian's early life, her terrified flight
from her mother and the man with 'beast's eyes'; her maddened
wandering along the French roads. But the significance of these
spaces is not restricted to Marian: Romney Hall becomes Romney
Hell when the homeless temporarily housed there burn it to
the ground; the Italian house is a magical space of fireflies and
stars where the binary oppositions personified in Aurora and
Romney—art and politics, woman and man, light and dark—are
reconciled with a dream of the new world delineated in *Revela-
tions*.

    Aurora Leigh is an extraordinary text. Barrett Browning's breadth
of reference enables her to confront the central myth about the
birth of the literary voice and to rewrite it with a place for the
feminine. In part this is done through the patterns of medieval
Christianity (Christ's body and wounds); in part by reference to a
body of Christian literature the Victorians associated with women.
The result is a self-assured verse which draws selectively on the
past because

> As dead as must be, for the greater part,
> The poems made on … chivalrous bones;
> And that's no wonder: death inherits death. (V. 197-99)

According to Harold Bloom, every text is forced to negotiate with
earlier textual voices in its attempt to create a new voice.[53] For the
woman poet, however, faced with literary traditions grounded on
a repression of the feminine, this negotiation is particularly demanding. One way of responding to this difficulty is to try to
establish a new voice;[54] another is to try to work within existing
conventions by altering the gender relations inscribed within
them. Barrett Browning's restless innovation testifies to the latter
course. She engages directly with the binary oppositions that
marginalize the feminine within revolutionary and reactionary
ideologies alike, displaying a consistent interest in the construction of the poetic *voices* of her texts as well as in the *content* of her
poems. *Aurora Leigh* is the supreme example: epic, novel, medieval romance, medieval debate are mixed together with Romantic
poetry and contemporary women's novels. *Aurora Leigh* is centrally
interested in setting up an alternative arena to that of a divisive
patriarchal politics, one in which art provides a model for a society based on relationships. But every text requires a renegotiation

of the same ground from the standpoint achieved in the last attempt. In *Casa Guidi Windows* (1851) Barrett Browning had attempted to construct a political poetry which *included* the feminine. Nine years later she returned to the problem with the overtly political *Poems before Congress* (1860) which provoked a storm of indignant protest from her critics.[55] I consider that many of the *Last Poems* (especially 'Bianca among the Nightingales') are, in part, vigorous responses to this critical disapproval.

Birds and Women: Passionate and Political Voices

The choice of the epic for *Aurora Leigh* is a deliberate move which simultaneously marks its desire to engage with large issues and its refusal to be restrained by the lyric, the form usually associated with women.[56] The two collections of political verse are equally interested in large issues but attempt different voices. *Casa Guidi Windows* marries the internal interest of the lyric with the politics of the external world. These areas of interest are mapped onto the topography of a poem which discusses Italian politics as 'the simple story of personal impressions' of 'a woman' looking out from the enclosed space and metaphoric security of her apartment through a window at the world. The imagery is familiar from earlier texts but here its association with a political world renders it both more immediate and less overtly intellectual. The poetic birds, which had previously served to integrate the present voice with the poetry and ladies of a distant past, and with the poet's own childhood, are here identified with the next generation:

> I heard last night a little child go singing
>   The same words still on notes he went in search
> So high for, you concluded the upspringing
>   Of such a nimble bird to sky from perch
> Must leave the whole bush in a tremble green… (I. 1-7)

This identification can be traced throughout the poem to its conclusion where the child is Barrett Browning's own child and the future one she shares with him. In the process of this change the heroic voice also accommodates the future. Once linked to classical literature (as in the flowerbed in 'Hector') and offset by a feminine/child-like medieval pattern (the gentle image of birds singing in a pear-tree), and then both integrated in the voice of

the bedridden woman, the voice of this poem aligns itself directly
with vulnerable, marginalized elements (with birds and children)
and the heroes of the *risorgimento*:

> And I a singer also, from my youth,
> Prefer to sing with these who are awake,
>   With birds, with babes, with men who will not fear. (I. 155-57)

Poetry's role likewise shifts from marginalized prophecy of
tragedy (Aeschylus's Cassandra/nightingale predicting a tragic
future) to prediction of a positive future:

> And I, who first took hope up in this song,
> Because a child was singing one…behold,
> The hope and omen were not, haply, wrong!
> Poets are soothsayers still, like those of old
> Who studied flights of doves—and creatures young
> And tender, mighty meanings may unfold. (II. 736-41)

Barrett Browning draws her son into the argument of the poem to
emphasise the connections between the political reality outside
the text and the poetic world constructed within it: between lyric
and political text. The poetic voice is gentle and reasoned—'this
world has no perdition if some loss' (II. 780);[57] that of *Poems before
Congress* however is not. The poems in this volume vary from gross
propaganda ('Napoleon III in Italy') to impassioned outburst ('A
Curse for a Nation').

The result was a critical furore. Leonid Arinstein notes that
'hardly any poet had suffered such an onslaught since Byron and
Shelley'.[58] In that onslaught Barrett Browning was unfavourably
compared with an individual whose name ironically conflates
Barrett Browning's Italian home with both poetic topos *and* iconic
silent woman—and who is equally misrepresented in the description:

> To bless and not to curse is woman's function and if Mrs Browning,
> in her calmer moments, will but contrast the spirit which has
> prompted her to such melancholy aberrations with that which
> animated Florence Nightingale, she can hardly fail to derive a
> profitable lesson for the future.[59]

Florence Nightingale was, of course, not only a nurse but was
considered a patriot for nursing the wounded in the Crimean war:
Barrett Browning compounded the sins of anger and direct

speech when she criticized her own country. 'An August Voice'
serves to illustrate her angry denunciation: a dramatic monologue
that leaves aside any reference to the femininity of the poetic
voice. It moves directly into the political arena, its wordplay driven
by sarcasm—as a single stanza demonstrates:

> You'll take back your Grand-duke?
>   I promised the Emperor Francis
> To argue the case by his book,
>   And ask you to meet his advances.
> The Ducal cause, we know
>   (Whether you or he be the wronger),
>
>   Has very strong points;—although
>   Your bayonets, there, have stronger.
> You'll call back the Grand-duke. (stanza ii)

'A Curse for a Nation', which closes the collection, *does* foreground the gender of the speaker, but this does not soften but
increases the transgressive sting of the political diatribe. When an
angel asks a woman for a curse she refuses:

>   To curse choose men.
> For I, a woman, have only known
> How the heart melts and the tears run down. ('Prologue', x)

But the initial refusal only renders her final curse more bitter as it
attacks Britain for refusing to intervene in the Austro-Italian conflict:

> Because yourselves are standing straight
>   In the state
> Of Freedom's foremost acolyte,
> Yet keep calm footing all the time
> On writhing bond-slaves,—for this crime
>   This is the curse. Write. ('The Curse', II)

Yet Barrett Browning was not accused of writing propagandist
poems but of composing *unwomanly* ones. It was a charge which
brought her face to face with the repressive norms against which
she had been struggling to define a new voice and poetry. She
responded by writing poems which dealt directly with this attack
(published posthumously the following year). The final section of
this chapter will discuss three representative pieces, 'Lord Walter's
Wife', 'Where's Agnes?' and 'Bianca among the Nightingales': the

first two briefly because they are more general in their response; the third in far greater detail. Each of these poems has a bitter edge not seen in the earlier work. Each interrogates the idealized figure of the passive and silent woman caught up in poetry and gender stereotypes. 'Bianca' is the most powerful of the three, for the nightingales both personify and magnify the multiple repressive forces against which the figure of Bianca must struggle for her voice.

'Lord Walter's Wife' and 'Where's Agnes?'

In the first poem a woman turns the tables on a man who tries to implicate her in his seduction fantasy. Because his fantasy denies—in fact demands—that she have no volition, when she appears to concur willingly with his desire he is horrified and falls back onto the image of the angel:

> 'But you,' he replied, 'have a daughter,
>   a young little child, who was laid
> In your lap to be pure: so I leave you:
>   the angels would make me afraid.' (v. viii)

> 'Oh, that,' she said, 'is no reason.
>   The angels keep out of the way'; (v. ix)

Where Barrett Browning works from within masculine patterns in shaping her poetry, in this text the strategy is dramatized as the content. Lady Walter is offered a grossly distorted fantasy of herself as sexually available: her response is not to internalize it—and feel guilt and shame—but to act out the role she is offered. The would-be seducer is repulsed by the apparent availability of the sexual liaison with which he had been playing quite happily.

> At which she laughed out in her scorn.—
>   'These men! Oh, these men over-nice,
> Who are shocked when a colour not virtuous,
>   is frankly put on by a vice.' (v. xi)

The poem is overwhelmingly interested in the relation of language to power games and works to expose the gap between words and meanings:

> 'If a man finds a woman too fair, he
>   means simply adapted too much

> To uses unlawful and fatal. The praise!
> —shall I thank you for such?' (v. xv)

But the incident is deliberately not personalized, but seen as a index of a wider corruption of language:

> '...since, when all's said, you're too noble
> to stoop to the frivolous cant
> About crimes irresistible, virtues
> that swindle, betray and supplant.' (v. xxii)

As in 'Caterina', the speaker is seen only in relation to the male figures: she has no name and her words repeat and magnify those of the would-be seducer. Yet again, as in the earlier poem, the action of voicing another's words means that they must be revalued:

> 'I determined to prove to yourself that,
> whate'er you might dream or avow
> By illusion, you wanted precisely no
> more of me than you have now.' (v. xxiii)

Language is used against itself to destroy fantasies rooted entirely in language: the woman's voice emerges from out of that which represses her.

'Where's Agnes?' is almost the mirror-image of 'Lord's Walter's Wife'. Where the former poem showed a man switching from idolization to repudiation, from one extreme to the other, in a few short lines, in this poem the man is faced with the loss of his dream of perfect chastity through an actual infidelity. Because his very being and stability is defined through this chastity, the angel becomes demon: 'She, who scarcely trod the earth, / Turned mere dirt?' (stanza xviii) The door that he thought led to heaven is suddenly seen differently:

> That door could lead to hell?
> That shining merely meant
> Damnation? What! She fell
> Like a woman, who was sent
> Like an angel, by a spell? (stanza xvii)

The speaker is forced to recognize his own role in projecting his dream onto a face which was as 'blank' to him as if it were dead— and which he would prefer to be dead so that his beloved fantasy could continue to live. As it is he is driven to question just what has been destroyed by Agnes' actions:

> Who's dead here? No, not she:
>   Rather I! or whence this damp
> Cold corruption's misery? (stanza xxi)

As in 'Lord Walter's Wife' and 'Where's Agnes?', 'Bianca among the Nightingales' deals with abandonment and delusion. Like these two poems, it too is deeply interested in the way that individual fantasy is grown out of accepted norms of 'reality'—in these cases sexual fantasies which depend on the untouchable beloved for their erotic charge. The two poems discussed so far draw out the power games inherent in the construction of the chaste silent woman as a site of masculine desire. Should the woman show any desire of her own she disrupts the ability of the male to dominate her and calls up the hatred that seeks to defend the fantasy—not the real woman on whom that socially constructed fantasy is projected:

> 'Why, now, you no longer are fair!
> Why, now, you no longer are fatal, but
>   ugly and hateful, I swear.' ('Lord Walter's Wife', x)

'Bianca' however has an additional resonance for it draws on the *literary* figure of the nightingale and its multiple associations with class and gender. The intricate web of literary references which forms the backdrop to the poem points to its wider preoccupations. Though the two linked parts of the poem's title recall the opposed figures of earlier debate poetry, the interest of this monologue lies in the individual self of the speaker. Barrett Browning depicts an obsession which distorts Bianca's world into a maze of incestuous symbols from which she cannot escape. Bianca's jealousy and her sense of humiliation are exacerbated by confusions, her mind constantly circling around questions of truth and betrayal, of the sanctity of religious vows, of God and the Virgin: all rooted in the lost meaning of her lover's words. The nightingale chorus forms a kaleidoscopic mirror to both imprison and reflect her: the mingled passion and pain of her own voice marking her as yet one more of the massed warring voices which call within and without her.

Bitter Confusions: 'Bianca among the Nightingales'

I briefly mentioned 'Bianca' earlier in the chapter and discussed it as a paradigmatic Victorian poem in the previous one. Here I want to move within the text and examine it in more detail as an extended analysis of all the elements discussed so far in this chapter.

Like *Casa Guidi Windows* and *Poems before Congress*, this poem is deeply concerned with Italian politics: Barrett Browning wrote of how she kept flying into 'cold stages of anxiety, and white heats of rage' until she was 'scarcely of sane mind'[60] as she considered that Italy had been betrayed by Napoleon III under pressure from a scheming English government. It dramatizes a struggle between the two nations in a seething monologue with a semi-novelistic plot: an Italian woman raging at the cold Englishwoman who has stolen her lover. Each woman symbolizes a different country, the conflict focusing opposing attitudes and ideals: Bianca refuses the role of the conventional female victim and follows them both to the seeming freedom of England—cuttingly summed up as 'free to die in'—while the unnamed English lady typifies the sensual corruption of the aristocracy, personified in *Aurora Leigh* by Lady Waldemar.

Discussing the importance of symbolic countries to nineteenth-century women poets (Barrett Browning and Christina Rossetti in particular), Sandra Gilbert concludes that they transform a feminine passionate Italy, a motherland to be defended against the overbearing patriarchal rule of Austria, 'from a political state to a female state of mind... Redeeming and redeemed by Italy, they imagine redeeming and being redeemed by themselves.'[61] In that the 'literary vision of Italy had always emphasized passion and sensuality' (compare Mme de Staël's *Corinne*), she claims that they set the emotiveness of this motherland against 'the icy artifice of the Victorian culture in which they had been brought up'. The characterization of Italy as a sensuous motherland is certainly true for *Aurora Leigh*, though I consider that the figures of a chaste Marian and a pure Aurora demonstrate Barrett Browning's ambivalence about this 'sensuality'. Gilbert's reading focuses on the figure of Bianca, seeing her as one of a number of 'ennobled versions of *Jane Eyre*'s Bertha Mason Rochester: large, dark, passionate foreigners who are wholly at ease—even at one—with the Vesuvius of female sexual creativity'.[62] In this case I think that the concern with female eroticism is positively misleading. Though Bianca's sexuality is certainly central, she is consumed with jealousy, frustration and pain, a mental torture driving her from her warm and harmonious Italian home to a cold, dead England that closely resembles the Catholic state of Limbo. It is significant that Gilbert's reading should omit the nightingales which counterbalance Bianca's name in the title and which populate the insistent refrain. As I note above, the references to the nightingale in *Aurora Leigh* express both loss and a dangerous sensuality. Barrett Browning does far more here than present a woman and her sexuality. The poem depicts the necessity for clarity of language and the bitter confusions that result from betrayal when words such as 'soul', 'love' and 'freedom' are 'prophaned'. Interested in her wider argument, Gilbert does not mention the terrible sense of constriction and suffocation that envelopes the monologue. Bianca is burning up inside a sheet of flame represented and created by the nightingales as much as by herself: trapped in symbolic icy England, she is far from being 'at ease...[with her] female sexual creativity'.

Weaving Confusions: The Text of 'Bianca'

The first three stanzas of 'Bianca' establish Italy with its fireflies and nightingales as a place where earth and soul, sex and religion mingle. Every line is marked by a tremendous erotic power: the couple's passion depicted in a vision of intense gold light, the dark olives crystallizing within the vales (enclosed spaces, hence feminine) and the (masculine) hills erecting themselves like the thrusting cypress which reaches up 'like a church' into the sky, sanctifying passion by its intensity. Because of this Bianca implies that she and Giulio are bound in the sight of God ('God's Ever guarantees this Now', l. 22).

In line with its status as a dramatic monologue, the poem is structured like a small play. The opening stanza presents an archetypal scene against which the impermanence of a specific time and an individual emotion ('that night we felt...') is frozen momentarily in eerie light. Throughout the rest of the poem the memory of this night tantalizes Bianca with its promise of permanence, yet the cypress's traditional connotations of sorrow and death, already used in 'Caterina', suggest loss even in this beginning:

> The cypress stood up like a church
> That night we felt our love would hold... (i, 1-2)

The moon's associations with erotic love (even if unconsummated as in the associations with the chaste goddess of Diana) are daringly translated into religious terms by the adjective 'saintly' and the implications of purifying and cleansing. If the cypress reaches upwards in passion, the moon stoops to earth as:

> ...[the] saintly moonlight seemed to search
> And wash the whole world clean as gold... (i, 3-4)

Erotic impulses compose this 'whole world', fusing the passionate couple with their surroundings, the cleansing fire balanced by the sensual song:

> The fire-flies and the nightingales
> Throbbed each to either, flame and song. (i, 7-8)

Yet the exclusive concentration on the earthly birds in the last line ('the nightingales, the nightingales') shatters this delicate balance—leaving out the holy fire to pick up the underlying loss of the cypress of line 1. The stressed repetition of the birds focuses the full weight of the narrative voice. As memories, they are part of Bianca, and express her inmost longings.

But time cannot be fixed and the cypress's isolation and shadow are only harmonized at that precise moment:

> Upon the angle of its shade
> The cypress stood, self-balanced high;
> Half up, half down, as double-made,
> Along the ground, against the sky. (ii, 10-13)

The next line, with its desperately italicized '*we*', tries to catch an already doomed moment of mingled 'soul' and 'blood'. Like the cypress, the lovers are a mixture of the sacred and the earthly:

> *We* scarce knew if our nature meant
> Most passionate earth or intense heaven. (ii, 16-17)

The nightingale refrain catches this fragility, the singing birds now expressing leaping blood, *movement,* in a way which leads to the climax of sexual passion in stanza iii:

> We paled with love, we shook with love,
>> We kissed so close we could not vow... (iii, 19-20)

The sexual passion is so intense that Bianca feels their souls are entwined with their bodily desire. Giulio's words fix the transient moment into something eternal: 'God's Ever guarantees this Now' (1.22). But once spoken, these words vitalize the nightingales into something aggressive. The present tense continues to reverberate in her mind. Giulio speaks through them; they *are* Giulio:

> And through his words the nightingales
>> Drove straight and full their long clear call,
> Like arrows through heroic mails... (iii, 23-25)

—the erotic charge is heightened by the half-pun on the 'heroic mails' pierced by the nightingales' cries.[63] Considering the passivity usually associated with the nightingale as a female song-bird, the violence conveyed by the chivalric vocabulary ('arrows', 'mails') is startling. On the one hand it suggests a distant medieval world, attended by unhappy love-affairs, adultery and tragedy (the world for example of Chaucer's *Troilus and Criseyde*); on the other, it summons up the *patterns* of those stories. Lost and betrayed, Bianca looks back to past happiness, but the way she remembers it draws on literary forms which reflect the adulterous deceptions and unrequited love of her present.

From stanza iv onwards Bianca is in the present, in England and out of her element. Here the moonlight neither cleanses nor makes whole but separates, makes alien: Bianca sees the cold light descending from heaven to 'quench' the searing passions of earth, no longer complemented by holy fire but twisted to hellish flame:

> O cold white moonlight of the north,
>> Refresh these pulses, quench this hell! (iv, 28-29)

The 'coverture of death' which stretches 'across this garden-chamber' cuts off the upward movement associated with the enclosed spaces of earlier poems. These spaces are where the English nightingales sing: they also include the enclosed space of Bianca's heart and head. In this context she seems herself to have become one of them, for where the birds sang through Giulio's 'words', here they 'sing, through my head' (l. 44).

The separation of the 'earthly' present from the 'divine' past (the separation recorded in 'The Poet and the Bird') means that Bianca sees two kinds of nightingale: the English birds which represent the sexual impulse alone, and the original Italian ones which sang within and through the lovers and sanctified their desire. Though the confusion lies within her, it infects and distorts the way she interprets the world around her. Nothing makes sense anymore and this irrationality is demonstrated in her language: three sentences tail off inconclusively, the syntax is strained with exclamations, a bracketed, half-finished comment, and an abortive attempt at logic. What Bianca faces as a mirror of herself is an image of the ambivalence of that which is defined relative to the (masculine) centre—in her case Giulio—for the birdsong becomes simultaneously a memory of purity and a mockery of that memory. These nightingales not only reflect back the meanings that she projects onto them, trapping her within a world of betrayal and pain, but they carry cultural meaning, the pressures encoded in literary forms that silence and repress feminine desire. Bianca speaks her desire but can only express it through semi-hysterical incomprehension. Giulio deserted her despite his vow of eternal love. Language is split off from any connection with reality when 'we two / Are sundered'. The source of this metaphysical corruption is a suffocating England whose language and ethics are fatally compromised:

> ...what have nightingales to do
> 　In gloomy England, called the free...
> (Yes, free to die in!...) when we two
> 　Are sundered, singing still to me? (iv. 32-35)

In the first two stanzas the singing of the nightingales seem to be given a stable meaning, combining the patterns of sacred and romantic love; Giulio and the cypress tree provide seemingly solid reference points (though the figurative cypress is associated with death); in stanza iii that illusory stability starts to shift and the birds are associated with the chivalric—and repressive—mores of courtly poetry. In this fourth stanza, they are revealed as alien creatures without connection or significance to the civilized human world. They continue to sing whatever the setting, their

nature revealed as animalistic, almost predatory. But Bianca is
desperate to reject this meaning, for it reveals the undercurrent
of lust not only in Giulio's attraction to the calculating English
woman but also in the power which draws her unerringly after
him. The nightingales in this aspect draw her into their natural
world. Her response is to try to throw off her passion, to oppose
the nightingales with logic, to make a reasoned case:

> Each man has but one soul supplied
>   And that's immortal. Though his throat's
> On fire with passion now, to *her*
>   He can't say what to me he said!
> And yet he moves her they aver. (v. 39-43)

Bianca's frustration is expressed through her confused language:
because Giulio had claimed divine sanction for their love she sees
his words as expressing an eternal truth. The fact that he has
broken his word thus spreads doubt into every area of her life.
Where 'Hector in the Garden' posits a childhood world of magical language, and Caterina redefines her lover's words in his absence, projecting herself into an absolute world beyond the grave,
'Bianca' presents a world in which language has only relative
value—and which threatens to fall apart when its illusory centre
breaks up. As in *The Floure and the Leaf*, the absence of a central
(phallic) signifier—associated with the nightingale—leads the collapse of the company which lacks a masculine component (the
flower company; Bianca) into chaos and meaninglessness.

The nightingales and fireflies establish the poles of song and
flame which dominate the poem. Bianca sees her love as sanctified by holy fire, but the meaning of that fire shifts when Giulio
breaks his word. She struggles to keep that sanctified flame free of
the lust that she now accuses him of experiencing and she tries to
control his words by retreating to the script of a novel with a
passive and inarticulate heroine:

> Though his throat's
> On fire with passion now, to *her*
>   He can't say what to me he said! (v. 40-42)

Bianca's passion is so caught up with the nightingales that her
perception of any relationship that Giulio could have with another woman is tainted by them also:

> I think I hear him, how he cried
> 　'My own soul's life!' between their notes... (v. 37-38)

In a corrupt England different nightingales sing: during the nine-teenth century a 'nightingale' was a slang name for a prostitute—one who sold 'love' at night.[64] Bianca sees her rival is a temptress, a Siren-like nightingale, and Giulio's words a form of payment—of one sort or another. He 'would not name his soul' but

> ...rather pays her cost
> 　With praises to her lips and chin.
> Man has but one soul, 'tis ordained,
> 　And each soul but one love, I add;
> Yet souls are damned and love's profaned... (vi. 47-52)

Yet, against her wishes, the nightingales that 'sing her mad' include her own desiring self. She tries to exonerate him from blame by displacing all of her confusions onto her rival. She sees the English aristocrat as a parasite, sucking up Giulio as her land sucks up fogs, drawing him into a relationship of pure lust, one with neither flame nor song. Bianca's 'England' reveals the role that perception plays in constructing meaning: she describes it as covered with low earth-bound bushes and lacking the spiritual and erotic implications of thrusting Tuscan cypresses, but, to her total incomprehension and like the insidious birds that sing there, Giulio seems content with the change: 'There's little difference, in their view (l. 44)'.

Because Bianca's present is dominated by her past, she can have no future, yet because the past has been betrayed it can never be recovered. She is locked into the destructive patterns expressed in her horrified obsession with the nightingales: in England, Bianca thinks of Italy; in the present she looks back to the past. The nightingales that sing everywhere seem to fuse into a single chorus because they form the only link between such disparate spaces and times. But the link has no substance, it is purely arbi-trary: nightingales sing according to seasonal change and have no human message. The only significance they can have is that pro-jected upon them—and what Bianca sees in them is a kaleido-scope of different literary references and allusions all warring with each other in a cacophony of cries. Caught in an impasse, her reflections on 'gloomy England' throw her onto memories of her native Florence. She remembers a day which combined passion and spirituality: the 'luminous city, tall with [the] fire' of shooting rockets; the day that the Englishwoman entered her life. The river was filled with skimming 'birdlike' boats at a religious festival, then (slipping into the historic present to indicate how the moment is continually re-enacted in Bianca's mind) 'a boat strikes flame into our boat':

> ...The shock had flashed
> A vision on us! (ix. 77-78)

The nightingales singing in this stanza depict the Englishwoman's sexual attraction, mocking Bianca by their memory. Like her aristocratic predecessor in *Aurora Leigh* or like Keats's *femme fatale* in 'La Belle Dame Sans Merci' of *Lamia*, this woman is predatory. She appears like an angel 'with her loosed / Gold ringlets' (l. 87), sweetening the Italian tongue so that the very nightingales seem to sing from it. Bianca describes her attraction as purely sexual, seeing her as the tempter, the snake with a 'fine tongue' who corrupts God-given nature, drawing her lover—and herself—to a blasted land whose 'very nightingales...torture and deride' (ll. 97-98). Bianca's present is twisted, the world about her poisoned by the tempter's tongue: the English coasts are not washed clean but, like Bianca, 'left bitter by the tide'. Intent on creating differences which give her ethical superiority in a world of meaningless flux, Bianca further undermines the stability of language: the 'gold' of her rival has nothing to do with God and moonlight; sex must be divorced from spirituality; 'true' beauty must be distinguished from 'false':

> A worthless woman; mere cold clay
> As all false things are: but so fair,
> She takes the breath of men away
> Who gaze upon her unaware. (xii. 100-104)

By this point the nightingales have lost all connection with romance: in stanza xi they 'tortured', by the end of xii their song becomes the poisonous salivation of the snake-like Englishwoman herself:

> ...she lied and stole,
> And spat into my love's pure pyx
> The rank saliva of her soul. (xii. 105-107)

The imagery of snakes and spiders turns the poem back towards

Bianca's 'garden-chamber' and the sacred, enclosed, 'altar's wood' which is the lost Eden of her love—and the usual place for a songbird. At the same time the salivating spider hunts in the garden (for *fireflies?* for the fly-like lovers caught by the snake's 'fine tongue'?) summoning up the poisonous spider in Donne's 'Twick'nham Garden'.

Stanzas xii–xiii mark the climax of both the spiritual and the earthly imagery, with the birds turned to snakes and spiders (things that creep and crawl), and the woman as primal temptress: an image from which Bianca is desperate to dissociate herself

> I would not...
> ...
>   For life itself, though spent with him,
> Commit such sacrilege, affront
>   God's nature which is love, intrude
> 'Twixt two affianced souls, and hunt
> ... in the altar's wood. (xiii. 109-16)

What fuels Bianca's rage is a sense of impotence and jealousy that Giulio should prefer the golden image—'her white and pink... her grace of limb'—to her own passionate reality. The violence of the 'gentler' ways that Bianca says the Englishwoman could have employed and caused her less pain:

> She might have pricked out both my eyes,
> ...
> —Or drugged me in my soup or wine... (xiv. 120, 122)

—apart from unavoidably summoning up images of the Gothic novel—suggests ways in which Bianca would like to revenge herself. As a figure with no stability, Bianca depends on her paranoid world to give her shape—the nightingales, Giulio's absence, her memories of her loss. At the same time the passage recalls the obsession with revenge with which Philomela was credited by early medieval interpreters who believed the nightingale called out 'occi' as a demand for the death of her betrayer.

Stanza xiv's version of the refrain '(our Lady hush these nightingales)', spoken *sotto voce*, recognizes this urge for vengeance and appeals for divine protection against the nightingales that summon up memories that bubble up inside (Bianca's soul has been poisoned). Yet, because there is a Christian tradition of the nightingale, the appeal to the Virgin cannot free Bianca from the birds

whose calls haunt her at every turn—as seen in Chapter 2, one of
the pseudo-Lydgate's nightingale poems actually combines vengeance with Christianity. Bianca's attempt to set the religious bird
against the secular is thus doomed: her world is composed of
nightingales, bewildering her in their many different guises until
she cannot separate those which sing through her from her past,
from those which sing through Giulio's words of love, from those
which sing poisonously through the enmeshing Englishwoman:

> ...Let her pass.
>   I think of her by night and day.
> Must *I* too join her...out, alas!...
>   With Giulio, in each word I say?
> And evermore the nightingales! (xv. 31-35)

The final stanza is tremendous. The sensuality of the nightingales,
initially sanctified by divine forces in a context which includes
both natural and social worlds (the valleys, the hills: the tree, the
fireflies; the saintly moonlight; the implied marriage; the river in
Florence on a religious festival day) has become detached from all
into a sheet of flame both surrounding and consuming Bianca.
The underlying touches of medievalism (the 'heroic mails'; the
rival as Siren; the reference to the Virgin) culminate in the five
lines which refer directly to the debate of *The Owl and the Nightingale* in which the Owl's attacks on the Nightingale's courtly
associations are countered by accusations that the Owl is spiteful
and that her mournful cry is an omen of death. Bianca, in the
grip of her terrible obsession, suddenly throws the Nightingale's
accusations back into her own face:

> —Oh, owl-like birds! They sing for spite,
>   They sing for hate, they sing for doom,
> They'll sing through death who sing through night,
>   They'll sing and stun me in the tomb—
> The nightingales, the nightingales! (xvi. 140-45)

Bianca among the Nightingales is a strange, melodramatic poem,
one which draws on the figurative bird in a totally new way, transforming it from a passive to a dynamic symbol. Compressing many
different literary allusions within itself, it stands out among the
host of nightingale poems which I have discussed throughout this
book, by engaging critically with both classical myth and medieval
literature—not by refusing the patterns but by throwing them up

in such profusion that they enact the repressions hidden when a single meaning is assigned to a symbolic figure. The nightingale of the courtly lyric has a different function to that of the debate—as does the nightingale in a lyric by Alcuin to one in the *Carmina Burana*—as does the nightingale in *Agamemnon* to that of Pliny: each of these figures reflect historically specific marginalities, which stabilize their particular ideological systems. By summoning up these various nightingale figures and setting them against each other, Barrett Browning destabilizes the myth of the stability of any given system. She inverts the practice of producing a single (masculine) meaning by marginalizing (feminine, class, natural) differences and produces a single *feminine* voice against a kaleidoscope of past references.

Whether or not Barrett Browning intended any direct reference to Florence Nightingale can only be conjecture. That this vibrant and capable woman, whose name ironically summons up such powerful literary and cultural associations, should have been held up as an example of correct feminine behaviour to a poet who had assiduously avoided using the symbol all her prolific life, stuns through its coincidence. A consideration of the implications of such an attack prompted this chapter and, in effect, the argument of this whole book.

Appendix I
Nightingales in Classical Literature[1]

Greek Literature[2]

Homer (Eighth Century BCE)

Penelope: But to me has a god given sorrow that is beyond all measure, for day by day I find my joy in mourning and lamenting, while looking to my household tasks and those of my women in the house, but when night comes and sleep lays hold of all, I lie upon my bed, and sharp cares, crowding close about my throbbing heart, disquiet me, as I mourn. Even as when the daughter of Pandareus, the nightingale of the greenwood, sings sweetly, when spring is newly come, as she sits perched amid the thick leafage of the trees, and with many trilling notes pours forth her rich voice in wailing for her child, dear Itylus, whom she had one day slain with the sword unwittingly, Itylus, the son of the king Zethus; even so my heart sways to and fro in doubt, whether to abide with my son and keep all things safe, my possessions, my slaves, and my great, high-roofed house, respecting the bed of my husband and the voice of the people, or to go now with him whosoever is the best of the Achaeans...

(*The Odyssey*, trans. A.T. Murray, vol. II, 1919, 19.511-28)

Hesiod (Eighth Century BCE)

Now I will tell you a fable for princes who themselves understand. Thus said the hawk to the nightingale with speckled neck, while he carried her high up among the clouds, gripped fast in his talons, and she, pierced by his crooked talons, cried pitifully. To her he spoke disdainfully: 'Miserable thing, why do you cry out? One far stronger than you now holds you fast, and you must go wherever I take you, songstress as you are. And if I please I will make my meal of you, or let you go. He is a fool who tries to withstand the stronger, for he does not get the mastery and suffers pain besides

his shame.' So said the swiftly flying hawk, the long-winged bird.
> (*The Homeric Hymns and Homerica*, trans. Hugh
> G. Evelyn-White, 1914, 'Works and Days', ll. 203-11.)

Sappho (Sixth Century BCE)

... all night long... sing of the love between you and the violet-robed bride. Come, wake up: go [and fetch] the young bachelors of your own age, so that we may see [less] sleep than the clear-voiced [bird].

> (*Greek Lyric*, trans. David A. Campbell, 1982, vol. I, nos. 30, 79)

Why, Irana, does Pandion's daughter, the swallow, [wake] me?

> (ibid., nos. 135, 151)

The messenger of spring, the lovely-voiced nightingale.

> (ibid., nos. 136, 153)

Aesop (?620–564 BCE)

A sperehawk / Whiche dyd put hym within the nest of a nyghtyngale / Where he fond the lytyl and yong byrdes / the nyghtyngale came and perceyued hym / Wherefore she praid the sperehawke / Saying / I requyre and praye the as moche as I may / that thou haue pyte on my smal byrdes / And the sperehawke answerd and sayd / yf thow wilt that I graunte the thy request / thow must synge swetely after my wille and gree / And thenne the nyghtyngale beganne to synge swetely / not with the herte / but with the throte only / For he was too fylled of sorowe that otherwyse he myght not doo / The sperehawk sayd thenne to the nyghtyngale / This songe playseth me not / And toke one of the yonge byrdes and devoured hit... And as the sayd sperehawke wold haue devoured and eten the other came there a hunter whiche dyd caste a grete nette Upon the Sperehawke...

> (*Subtyll Historyes and Fables of Esope*, Westminster, 1483, III, v)

Aeschylus (?525–?456 BCE)

(i)

Clytemnestra: Well, if her speech be not strange and outlandish, even as a swallow's, I must speak within the compass of her wits and move her to comply.

> (*Aeschylus*, trans. Herbert Weir Smyth, vol. II, *Agamemnon*, l. 1050)

Chorus: Frenzied in soul thou art, by some god possessed, and dost wail in wild strains thine own fate, like some brown nightingale that never ceases making lament (ah me!), and in the misery of her

heart moans *Itys, Itys,* throughout all her days abounding in sorrow.
Cassandra: Ah, fate of the tuneful nightingale! The gods clothed
her in winged form and gave to her a sweet life without tears.

(ibid., ll. 1140-147)

(ii)
When our plaint greets his ear, he will fancy that he hears the voice
of Metis, the hawk-chased nightingle.

For she, constrained to
leave her green leaves, ever makes dolorous lament for her wonted
haunts, and blended therewith the tale of her own child's doom—
how that he perished, destroyed by her own hand, victim of the
wrath of an unnatural mother.

(ibid., vol. III, *The Suppliant Maidens*, strophe ii)

Sophocles (?496–406 BCE)

(i)
Antigone: Where we stand is surely holy ground;
A wilderness of laurel, olive, vine;
Within a choir of songster nightingales
Are warbling.
(*Sophocles*: trans. F. Storr, 1912, vol. I, *Oedipus at Colonus*, Prologue)

Chorus: ..a land of all lands the goodliest,
'Tis the haunt of the clear-voiced nightingale,
Who hid in her bower, among
The wine dark ivy that wreathes the vale,
Trilleth her ceaseless song

(ibid., strophe i)

(ii)
Chorus: Ah, when his mother, blanched with age and frail
Hears of his shattered reason, what wild wail
Will she upraise, a dirge of shrill despair,
(No plaintive ditty of the nightingale)

(ibid., vol. II, 1913, *Ajax*, strophe ii)

(iii)
Chorus: Ah, not far off, but nigh,
The woe that stirred my cry,
A boding wail
As of some shrill-voiced nightingale.

(ibid., *Trachiniae*, antistrophe ii)

Thucydides (?472–?395 BCE)

This Teres is not in any way connected with Tereus who took to
Athens to be his wife Procne the daughter of Pandion, nor indeed

did they come from the same Thrace. Tereus dwelt at Daulia in the land now called Phocis, which was then occupied by Thracians, and it was in that land that the women perpetrated their deed upon Itys. In fact many of the poets, when they refer to the nightingale, call it the bird of Daulia.

(*The Peloponnesian War*, trans. C. Foster Smith, 1919, vol. I, bk II, 29)

Euripides (?480–406 BCE)

(i)

Hecuba: My daughter, wasted are my words in air,
Flung vainly forth my pleadings for thy life.
If thou canst aught prevail beyond thy mother,
Be instant; as with nightingale's sad throat
Moan, moan, that thou be not bereft of life.

(*Euripides*, trans. Arthur S. Way, 1912, vol. I, *Hecuba*, strophe i)

Chorus: O, thou in thine halls of song abiding,
Under the greenwood leaves deep hiding,
    I hail thee, I hail,
Nightingale, queen by thy notes woe-thrilling
Of song-birds, come, through thy brown throat trilling
        Notes tuned to my wail.
        As of Helen's grief and pain
        And of Illum's daughters' tears.

(ibid., *Helen*, strophe i)

Aristophanes (?448–?380 BCE)

(i)

Hoopoe (calling to Nightingale):
Shake off thy slumbers, and clear and strong
Let loose the floods of thy glorious song,
The sacred dirge of thy mouth divine
For sore-wept Itys, thy child and mine;
Thy tender trillings his name prolong
With the liquid notes of thy tawny throat;
Through the leafy curls of the woodbine sweet
The pure sound mounts to the heavenly seat,
And Phoebus, lord of the golden hair,
As he lists to thy wild plaint echoing there,
Draws answering strains from his ivoried lyre,
Till he stirs the dance of the heavenly choir,
And calls from the blessed lips on high

Of immortal Gods, a divine reply
To the tones of thy witching melody.
   (The sound of a flute is heard within, imitating
   the nightingale's song.)
Euelpides: O Zeus and King, the little birdie's voice!
O how its sweetness honied all the copse!
   (*Aristophanes*, trans. B.B. Rogers, 1924, vol. II, *The Birds*, ll. 209-24)

(ii)
Chorus (to Hoopoe):
… O for the nightingale peerless in song,
  who chants in the choir of the Muses her lay;
Our sweetest and best, fetch her out of the nest,
  and leave her awhile with the Chorus to play
…
Chorus: O darling! O tawny-throat!
    Love, whom I love the best,
    Dearer than all the rest,
    Playmate and partner in
       All my soft lays,
    Thou art come! Thou art come!
    Thou hast dawned on my gaze,
    I have heard thy sweet note,
    Nightingále! Nightingále!
Thou from thy flute
Softly-sounding canst bring
Music to suit
With our songs of the Spring:
    Begin then I pray
  Our own anapaestic address to essay.

with Nightingale: Ye men who are dimly existing below,
  who perish and fade as the leaf,
Pale, woebegone, shadowlike, spiritless folk,
  life feeble and wingless and brief,
Frail castings in clay, who are gone in a day,
  like a dream full of sorrow and sighing.
                 (ibid., ll. 677-88)

(iii)
Lysistrata: 'Soon as the swallows are seen
  collecting and crouching together,
Shunning the hoopoes' flight
  and keeping aloof from the Love-birds,
Cometh a rest from ill,
  and Zeus the Lord of the Thunder

Changeth the upper to under.'
Woman: Preserve us, shall *we* be the upper?
Lysistrata: 'Nay, but if once they wrangle,
   and flutter away in dissension
Out of the Temple of God,
   then all shall see and acknowledge,
Never a bird of the air
   so perjured and frail as the swallow.'
(ibid., 1924, vol. III *Lysistrata*, ll. 770-80)

Plato (?427–?347 BCE)

(i)
Socrates: But men..do not consider that no bird sings when it is hungry or cold or has any other trouble; no, not even the nightingale or the swallow or the hoopoe which are said to sing in grief or lamentation.
(*Plato*, vol. I, trans. H.N. Fowler, 1914, *Phaedo*, p. 295)

(ii)
...He saw the soul of Thamyras choosing the life of a nightingale...
(ibid., vol. II, trans. Paul Shorey, 1935, *The Republic*, p. 515)

Aristotle (384–322 BCE)

At the beginning of spring...the nightingale [lays] five or six eggs: it goes into hiding from autumn until spring.
(*Aristotle*, trans. A.L. Peck, 1970, vol. II, Historia Animalium, V, ix,
542.b. Also descriptive references: IV, ix; IX, xv; IX, il)

Theocritus (?310–?250 BCE)

(i)
The Dirge: Two testers they have plight ye, with
   dainty dill well dressed,
Whereon, like puny nightingales that flit from bough
   to bough
Trying their waxing wings to spread, the Love-babes
   hovering go.
(*The Greek Bucolic Poets*, trans. J.M. Edmonds, 1912, *Idyll XV*,
'The Women at the Adonis Festival', p. 193)

(ii)
...in spring the blackbirds cry their lisping medleys of clear-toned song, and the babbling nightingale's cry them back their warblings with the honey voice that sings from their tuneful throats.
(ibid., Inscription IV, p. 367)

Anon (Once Attributed to Moshus) (Late Second Century BCE)[3]

> You nightingales that complain in the thick leafage, tell to
> Arethusa's fountain of Sicily that neatherd Bion is dead, and with
> him dead is music, and gone with him likewise the Dorian poesy
> ...
> Never so woeful was the lament of the Siren upon the beach, never
> so woeful the song of that Nightingale among the rocks, or the
> dirge of that Swallow amid the long hills
> ...
> The nightingales and all the swallows, which once he delighted,
> which once he taught to speak, sat upon the branches and cried
> aloud in antiphons, and they that answered said 'Lament, ye
> mourners, and so will we'.
>
> (ibid., 'The Lament for Bion', pp. 445-49)

Callimachus (?305–?240 BCE)

> They told me Heraclitus, they told me you were dead,
> They brought me bitter news to hear and bitter tears to shed.
> I wept as I remembered how often you and I
> Had tired the sun with talking and sent him down the sky.
>
> And now that thou art lying, my dear old Carian guest,
> A handful of grey ashes, long, long ago at rest,
> Still are thy pleasant voices, thy nightingales, awake,
> For death, he taketh all away, but them he cannot take.
>
> (*Greek Literature: An Anthology*, chosen by Michael
> Grant, 1976, Epigram 2, trans. William Cory)

Latin Literature

Catullus (?84–?54 BCE)

> ...elegies of loss
> plaintive as Procne crying under the shadow of the
>   cypress
> for lost Itylus.
>
> (*The Poems of Catullus: A Bilingual Edition*, trans. Peter Whigham,
> 1966, no. 65, p. 161)

Virgil (70–19 BCE)

(i)

On Silenus:

...he told of Tereus' changed form, what feast, what gifts Philomela
made ready for him, in what wise she sped to the desert, and with

what wings, luckless one! she first hovered above her home.

> (*Virgil,* trans. H. Rushton Fairclough, rev. edn. 1935, vol. I,
> *Eclogue* 6, p. 47)

(ii)
...Procne, with breast marked by her blood-stained hands.

> (ibid., *Georgic IV*, 197)

(The story of Scylla is closely linked with that of the 'Daulian maids'
[ll. 199-200], related also by blood:)
(iii)
...Ye, if ye that meet me are of human stock, ye discern me: I am
Scylla, of blood akin to yours (of thy grace may I say this, O
Procne!)

> (ibid., rev. edn 1934, vol. II, 'Ciris', ll. 409-10, p. 437)

Ovid (43 BCE–?17 CE)
(i)
...only the Daulian bird, most mournful mother who wreaked
unholy vengeance on her lord, laments in song Ismarian Itys. The
bird sings of Itys, Sappho sings of love abandoned—that is all.

> (*Ovid,* trans. Grant Showerman, 1921, vol. I, *Heroides*, XV, ll.154,
> 155, p. 191)

(ii)
If you Philomela, are lamenting the deed of the tyrant Ismarus,
that lament has been fulfilled by its term of years; turn aside to the
hapless funeral of no common bird—great cause for grief is Itys,
but belongs to the ancient past.

> (ibid., *Amores*, II.vi, ll. 6-7, p. 399)

(The ready availability of Ovid's version of the Philomela myth in the
Metamorphoses (6. 400 ff) means that it is unnecessary to quote it in full
here.)

Martial (?40–?104 CE)

...the Attic adulteress mourns for Thracian Itys

> (*Martial,* trans. Walter C.A. Ker, 1920, vol. II, *Epigrams*, X, no. 51,
> p. 195)

Philomela laments the crime of incestuous Tereus: she who was a
silent maiden is acclaimed as a bird of song.

> (ibid., XIV, no. 75, p. 467)

Pliny the Elder (23–79 CE): 'The locus classicus *for the Nightingale's song'.*[4]

Nightingales pour out a ceaseless gush of song for fifteen days and nights on end when the buds of the leaves are swelling—a bird not in the lowest rank remarkable. In the first place there is so loud a voice and so persistent a supply of breath in such a tiny little body; then there is the consummate knowledge of music in a single bird: the sound is given out with modulations, and now is drawn out into a long note with one continuous breath, now varied by managing the breath, now made staccato by checking it, or linked together by prolonging it, or carried on by holding it back; or it is suddenly lowered, and at times sinks into a mere murmur, loud, low, bass, treble, with trills, with long notes, modulated when this seems good—soprano, mezzo, baritone; and briefly all the devices in that tiny throat which human science has devised with all the elaborate mechanism of the flute, so that there can be no doubt that this sweetness was foretold by a convincing omen when it made music on the lips of the infant Stesichorus. And, that no one may doubt its being a matter of science, the birds have several songs each, and not all the same but every bird songs of its own. They compete with one another, and there is clearly an animated rivalry between them; the loser often ends her life by dying, her breath giving out before her song. Other younger birds practise their music, and are given verses to imitate; the pupil listens with close attention and repeats the phrase, and the two keep silence by turns: we notice improvement in the one under instruction and a sort of criticism on the part of the instructress. Consequently they fetch the prices that are given for slaves, and indeed larger prices than were paid for armour bearers in old days. I know of one bird, a white one it is true, which is nearly unprecedented, that was sold for 600,000 sesterces to be given as a present to the emperor Claudius's consort Agrippina. Frequent cases have been seen before now of nightingales that have begun to sing when ordered, and have sung in answer to an organ, as there have been found persons who could reproduce the bird's songs with an indistinguishable resemblance by putting water into slanting reeds and breathing into the holes or by applying some slight check with the tongue. But these exceptional and artistic trills after a fortnight gradually cease, though not in such a way that the birds could be said to be tired out or to have had enough of singing; and later on when the heat has increased their note becomes entirely different, with no modulations or variations. Their colour also changes, and finally in winter the bird itself is not seen. Their tongues do not end in a point like those of all other birds. They lay in early spring, six eggs at most.

(*Pliny: Natural History*, trans. H. Rackham, vol. III,
Bks VIII-XI; X, 43, 345-47.)

Pausanius (Second Century CE)

Not far [from the tomb of Hippolyte] is the grave of Tereus, who married Procne, the daughter of Pandion. According to the Megarians, Tereus reigned at Pagae in Megaris. But my belief, supported by evidence which is still extant, is that he reigned over Daulis, which lies beyond Chaeronea; for of old the greater part of what is now called Greece was peopled by barbarians. When the women had retaliated on Itys for the deed which Tereus had wrought on Philomela, Tereus could not catch them. He died by his own hand at Megara; and the people immediately raised a barrow to him, and they sacrifice every year, using gravel in the sacrifice instead of barley groats. And they say that the hoopoe first appeared here. But the women went to Athens, and there, mourning both their wrongs and their revenge, they wept themselves to death. The fable that they were turned into a nightingale and a swallow was suggested, I suppose, by the plaintive and dirge-like song of these birds.

(*Pausanias's Description of Greece*, trans. J.G. Frazier, 2nd edn, 1913,
vol. I, 'Attica', Bk I, chapter 41.8, p. 63)

Appendix II
Christian Latin Poems

Paulinus of Nola (353–451 CE)

    adnue, fons verbi, verbum Deus, et velut illam
    me modo veris avem dulci fac voce canorum,
    quae viridi sub fronde latens solet avia rura
    multimodis mulcere modis linguamque per unam
    fundere non unas mutato carmine voces,
    unicolor plumis ales, sed picta loquellis.
    nunc teretes rotat illa modos, nunc sibila longis
    ducit acuta sonis, rursum quasi flebile carmen
    inchoat et subito praecidens fine querellam
    adtonitas rupto modulamine decipit aures.[1]

Eugenius of Toledo (d. 658 CE)

    vox, philomela, tua cantus edicere cogit,
        inde tui laudem rustica lingua canit.
    vox, philomela, tua citheras in carmine vincit
        et superas miris musica flabra modis.
    vox, philomela, tua curarum semina pellit,
        recreat et blandis anxia corda sonis.
    florea rura colis, herboso caespite gaudes,
        frondibus arboreis pignera parva foves.
    cantibus ecce tuis recrepant arbusta canoris,
        consonat ipsa suis frondea silva comis.
    iudice me cygnus et garrula cedat hirundo,
        cedat et inlustri psittacus ore tibi.
    nulla tuos umquam cantus imitabitur ales,
        murmure namque tuo dulcia mella fluunt.
    dic ergo tremulos lingua vibrante susurros

et suavi liquidum gutture pange melos.
porrige dulcisonas attentis auribus escas;
   nolo tacere velis, nolo tacere velis.
gloria summa tibi, laus et benedictio, Christe,
   qui praestas famulis haec bona grata tuis.[2]

Aldhelm (c. 650–709 CE)

Vox mea diversis variatur pulcra figuris,
Raucisonis nunquam modulabor carmina rostris,
Spreta colore tamen, sed non sum spreta canendo.
Sic non cesso canens, fato terrente futuro;
Nam me bruma fugat, sed mox aestate redibo.[3]

Alcuin (c. 735–c. 804 CE)

quae te dextra mihi rapuit, luscinia, ruscis,
   illa meae fuerat invida laetitiae,
tu mea dulcisonis implesti pectora musis,
   atque animum moestum carmine mellifluo.
quapropter veniant volucrum simul undique coetus,
   carmine te mecum plangere Pierio.
spreta colore tamen fueras non spreta canendo;
   lata sub angusto gutture vox sonuit,
dulce melos iterans vario modulamine Musae,
   atque creatorem semper in ore canens.
noctibus in furvis nusquam cessavit ab odis
   vox veneranda sacris, o decus atque decor.
quid mirum cherubim, seraphim si voce tonantem
   perpetua laudent, dum tua sic potuit?
felix o nimium, dominum noctemque diemque
   qui studio tali semper in ore canit.
non cibus atque potus fuerat tibi dulcior odis,
   alterius volucrum nec sociale iugum.
hoc natura dedit, naturae et conditor almus,
   quem tu laudasti vocibus assiduis,
ut nos instrueres vino somnoque sepultos
   somnigeram mentis rumpere segnicem.
quod tu fecisti, rationis et inscia sensus,
   indice natura nobiliore satis,
sensibus hoc omnes magna et ratione vigentes
   gessissent aliquod tempus in ore suo.
maxima laudanti merces in secla manebit
   aeternum regem perpes in arce poli.[4]

Paulus Albarus (*fl. 850 CE*)

vox, filomela, tua metrorum carmina vincit
    et superat miris flamina magna modis.
vox, filomela, tua dulcis super organa pergit,
    cantica nam suabe fulgide magna canit.
vox, filomela, tua superat sic guttere Musas,
    ut citheras vincat sivila 'ter tua, ter.'
sicque liras dulces cordarum pollice ductas
    excellis mulcens, corda fobens hominum.
cedat omnigena, tivi vox quoque garruls cedat,
    iudice me carmen fulgeat omne tuum.
nulla certe tivi equeter nunc cantibus ales:
    et victrix hominum voce feras superum.
dic ergo varias blande modulamine voces
    et funde solite guttere sepe melos.
porrige dulcissonum gaudenti pectore plectrum
    et dulce tibias guttere clange sonans.
gloria summa deo dico per secula Christo,
    qui nobis famulis gaudia tanta dedit.[5]

Sedulius Scottus (*fl. 848–874 CE*): Carmen Paschale

Surrexit Christus sol verus vespere noctis,
    surgit et hinc domini mystica messis agri.
nunc vaga puniceis apium plebs laeta labore
    floribus instrepitans poblite mella legit.
nunc variae volucres permulcent aethera cantu,
    temperat et pernox nunc philomela melos.
nunc chorus ecclesiae cantat per cantica Sion,
    alleluia suis centuplicatque tonis.
Tado, pater patriae, caelestis gaudia paschae
    percipias meritis limina lucis: ave.[6]

Ecbasis captivi (*c. 940 CE*)

Concentu parili memoratur passio Christi.
passer uterque Deum cesum flet, verbere lesum,
exanimis factus, claudens spiranima flatus;
commutat vocem, dum turbant tristia laudem,
organa divertit, dum Christi vulnera plangit,
solvitur in luctum, recolens dominum crucifixum,

squalet se cinere, dum fertur mocio terrae,
offuscat visum, memorans solem tenebratum.
hii gemini trepidas pressere ad pectora palmas;
unicus ut matrem, sic deflent hii pacientem.
his avibus motis stupuit milicia regis;
turbatur pardus, tam gratum perdere munus.[7]

Fulbert of Chartres (c. 975–1028 CE)

cum telluris vere novo, producuntur germina,
nemorosa circumcirca frondescunt et brachia:
fragrat odor cum suävis florida per gramina,
hilarescit Philomela, dulcis sonûs conscia,
et extendens modulando gutturis spiramina,
reddit veris et aestivi temporis praeconia.
   (instat nocti et diei voce sub dulcisona,
     soporatis dans quietem cantûs per discrimina,
     necnon pulchra viatori laboris solatia.)
vocis eius pulchritudo clarior quam cithara;
vincitur omnis cantando volucrum catervula:
implet sylvas atque cuncta modulis arbustula,
gloriosa valde facta veris prae laetitia.
   (volitando scandit alta arborum cacumina,
     ac festiva satis gliscit sibilare carmina.)
cedit anceps ad frondosa resonans umbracula,
cedit olor et suävis ipsius melodia;
cedit tibi tympanistra et sonora tibia;
quamvis enim videaris corpore permodica,
tamen cuncti capiuntur hac tua melodia:
nemo dedit voci tuae haec dulcia carmina,
nisi solus rex coelestis qui gubernat omnia.[8]

? Eugenius Vulgarius (Tenth Century CE)

(i)
Anacreunti carmine
telam libet contexere,
pedam pedi lentiscere
et tramitem transducere.

(ii)
sunt saecla praeclarissima,
sunt prata vernantissima,
formosa gaudent omnia,
sunt grata nostri moenia

(iii)
laetentur ergo somata
et rideant praecordia,
amor petens finitima
sint cuncta vitulantia.

(iv)
Phoebus rotat per tempora
torquens polorum lumina;
somnum susurrant flumina,
aves canunt et dulcia.

(v)
turtur prior dans oscina,
rauce sonat post ardea;
sistema miscens merula,
olos implet croëmata.

(vi)
myrto sedens lusciola,
'vos cara', dicens, 'pignora,
audite matris famina,
dum lustrat aether sidera.

(vii)
'cantans mei similia,
canora prolis germina,
cantu deo dignissima
tractim refrange guttera.

(viii)
'tu namque plebs laetissima,
tantum dei tu psaltria
divina cantans cantica
per blanda cordis viscera.

(ix)
materna iam nunc formula
ut rostra vincas plumea,
futura vocis organa
contempera citissima.'

(x)
hoc dixit et mox iubila
secuntur subtilissima;
melum fit voce tinnula
soporans mentis intima.

(xi)
densantur hinc spectacula,
accurrit omnis bestia,
leaena, lynx et dammula,
caudata stans vulpecula.

(xii)
pisces relinquunt aequora
et vada sunt retrograda;
pulsando Codrus ilia
praegnas adest invidia,

(xiii)
auro sedat rex aquila,
circum cohors per agmina,
gemmato pavo tergora,
cornix subest et garrula.

(xiv)
corvina quin centuria,
ardet phalans et milvea;
de marte tractant omnia,
vincatur ut lusciola.

(xv)
palumbes at iuvencula
praesumit e victoria;
gallus prior cum merula
disrumpta plangunt ilia;

(xvi)
cicadis inflans iecora
campo crepat misellula;
palmam tenet lusciola
versus trahens per sibila.

(xvii)
turbata gens tum rostrea,
exsanguis hinc et aquila;
frigescit, in praecordia
virtusque cedit ossea.

(xviii)
praeco fugae fit ulula
urgens gradi per abdita,
pudore mens ne conscia
poenas luat per saecula.

(xix)
tunc versa castra plumea
sparsim legunt aumatia
auraeque fissa flamina,
petuntur tecta silvea.[9]

Translations

Paulinus of Nola

Look favourably, source of the word, the word that is God, and make me tuneful, with a sweet voice, just like the bird of spring, she who, hiding beneath the green leaves, is accustomed to delight the pathless fields with harmonious melodies, and to pour forth from a single throat many voices in changeful song, an insignificant brown bird [nightingale/singer], brilliantly coloured by her voice: now she utters the smooth measures of her song, now she shapes her penetrating whistle into long notes, once more begins a song which seems mournful, then cutting short her complaint with a sudden close, deceives the awestruck ear with interrupted melody.[10]

Eugenius of Toledo

Your voice, my nightingale, makes everyone a singer:
so people in the country sing your praise.
Your voice is an instrument finer than a zither;
more hauntingly than wind-music it plays.

Your voice, my nightingale, uproots the seeds of sorrow;
its silken tones can soothe a troubled mood.
Your home is among flowers, you love a grassy meadow;
in leafy trees you tend your infant brood.

Hear how your melodies re-echo in the thicket:
even the rustling branches harmonize.
The swan, the twittering swallow, the gaudy-headed parrot
can never hope to match you in my eyes.

No bird can imitate the sweetness of your singing;
there's honey in your fluent rippling note.
Speak with your vibrant tongue, then, in soft shivery
    warbling,
pouring the liquid sounds from your smooth throat.

Feed our expectant ears with your song's delicious flavour;
never be silent, never silent, please!
Glory and blessing and praise to Christ our Saviour
who grants his servants pleasures such as these![11]

Aldhelm

My beautiful voice is varied in diverse phrases: I shall never
modulate my songs with a hoarse throat, even though I have
spurned decoration, I have not spurned singing. And though a
terrifying future is to come, I shall not stop my singing, for though
the depths of winter drive me away, I shall return in summer.[12]

Alcuin

Whoever stole you from that bush of broom,
   I think he envied me my happiness,
O little nightingale, for many a time
    You lightened my sad heart from its distress,
    And flooded my whole soul with melody.
And I would have the other birds all come,
    And sing along with me thy threnody.

So brown and dim that little body was,
    But none could scorn thy singing. In that throat
That tiny throat, what depth of harmony,
    And all night long ringing thy changing note.
    What marvel if the cherubim in heaven
Continually do praise Him, when to thee,
    O small and happy, such a grace was given?[13]

Paulus Albarus

Your voice, O nightingale, is better than rhymed song,
With its wonderful strains, it overcomes [the] great winds.
Your sweet voice, O nightingale, exceeds that of the organ,
For it sings its solo so melodiously in great splendour.
Your voice, O nightingale, so surpasses the Muses in song,
As your fluting 'ter, ter, ter' surpasses the lyre.
And thus you excel, in sweetness, the melting lyre [melody] of
Strings struck with the thumb, sustaining the hearts of men.
All sound, any [mere] chattering voice, gives way to you,
In my judgement your song should outsing all.
Surely no bird is now your equal in song?
And you surpass as victor the voice of mankind.
Therefore cry forth your varied song with delightful melody,
And let flow your song constantly from your eager throat.
Pour forth your sweet-sounding lyric from a joyful breast
And from your sweet throat sound the ringing trumpets.

Glory to Christ our Lord in the highest, I say, through the ages
Christ who gives to us, his servants, such great joys.[14]

Sedulus Scottus: Easter Sunday

Last night did Christ the Sun rise from the dark,
　The mystic harvest of the fields of God,
And now the little wandering tribes of bees
　Are brawling in the scarlet flowers abroad.
The winds are soft with birdsong; all night long
　Darkling the nightingale her descant told,
And now inside church doors the happy folk
　The Alleluia chant a hundredfold.
O father of thy folk, be thine by right
The Easter joy, the threshold of the light.[15]

Ecbasis captivi: 'The Escape of the Captive'

Christ's passion is remembered in a two-part song,[16]
Each bird [sparrow[17]] grieves for the God fallen, injured
　by the lash,
Rendered lifeless as he breathes his last.[18]
She changes her melody while she weeps for the wounds of
　Christ,
She dissolves in grief, recalling our Lord crucified,
And soils herself with ashes when the earthquake moves
　the earth,
She hides her face, remembering the clouded sun.
These two [birds] press trembling wings to their breasts;
They mourn him who suffered, as the mother mourns her
　only son.
After the birds have gone, the soldiers of the King stand stupefied;
The panther is distressed to lose such a gracious gift.[19]

Fulbert of Chartres

When the earth with spring returning buds again,
And the branches in the woods again are green,
And the sweetness of all flowers is in the grass,
Lilts the nightingale all passionate with song,
With the thrilling of her tiny swelling throat,
Flings the prophecy of spring and summer tides.
Beyond all birds that sing, clearer than flutes....

Filling the woods and every little copse,
Most glorious with the rapture of the Spring....
The snarer in the green woods holds his peace,
The swan falls silent, and the shrilling flute.
So small art thou, to take us all with singing,
None gave that voice, unless the King of Heaven.[20]

? Eugenius Vulgarius

We live in splendid times: the fields
are rich and blossoming with spring;
our city is a pleasant place;
there's joy in every living thing.

So let our bodies take their ease,
and hearts enjoy this happy state;
with 'love thy neighbour' as the theme
all creatures ought to celebrate.

The heavens wheel about the earth
with sun by day and stars at night;
the rivers whisper sleepily,
and singing birds express delight.

The cooing turtle-dove is first;
the heron follows with a squawk;
the blackbird joins the chorus; next
the swan contributes to their talk.

Then sitting on a myrtle branch
the nightingale instructs her young:
'Now while the stars are bright, my dears,
take lessons in your mother-tongue:

'copy my song; I want to hear
the younger generation's notes
in seemly hymns of praise to God
emerging from your little throats.

'We are a joyful tribe of birds,
the Lord's musicians and his choir.
So let him hear your instruments:
make every tiny chest a lyre.

'Tune up your growing vocal chords
for instant use; adopt my skills
and we'll outdo what pass for songs
from other birds' inferior bills.'

The youngsters do as they are told;
And soon their sweetly piping art
is mingled with their mother's tune
in melodies to stun the heart.

At this their audience expands,
as all the creatures flock to hear:
the little fox with bushy tail,
the lioness, lynx, and fallow deer.

Even the fishes leave the sea,
the rivers find their flow reversed;
the poet Codrus tears his hair,
so full of envy he could burst.

The eagle on a golden throne
presides above his marshalled rows
of peacocks dressed in jewelled gear,
and companies of chatty crows,

squadrons of kites, battalions
of ravens, all exchanging views
about the contest and its odds,
keen that the nightingale should lose.

But no: the ringdove has withdrawn,
despairing of the victory;
the cock and blackbird, ruptured both,
can only squeak in misery.

The cricket-bird inflates her lungs
and bursts with a pathetic pop.
The nightingale, with staying-power
to match her skill, comes out on top.

Dismay confounds the other birds;
the eagle's face is almost pale:
a ghastly chill invades his bones;
his very heartbeat seems to fail.

The screech owl signals the retreat,
urging the birds to slip away,
or else the shame will haunt their minds
tormenting them till Judgement Day.

And so the feathered ranks disperse;
their whistling wings divide the air
as each escapes to find his own
secluded nook or leafy lair.[21]

Notes

Unless otherwise stated, place of publication is London, and classical texts are taken from the Loeb Classical Library (London: Heineman; Cambridge, MA: Harvard University Press).

Introduction
Reflecting on the Nightingale

1.   Mechthild of Magdeburg, taken from *The Medieval Lyric* (trans. P. Dronke; Hutchinson, 1968), p. 85.

2.   Elizabeth Barrett Browning, 'Bianca among the Nightingales', in *Last Poems* (1862); text taken from *Selected Poems* (ed. Malcolm Hicks; Manchester: Carcanet/Fyfield, 1983).

3.   *Voice Terminal Echo: Postmodernism and English Renaissance Texts* (Methuen, 1986), p. 14; 19.

4.   'The Nightingale in Greek and Latin Poetry', *Classical Journal* 30 (1934), pp. 78-84 (78).

5.   *EOS: An Inquiry into the Theme of Lovers' Meetings and Partings at Dawn in Poetry* (ed. A.T. Hatto; Mouton: The Hague, 1965), 'Appendix I, "The Nightingale"', pp. 792-93.

6.   Hatto, *Inquiry*, p. 797.

7.   S. Greenblatt, *Renaissance Self-Fashioning* (Chicago/London: University of Chicago Press, 1984), p. 174.

8.   H.W. Garrod, 'The Nightingale in Poetry', in *The Profession of Poetry and Other Lectures* (Oxford: Clarendon Press, 1929), pp. 131-59.

9.   L. Norris, 'Nightingales', *Selected Poems* (Bridgend: Poetry Wales, 1986), pp. 44-45.

Chapter 1
Sorrowful Weaving: Nightingales in Greek and Latin Texts

1.   Geoffrey Hartman, 'Evening Star and Evening Land', in *The Fate of Reading and Other Essays* (Chicago: University of Chicago Press, 1975), p. 164.

2.   Garrod, 'The Nightingale in Poetry', p. 136.

3.   Patricia Klindiest Joplin, 'The Voice of the Shuttle Is Ours', *Stanford Literature Review* 1 (1984), pp. 25-53.

4.   W.R. Halliday, *Indo-European Folk-Tales and Greek Legend* (Cambridge: Cambridge University Press, 1933).

5.   R.M.C. Forbes Irving, *Metamorphosis in Greek Myth* (Oxford: Clarendon Press, 1990).

6.   Arthur Koestler argues that the rationalism advocated by Socrates, Plato and Aristotle should be viewed as a conservative response to ideological crises within the Athenian empire (*The Sleepwalkers: A History of Man's Changing Vision of the Universe* [Arkana, 1989]).

7.   'The Voice of the Shuttle: Language from the Point of View of Literature', in *Beyond Formalism: Literary Essays, 1958–1970* (New Haven: Yale University Press, 1970) (pp. 337-55).

8.   Joplin opens her article by nominating 'the voice of the shuttle' for the putative status of an archetypal metaphor. Though it will be clear that I disagree with Joplin's conclusions, I found her article stimulating and my own discussion has been enriched through argument with her work.

9.   Forbes Irving, *Metamorphosis*, p. 107.

10.   See Forbes Irving, *Metamorphosis*, pp. 103-105, on the relation of the unnatural appetite of incest to that of cannibalism.

11.   Joplin, 'Voice', comments that 'once raped, Philomela stands radically outside all boundaries: she is exiled to the realm of 'nature' or what Girard calls undifferentiated violence; she is imprisoned in the woods' (p. 42); for a general discussion of the mechanism of scapegoating, see pp. 35-42.

12.   Joplin, 'Voice', p. 34.

13.   'Myth, like literature and ritual, abets structure by giving the tale a dead and deadly end... The sisters are said to trade murder and dismemberment of the child for rape and mutilation of the woman' (Joplin, 'Voice', p. 45).

14.   But see Eva C. Keuls's fascinating discussion of the dual role of weaving in Greek society: 'a major element in the enculturation of the female... second in importance only to... marriage... On the other hand textile-making imagery also reflected man's awe and fear of his incarcerated female'. She points out that weaving and spinning fixed the position of women within their social place: 'home textile-working was and, in some parts of the world, still is a mechanism for the restriction of women to private quarters ('Attic Vase-Painting and the Home Textile Industry', in Warren G. Moon [ed.], *Ancient Greek Art and Iconography* [Madison, WI: University of Wisconsin Press, 1983], pp. 209, 210).

15.   Charles Altieri claims that 'on the psychological level the single plot denies the priority of fictions; it claims that literature is always referential and that the present phenomena are never adequate but must be verified by some kind of reality testing' ('Ovid and the New Mythologists', *Novel* [Fall 1973], pp. 31-40 [39]).

16.   Keuls's remark that 'women were commonly locked up in their quarters' (p. 216) seems particularly pertinent to Joplin's approach: an approach which clearly rests on moral grounds themselves further illuminated by

Altieri. Against the structural difference of gender Altieri posits the opposition of artist to moralist: '...the plot is also a trick and the centered symbolic plot of the moralist writer is a restriction of *human* freedom' ('Vase Painting', p. 38; my emphasis).

17.   'Perhaps the most important thing is that the birds' main punishment comes during their human lifetime and their bird state is not actually a period of suffering ... the position of these transformations at the end of their story, and the fact that they will last for ever, removes any sort of urgency about the heroes' behaviour or state of mind as birds' (Forbes Irving, *Metamorphosis*, p. 112).

18.   Beryl Rowland, *Birds with Human Souls: A Guide to Bird Symbolism* (Knoxville, TN: University of Tennessee Press, 1977).

19.   Joplin, 'Voice', p. 42.

20.   Forbes Irving notes that Tereus 'becomes a bird that is opposed to all human civilisation: the hoopoe lives as far away from men as possible and covers its nest with excrement to keep away human beings'; he quotes Pliny as saying that it is a bird that eats filth (*Metamorphosis*, pp. 103, 105). J.R.T. Pollard also notes Aelian's belief that the hoopoe detests the female sex (*Birds in Greek Life and Myth* [Thames and Hudson, 1977], p. 46).

21.   'The Web of Song: Weaving Imagery in Homer and the Lyric Poets', *Classical Journal* 76 (1981), pp. 193-96.

22.   'Sappho, Pindar and Bacchylides may all be said to have conceived of their craft as a process of 'weaving' a patterned tapestry of song' (Snyder, 'The Web of Song', p. 193).

23.   Snyder, 'The Web of Song', p. 193.

24.   Snyder, 'The Web of Song', pp. 193-94.

25.   A variant of the Philomela myth; recorded in J.R.T. Pollard, '*The Birds* of Aristophanes: A Source Book for Old Beliefs', *American Journal of Philology* 69 (1948), pp. 353-76 (356-59); see also Forbes Irving *Metamorphosis*, pp. 100-101.

26.   Keuls remarks on the confusion of loom and lyre in vase painting ('Vase-Painting', p. 219). Perhaps this similarity could be seen as connecting the two activities which bind a community together: the material and gendered weaving process at its heart and the creative connections allowed through narrative and art which provide the metaphoric frame.

27.   Critias fr. 8, 1-2, quoted in Snyder, 'The Web of Song', p. 196 (taken from E. Diehl. 'Fuerunt ante Homerum poetae', *Rheinisches Museum für Philologie* 89 [1940]).

28.   Pointed out to me by Mr Francis Warner.

29.   *A Glossary of Greek Birds* (Oxford: Clarendon Press, 1895), pp. 13-14. Thompson details all references to the nightingale in extant Greek literature (pp. 10-14).

30.   There were many theories that attempted to explain the disappearance and reappearance of migratory birds: Aristotle thought that some birds migrated but that others, including the swallow, hibernated in holes. The

debate continued up until the early nineteenth century with Georges Cuiver rehearsing an old argument in his claim (1817) that swallows become torpid in cold weather and spend the winter at the bottom of marshes (Jean Dorst, 'Old Explanations of Bird Migrations', in *The Migrations of Birds* [trans. Constance Sherman; Heinemann, 1962]).

31.   Charles Swainson considers that 'Primitive peoples are not interested aesthetically in bird songs... A bird's supposed magical power or its significance as an omen is that which raises its status' (*The Folklore and Provincial Names of British Birds* [E. Stock, 1886 (repr. 1956)], p. 187). Once fixed in this way the significance of the bird as omen is translated into narrative.

32.   Thompson, *Glossary of Greek Birds*, p. 13.

33.   A fascinating study of 'a modern Greek folksong of ritual character ...generically known as the 'swallow song' provides a pertinent example of a structuralist interpretation of a similarly defined group of associations around the swallow. Michael Herzfeld sees the swallow song (the name is a modern invention) as part of a *rite de passage*: 'the central opposition, clearly expressed by the terms of the ritual... is that between summer and winter: indeed the name "swallow song" is a misnomer, since it refers not to this central opposition but to a particular symbol on one side of the structural divide' ('Ritual and Textual Structures: The Advent of Spring in Rural Greece', in *Text and Context: The Social Anthropology of Tradition* [ed. R.K. Jain; Philadelphia: Institute for the Study of Human Issues, 1977], pp. 29-50 [29]; I am indebted to Dr Margaret Kenna for drawing my attention to this article.) Of course the difference that I am suggesting between the two systems lies in the introduction of art, of ambiguity into a system of balances which then becomes interpretative (i.e. an object of art) rather than reflective of or responsive to seasonal change.

34.   Pollard, *Birds in Greek Life and Myth*, p. 165; Halliday, *Folk Tales and Legend*, p. 92.

35.   'The Nightingale', pp. 78-84.

36.   See the entrancing discussion of 'The Drama of Logos' in Simon Goldhill's *Reading Greek Tragedy* (Cambridge: Cambridge University Press, 1986), pp. 1-32. As Goldhill points out, the Cassandra scene is the longest scene of the play and of corresponding importance.

37.   This argument is influenced by Jacques Derrida's concept of the supplement (*Of Grammatology* [trans. Gayatri Chakravorty Spivak, Baltimore/The Johns Hopkins University Press, 1976]).

38.   Garrod, *The Profession of Poetry*, p. 136 note; Halliday, *Folk Tales*, p. 100.

39.   Forbes Irving, *Metamorphosis*, p. 112.

40.   Chandler, 'The Nightingale', p. 80.

41.   Anne Carson, *Eros the Bittersweet* (Princeton: Princeton University Press, 1986).

42.   The word *idyll* is itself based on Theocritus's depiction of an idealized rural life.

43.   Milton's self-alignment with the nightingale is well known, not just in his first sonnet ('O Nightingale'), but throughout his work, and has been the subject of many critical accounts. Shelley's metaphoric association of poetry and nightingale in his 'Defence of Poetry' is famous and can be succinctly quoted here: '...a poet is a nightingale, who sits in darkness and sings to cheer its own solitude with sweet sounds; its auditors are as men entranced by the melody of an unseen musician, who feel that they are moved and softened, yet know not whence or why' (*The Complete Works of Shelley* [ed. R. Ingpen and W.E. Peck; New York: Gordian Press, 1965], VII, p. 116).

44.   Plato rejects lyric and epic because of the power of their emotional content: '...you will know that the only poetry that should be allowed in a state is hymns to the gods and paeans in praise of good men; once you go beyond that and admit the sweet lyric or epic muse, pleasure and pain become your rulers instead of law and the rational principles commonly accepted as best'. But, in recognizing that 'we are bound to love poetry', his objections shift to a different ground, strategically denying its political implications: 'Our theme shall be that such poetry has no serious value or claim to the truth' (*The Republic* [trans. Desmond Lee; Harmondsworth: Penguin, rev. edn, 1974], pp. 437, 439).

45.   See Pollard, *Birds in Greek Life and Myth*, p. 168, for the myth of the daughters of Minyas. They draw lots in terror, looking for a victim to placate the god. One of the women has a son Hippasos, whom they cut to pieces before joining the Bacchantes to celebrate the rites of Dionysus. Pollard does wonder, however, if this tale is influenced by Euripedes' *Bacchae*; if so it is possibly yet another twisting of the web of Philomela references.

46.   Joplin, 'Voice', p. 41.

47.   Thompson, *Glossary of Greek Birds*, p. 11.

Chapter 2
Christian Nightingales: Transforming the Classical to the Christian; the Sacred to the Erotic

1.   'Flowres of Sion', sonnet xxiii, in L.E. Kastner (ed.), *The Poetical Works of William Drummond of Hawthornden* (Edinburgh: Manchester University Press, 1913), II, p. 13.

2.   I draw on Hodge's discussion of 'turning points' in 'Literature and History', *Literature as Discourse* (Cambridge: Polity Press, 1991), pp. 204-205. There is of course considerable conflict among historians over the relative importance of the Renaissance, the twelfth century and the eleventh (to name but a few) in terms of their status as significant transformative moments in European history.

3.   I find J.T. Jackson Lears's deliberation on 'The Concept of Cultural Hegemony' very suggestive both here and in the whole of the chapter. He notes that 'Gramsci realised that a class interpretation of history does not entail a fixation on the struggle between oppressors and oppressed; rather,

as Eugene Genovese has observed, "it may reveal a process by which a ruling class successfully avoided such confrontation", and the source of that success may well be in the realm of culture' ('The Concept of Cultural Hegemony', *American Historical Review* 90 [1985], p. 572). This assessment provided the basis for the ideas of class/genre transgression that I attempt to trace within the various texts under consideration. The problem with it is that it appears to see the 'ruling class' as synonomous with 'the oppressors' in single opposition to 'the oppressed'. I see this opposition as complicated by other elements (e.g. the introduction of Christianity and the problem of constructing a Christian identity; the emergence of the twelfth-century secular clerisy), all competing for supremacy. It is only in such a complicated vision that there can be place for that other element so frequently absent in Marxist thought—the role of gender.

4.   I am influenced by Hodge's subtle discussion of the interrelation of 'Genre and Domain', in *Literature as Discourse*, pp. 21-47, esp. pp. 36-38.

5.   Roger Collins stresses the refusal of Christians to take part in the rituals which defined the state (*Early Medieval Europe* [Macmillan, 1991], pp. 12-13, 21).

6.   Marina Warner, *Alone of All her Sex: The Myth and Cult of the Virgin Mary* (Picador, 1985), p. 71.

7.   See excerpts from Perpetua's prison diary translated in Peter Dronke, *Women Writers of the Middle Ages* (Cambridge: Cambridge University Press, 1984), pp. 1-36, especially p. 22.

8.   For example, Jerome who fumed against the poetry he loved: 'poetry, the wisdom of the world, the pompous eloquence of the orators, this food of devils' (*Epistles* 21.13, quoted in F.J.E. Raby, *Christian Latin Poetry* [Oxford: Clarendon Press, 1927], p. 6). Hereafter *CLP*.

9.   *Women Writers*, discussed p. 1 n. 7.

10.   Collins, *Early Medieval Europe*, pp. 18-21.

11.   *CLP*, p. 6.

12.   'Before the middle of the third-century, there is no definite trace of Latin Christian poetry, and the earliest extant Latin hymns belong to the fourth-century.' Raby also remarks, though without analysis, that 'the age that saw the beginnings of Christian literature saw also the beginnings of Christian art' (*CLP*, pp. 3-4, 7). 'There is no clear evidence that the popular verse of the Romans was other than quantitative; rhythmical verse in the West was entirely a Christian possession and it was never employed by pagan writers' (*CLP*, p. 21). Detailed discussion and examples: pp. 20-28.

13.   See Raby's discussion of the teaching methods in the schools (*CLP*, pp. 4-5). Also Peter Dronke's discussion of rhetoric and Christian writers: *The Medieval Poet and his World* (Rome: Edizione di Storia e Letteratura, 1984), p. 2. Augustine's fascination with the entrance to another world through education is expressed in erotic terms: 'truly over the door of the grammar school there hangs a curtain, yet is that curtain the shroud of falsehood, not the veil of mysteries' (*Confessions* 1.13; quoted *CLP*, p. 7). Jerome's anxiety

about the temptations of classical literature is deeply caught up in anxieties about his own identity: Raby recounts Jerome's dream of being judged 'a Ciceronian, not a Christian' on Judgment Day (*Epistles* 22.30: quoted *CLP*, p. 6).

14. Personal accounts of martyrdom indicate the actual martyrs' willing—and humble—acceptance of their sacrificial role. Hagiographers of the fourth century and after attempted to reclaim the ground of control: '... the new conception of the martyr, which was to dominate the whole middle ages, was the creation of the post-Constantinian Church... The martyr [became] the aggressive soldier of the faith. Fearless, uncompromising, proud and violent, he is always master of the situation. He is strong; his enemies are feeble' (*CLP*, p. 51).

15. That Augustine's *City of God* should seek to vindicate—and to separate out—the operations of the Christian church from those of the corrupt polis illustrates the difficulty of relating church to state (pp. 413-26).

16. *CLP*, p. 101.

17. See Raby for a history of the attempt to control types and kinds of music as central to the struggle for authority amongst competing groups. Fascinatingly he joins in, condemning the 'sweet sensuous poison' of oriental hymnody (*CLP*, pp. 31-32).

18. See Dronke's fascinating chapter on colour imagery in *Medieval Poet*, pp. 55-108 (59).

19. Often discussed but see the Introduction of J. Hollander, *The Untuning of the Sky* (Princeton: Princeton University Press, 1961).

20. See J. Ferrante's discussion of the importance of Neoplatonic ideas in her chapter on medieval allegory, especially in relation to medieval perceptions of gender (pp. 38-64). (*Woman as Image in Medieval Literature* [New York: Columbia University Press, 1975]).

21. Where monks were able to move from monastery to monastery around Europe rather than being fixed in one place, the secular nobility were associated closely with their lands—and after the sixth century grew increasingly hostile towards literacy. (See Alexander Murray, *Reason and Society in the Middle Ages* [Oxford: Clarendon Press, 1978], p. 215.)

22. Warner notes that by the twelfth-century monks were classed socially with women (*Alone of All her Sex*, p.188).

23. I am drawing on Lee Patterson's general argument and its conclusion in the rhetorical association of psychological interiority with the feminine: '... throughout the Middle Ages women were denied social conceptualisation—even existence as social—and historical—beings... If women were denied social definition, did this not mean that the realm of the *asocial*—of the internal, the individual, the subjective—was peculiarly theirs?' (*Chaucer and the Subject of History* [Routledge, 1991], p. 282).

24. John Marenbon claims that 'between the death of Boethius and the time of Alcuin, there is no evidence of... active philosophical speculation... Of an active interest in logic or metaphysics there are few traces'. Along with

many others, Marenbon characterizes the period between Boethius and the ninth century as 'an age that had been without philosophers' (*From the Circle of Alcuin to the School of Auxerre: Logic, Theology and Philosophy in the Early Middle Ages* [Cambridge: Cambridge University Press, 1981], pp. 2, 5.)

25.   F.J.E. Raby, *Secular Latin Poetry in the Middle Ages* (2 vols.; Oxford: Clarendon Press, 1934), I, p. 150. Hereafter *SLP*.

26.   For the other side of the story see Murray's superb analysis of both the decline in numeracy from the classical past into the early Middle Ages— leading to a greater emphasis on the liberal arts—and the psychological changes that accompanied its growing ascendancy into the twelfth century. See esp. chapter 6, 'The Dark Age of European Arithmetic', in *Reason and Society*.

27.   Murray, *Reason and Society*, pp. 151-54.

28.   First evident in Isidore of Seville's *Etymologie*, in which the Latin name *Luscinia* is analysed for the meaning of the actual bird: 'Quod cantu suo significare solet diei surgentis exortum, quasi Luscinia' (quoted in F.J.E. Raby, 'Philomena Praevia Temporis Amoeni', in *Mélanges Joseph de Ghellinck, S.J.* [Gembloux: J. Ducolot, 1951], pp. 435-48).

29.   Raby considers him to be 'on the whole...a mediocre poet' whose 'talents lay elsewhere' (*CLP*, p. 162). I would argue that his writing is not an offshoot of his teaching but a central part of it.

30.   Garrod, *Profession of Poetry*, p. 139, considers this to be an odd, personal reading, but it is possible that the excellent library of both profane and sacred texts at Canterbury may have suggested this interpretation and hence a direct link with the submerged associations with the *adonia*.

31.   There are two Christian poets called Sedulius—and some disagreement over which is the author of the *Carmen Paschale*. Helen Waddell considers that it is Sedulius Scottus (*Mediaeval Latin Lyrics* [Constable, 1929], p. 118 [text]; pp. 319-20 [discussion]. Hereafter *MLL*). Raby thinks that it is the fifth-century writer Caelius Sedulius (*CLP*, pp. 108-10). I use Waddell's text and conclusions in part because my arguments seem to indicate a fairly settled Christian ideology in that the sacred place of the church is taking over from that of an idealized God-created nature.

32.   *SLP*, I, p. 274. Subsequently in discussion of a later text Raby clarifies the significance of the allusion: 'We have in this poem, not merely the association of the nightingale with Christ's Passion, but the suggestion that the singer wishes to die for very grief' ('Philomena Praevia', p. 439). Echoes of the Philomela myth seem inescapable.

33.   *SLP*, I, pp. 269-76.

34.   *SLP*, I, p. 274.

35.   *SLP*, I, p. 276.

36.   'Philomena Praevia', p. 439.

37.   See Murray, *Reason and Society*, pp. 63-64, 81-109, on the disruption caused within the church by the relatively new vices of simony and ambition.

See also the summary of Eugenius's brief foray into contemporary papal intrigue and murder in *MLL*, pp. 325-6.

38. See Dronke's discussion of the sequence form in *Medieval Poet*, pp. 115-44.

39. Helen Waddell, *More Latin Lyrics* (Gollancz, 1976), p. 226. Hereafter *More LL*.

40. Warner's chapter on 'Maria Regina' indicates how such an appropriation of the divine by the ruling elite 'fortified the special relation between the court of heaven and the court on earth' (*Alone of All her Sex*, p. 111).

41. See R.I. Moore, *The Formation of a Persecuting Society* (Oxford: Blackwell, 1990), pp. 16, 142.

42. *CLP*, p. 263.

43. *More LL*, p. 226.

44. Dronke, *Medieval Lyric*, p. 143. The implications of Dronke's comment may be expanded to include gender when the significance of the learning of Latin is associated with the age at which it was learnt. Though Walter Ong's study of 'Latin Language as a Renaissance Puberty Rite' (*Studies in Philology* 56 [1959], pp. 103-24), obviously deals with a different period, he points to a sociological principle—the relation of learning the Latin language to a position of social privilege, one which excluded both women and the language associated with women. The principle generates a model in which languages are divided into a gendered hierarchy: the intellectual, learnt language associated with powerful men; the emotive vernacular associated with the disempowered—women and powerless men. In this context, it is to be expected that vernacular texts should display different characteristics to ones written in Latin.

45. See Lee Patterson's magnificent chapter on Chaucer's *Merchant*. He concludes that 'lacking an ideology that would legitimize his commercial life and secure his participation in the political world of events, the bourgeois turns instead to the inner world of the self as the space of self-definition' (*Chaucer*, p. 338). Though his analysis refers to the displacement of problems of class identity onto the site of marriage, his argument is equally valid for a displacement onto religion. After all he claims earlier that 'English mercantile culture was largely confected out of the materials of other cultural formations—primarily aristocratic but also clerical—and lacked a centre of its own' (p. 333).

46. *Selecta scripta S. Bonaventurae* (Quaracchi, 1898), p. 220; quoted and translated in *CLP*, p. 420.

47. The argument of the whole of Moore's *Persecuting Society*.

48. Eugene Vance, 'Love's Concordance: The Poetics of Desire and the Joy of the Text', *Diacritics* 5 (1975), pp. 40-52.

49. 'The nightingale makes merry by the blossom on the bough, and such great envy takes me that I cannot help but sing; but I know not of what, nor of whom, for I love not myself nor another. And I'm making great

efforts, for I can make good verse when I'm not in love!' ('Bernard de Ventadour', *Anthology of Troubadour Lyric Poetry* [ed. and trans. Alan R. Press; Edinburgh: Edinburgh University Press, 1971], pp. 72, 73).

50.   See Vance, 'Love's Concordance'. I consider Roger Boase's argument that Spanish courtly verse was inherently reactionary, part of a failing aristocracy's attempt to translate its ideological weakness into positive terms of courtly subservience and deference, to be equally valid for the genre as a whole (*The Troubadour Revival* [Routledge & Kegan Paul, 1978]).

51.   Central to the arguments of the following chapter.

52.   Again I refer to Patterson, whose discussion of 'The *Miller's Tale* and The Politics of Laughter' discusses how the peasant classes in part accepted their association with the land and sought to reverse the negative associations of marginality: 'The Miller's rehabilitation of nature is part of a political programme that turns against the governing classes one of its own instruments of ideological control' (*Chaucer*, p. 266). My argument is more to do with the different constructions of class ideology with relation to significant boundaries than an imposed identity. To a disempowered population the world of nature was more likely to be a place of work than an ambivalent oppositional space. This approach suggests a structural principle by which the common people would actively associate *themselves* with nature—not merely respond to aristocratic/clerical denigration—folk culture celebrating seasonal change (compare the *fêtes de mai*), even when they were not politically active and making claims for 'natural equality'.

53.   Peter Dronke, *Medieval Latin and the Rise of the European Love Lyric*. I. *Problems and Interpretations* (2 vols.; Oxford: Clarendon Press, 1965). See also Dronke's more recent discussion of the development of the sequence form in *Medieval Poet*, p. 140, in which he repeats the claim that written vernacular poetry was common in the seventh and eighth centuries despite the fact that little remains.

54.   *Medieval Lyric*, p. 87.

55.   *Medieval Lyric*, p. 81.

56.   'There was not a single institution or agency which had as its task the education of girls, even if education is defined as mere literacy' (Sara Lehrman, 'The Education of Women in the Middle Ages', in D. Radcliff-Umstead [ed.], *The Roles and Images of Women in the Middle Ages and Renaissance* [Pittsburgh: University of Pittsburgh Publications on the Middle Ages and the Renaissance, 1975], p. 133.)

57.   Janet Coleman, 'The *Owl and the Nightingale* and Papal Theories of Marriage', *Journal of Ecclesiastical History* 38.4 (October 1987), pp. 517-68.

58.   Warner, *Alone of All her Sex*, pp. 186-87.

59.   F. Heer comments that 'heterodox and heretic groups offered women much greater freedom than the church' (quoted in Ferrante, *Woman as Image*, p. 8 note). Of great interest is Ernest W. McDonnell's comprehensive study, *The Beguines and Beghards in Medieval Culture* (New York: Octagon Books, 1954): 'In the wake of Gregorian Reform Western Europe

was subjugated to continuous waves of religious excitement, sometimes assuming substantial proportions, sometimes of merely local significance' (Part One, 'A Case Study in the *Vita Apostolica*', p. vii). See also chapter 5: 'The Semi-religious under Discipline', pp. 59-70, on the continuing attempts of the Church fathers to enclose and control these establishments; also Part Two, 'The Extraregular in State and Society', chapter 1: 'Social Origins: The *Frauenfrage*', pp. 81-100, on the background to women's sects: 'In Frankfurt and Cologne, as well as in Strasbourg during the Thirteenth and Fourteenth Centuries, women from all classes, and not least from patrician families, dedicated their lives as *béguines* to divine service' (p. 82). More recently Ephraim H. Mizruchi discusses social control and the beguines in his *Regulating Society* (Chicago/University of Chicago Press, 1983), chapter 3, 'Beguines: Ambivalence and Heresy', pp. 48-65. There is a host of other writings on these semi-religious communities.

60. Moore, *Persecuting Society*, p. 26.

61. As in the German *wineleodas*, and the *Kharjas* quoted whole in eleventh and twelfth-century Spanish *cantigas de amigo*, discussed at length by Dronke in *Medieval Lyric*, chapter 3, esp. pp. 86-90

62. *Medieval Lyric*, p. 85.

63. 'The nightingale had...assumed in relation to the *fêtes de mai* a significance at once symbolical and mystical' (Gaston Paris, *Journal de Savants* [1891], pp. 669-86, quoted in *SLP*, II, p. 246).

64. David Lampe, 'Tradition and Meaning in *The Cuckoo and the Nightingale*', *Papers in Language and Literature* 3 (1967), pp. 49-62. That the two traditions overlapped forms the basis of Dronke's argument in the first volume of his magnificent *Medieval Latin and the Rise of the European Love Lyric*. I. *Problems and Interpretations* (2 vols.; Oxford: Clarendon Press, 1965).

65. Such as the delightful meditative poem written by an Irish monk on Pangur Bán, his cat, beautifully translated in Ted Hughes and Seamus Heaney's anthology, *The Rattle Bag* (Faber, 1982), p. 333.

66. Text in R.H. Robbins (ed.), *Secular Lyrics of the XIVth and XVth Centuries* (Oxford: Clarendon Press, 1952), p. xxxvi.

67. Text in Celia and Kenneth Sisam (eds.), *The Oxford Book of Medieval English Verse* (Oxford: Clarendon Press, 1970), p. 567.

68. *Medieval Lyric*, pp. 86-108.

69. Defined as 'in essence a dramatic lyric in which the pensive poet...overhears a dialogue or confession' (F.L. Utley, *The Crooked Rib* [Columbus: Ohio State University, 1944], p. 40). In line with his interest in the *querelle*, Utley sees the genre as rooted in women's songs.

70. E.K. Chambers and F. Sedgewick (eds.), *Early English Lyrics* (A.H. Bullen, 1907), pp. 267-70.

71. R.T. Davies (ed.), *Medieval English Lyrics* (Faber, 1963), p. 20.

72. For a fuller discussion of whether the genre derives from an aristocratic, scholarly or folk background, see *SLP*, II, pp. 332-34. Raby concludes

that 'the last word has hardly been said on the subject', though he supports the folk derivation.

73.   Wouldn't you like a shepherd boy, shepherd girl?'
       'I can very well herd alone, knight!
       I can very well herd alone, nightingale!'

       'Won't you let us sit in the shade, shepherd girl?'
       'The shade is damp with dew, knight!
       The shade is damp with dew, nightingale!'

       'Over there the ferns are dry, shepherd girl!'
       'Then go spend an hour there, knight!
       Then go spend an hour there, nightingale!'
   —From *Chants d'Auvergne* (orch. Canteloube)

74.   Especially common in German and Scandinavian tales (L.C. Wimberley, *Folklore in the English and Scottish Ballads* [repr.; New York: Dover, 1965 (1928)], p. 46. See note 52 above).

75.   Davies quotes R.L. Greene in his discussion of the poem as a 'battle of the sexes' (*Medieval English Lyrics*, p. 240): 'Holly and Ivy are common in English folk-songs, and the identification of holly with the male and ivy with the female is common in folk-customs' (*The Early English Carols* [Oxford: Clarendon Press, 1935]; see also Utley, *The Crooked Rib*, p. 43).

76.   Text in Wimberley, *Folklore*, p. 155. She also notes the Elysian nature of the nightingale, popinjay and thrush in Swainson, *Provincial Names*.

77.   The sermon 'unashamedly uses a popular metre...and the secular poet's rhetorical tricks' to reach its popular audience (*Medieval English Verse*, [ed. and trans. B. Stone; Harmondsworth: Penguin, 1964], p. 82).

78.   Text in F.J. Furnivall (ed.), *Political, Religious, and Love Poems*, (Early English Text Society, 1903), p. 131.

79.   Text in Eleanor Prescott Hammond (ed.), *English Verse between Chaucer and Surrey* (Durham, NC: Duke University Press, 1927).

80.   'With the exception of *Pervigilium Veneris*, the spring song hardly exists in Latin literature' (Helen Waddell, *The Wandering Scholars* [Constable], p. 22.)

81.   Especially that of Bernard de Ventadour (10 of 40 extant poems).

82.   Chambers and Sedgewick (eds.), *Early English Lyrics*, p. 270.

83.   Jethro Bithell, *The Minnesingers*. I. *Translations* (New York: Longman, Greene & Co., 1909), p. 16,

       Send out a song over the countryside,
       O Nightingale, to move my queen of pride.
       Sing wild, as though it were my passion cried
       For her sweet body and the love denied;

also pp. 5, 22, 36, 46, 48; see also E. Taylor, *Lays of the Minnesingers* (Longman, 1825), pp. 102, 133, 141-43, 145, 150-51, 156.

84. *Wine, Women and Song* (trans. J.A. Symonds; Chatto & Windus, 1907), pp. 31-32.

85. T.A. Shippey, 'Listening to the Nightingale', *Comparative Literature* 22 (Winter 1970), pp. 46-60.

86. 'Listening', p. 49.

87. Warner, *Alone of All her Sex*, p. 139.

88. Dronke cites a troubadour judgment that any lady (including an unmarried one) could be a *midon* (*Medieval Latin*, p. 47).

89. *Carmina Burana.*

90. See Moore's note on historians' adaptation of Mary Douglas's argument that 'anxiety about sexual power may be a means of expressing or focusing nervousness of those whose functions or value in society give them much greater importance than is reflected in their status or influence' (*Purity and Danger* [1966], pp. 140-58; as discussed and applied, Moore, *Persecuting Society*, p. 101).

91. Argued by Ingebor Glier on the late development of love poetry, 'Troubadours and Minnesang', *The New Pelican Guide to English Literature*. I.2. *The European Inheritance* (gen. ed. Boris Ford; 5 vols.; Harmondsworth: Penguin, 1982), pp. 167-87.

92. *Medieval Lyric*, p. 29.

93. Quoted in *Medieval Lyric*, p. 28.

94.
(v)

'Will you never stop that racket,
   overrated little bird?
Do you think your art surpasses
   all the singing ever heard?
Don't you know that other music
   is quite frequently preferred?

(ix)

Now a pause in the performance;
   but you're singing on the cheap:
out of all who listen to you,
   no one offers you a tip—
only God, perhaps, who made you
   with his special workmanship.

(xi)

But in summer, what relief! She
   gives her voice a little rest,
stupefied with admiration
   of the offspring in her nest.
And when winter comes, she's vanished,
   dead beneath the freezing mist.

Fleur Adcock 'The Virgin and the Nightingale' (Newcastle-upon-Tyne: Bloodaxe, 1983), pp. 31, 33. Full text and translations, pp. 30-35).

95.   Also mentioned by Lampe, its implications are highlighted by Rowland, *Birds with Human Souls.*

96.   Quoted by Shippey, 'Listening', p. 52. Where Shippey stresses the *situation*, other critics draw attention to the importance of the nightingale *itself*, seen as an example of Marie's use of a 'specific, concrete object as the centre of her *lai*'. R.D. Cottrell, for example, sees the bird as the 'central character' ('Le Lai de Laustic: From Physicality to Spirituality', *Philological Quarterly* 47 [1967], pp. 499-505). Robert T. Cargo draws attention to similarities between the fates of Marie's bird and lady and that of Ovid's Philomela ('Marie de France's *Le Laustic* and Ovid's *Metamorphoses*', *Comparative Literature* 18 [1966], pp. 162-66). Modern translation in *The Lais of Marie de France* (trans. with an introduction by Glyn S. Burgess and Keith Busby; Harmondsworth: Penguin, 1986).

97.   Patterson, *Chaucer*, p. 341, comments that 'we should remember that for the Middle Ages the disruptive desire of the female subject was seen as a threat precisely because it sought to locate itself outside and against all forms of cultural order'.

98.   It is alluded to in *The Owl and the Nightingale* (ll. 1049-60), the *Gesta Romanorum, Renard Contrafait* and Alexander Neckham's *De Naturis Rerum*, while its subversive implications (its subtle victory through the emphasis on the *symbolism* of the nightingale) are undermined in the explicitly sexual form it takes in Boccaccio's *Decameron* (V. iv).

99.   It appears infrequently in early Celtic nature poetry, e.g. with the blackbird, thrush and lark in Llywarch Hen's ninth-century poems of pleasure and love (Ifor Williams, *Lectures on Early Welsh Poetry* [ed. Rachel Bromwich; Cardiff: University of Wales Press, 1972]).

100.   Rachel Bromwich notes the heated exchange—ending in a challenge to a duel—between Dafydd and Gruffudd Gryg, representatives of the new 'love' and the older 'praise' poetry respectively (*Writers of Wales: Dafydd ap Gwilym* [Cardiff: University of Wales Press, 1974], p. 2). However, Kenneth Jackson discusses the possible influence of early Celtic nature poetry on the *Natureingang* of the troubadours in *Studies in Early Celtic Nature Poetry* (Cambridge: Cambridge University Press, 1935), pp. 150-59. But even if this is so the nightingale retains links with courtly lyrics.

101.   E.g. Jean de Condé, *La Messe des Oiseaux* (thirteenth century); text in B.A. Windeatt, *Chaucer's Dream Poetry: Sources and Analogues* (Cambridge: Cambridge University Press, 1982), pp. 104-19. Also the fifteenth-century English poem 'The Harmony of Birds'; text in *Two Early Renaissance Bird Poems* (ed. M. Andrew; Washington, DC: Folger Shakespeare Library; Associated University Presses, 1984).

102.   Thomas Parry, *Hanes Llenyddiaeth Gymraeg hyd 1900* (Cardiff: University of Wales Press, 1945), pp. 81, 88, 90.

103.   Jacques Ribard's reading of *Le Laüstic* sees the window as a frontier between the interior day world and the unreachable 'viergier amoureux' outside. He concludes that 'l'oiseau-emblème... en mourrant, symbolise

l'impossible communication de ces deux mondes', but that the spiritualized love of the couple is 'toujours préservé dans l'éternité du chant' (quoted in Edgar Sienert: *Les Lais de Marie de France: Du conte merveilleux à la nouvelle psychologique* [Paris: Librairie Honoré Champion, 1978], pp. 135-36).

104. D. Gray, *Themes and Images in the Medieval English Religious Lyric* (Routledge & Kegan Paul, 1972), poem quoted pp. 77-78.

105. See E. Walberg's introduction to his edition of the French version of Pecham's *Philomena*, 'le *Chant* que je reproduis ci-après, n'a... aucun rapport avec la suave mélodie du "confidant de l'amour". Il est une inspiration toute différente' (*Le Chant de Roussigneul* [Lund: C.W.K. Gleerup, 1942]), p. 5.

106. 'Philomena Praevia', p. 444.

107. Howden made the alternative version of his own poem for Eleanor, Henry III's wife. The French version of Pecham's poem, 'scriptum in villa Dolensi', is noted above.

108. O. Glauning (ed.), *Lydgate's Minor Poems: The Two Nightingale Poems* (Early English Text Society, 1900), p. xxxix.

109. 'Philomena Praevia', p. 444.

110. R. Woolf, *The English Religious Lyric in the Middle Ages* (Oxford: Clarendon Press, 1968), pp. 232-33 (translation).

111. Gray, *Themes and Images*, p. 77.

112. Murray, *Reason and Society*, pp. 9-13.

113. *Reason and Society*, p. 16 (references given).

114. Gray, *Themes and Images*, p. 11.

115. Text from Walberg (ed.), *Le Chant*.

116. Quote from Glauning (ed.), *Lydgate's Minor Poems*.

117. Sandison compares the dream vision with other genres: '...the French lyrics of adventure, almost without exception, tell of actual encounters. Even when they concern a symbolic character... a nightingale that offers sage advice, the Virgin... the recitals are realistic and matter-of-fact; there is no suggestion that the adventure is visionary.' Sandison discusses the importance of the woman's role in the *chanson dramatique*, a form of the *chanson d'aventure*: 'Either a woman's monologue forms the kernel of the *chanson dramatique*, or a dialogue or scene in which the woman's part is usually dominant, or—in a small group standing [related to the] *chansons de mai*—the song of the nightingale in praise of springtime and love' (p. 10). Helen E. Sandison, *The 'Chanson d'Aventure' in Middle English* (Bryn Mawr, PA: Bryn Mawr College, 1913), p. 22. The dream vision, on the other hand, deliberately distances itself from 'actual encounters' and therefore introduces elements of ambiguity and interpretation: elements that this text wishes to contain.

118. Sandison stresses the individual nature of the woman in the *chanson d'aventure* 'who sits *tote soule* under a tree' ('*Chanson d'Aventure*', p. 10).

119. Common in Persian literature. For examples see *Fifty Poems of Hafiz* (ed. and trans. A.J. Arberry; Cambridge: Cambridge University Press, 1953), nos. 5, 8, 25, 44.

Chapter 3
Debating Class and Gender: Medieval English Nightingales

1.   Though Abelard's teacher, Roscelin, had earned the hostility of the church authorities and professional theologians by bringing logic to bear on theology, it was Abelard who attempted to 'reconcile theology, hitherto firmly in the grips of naïve realism, to a "nominalist" theology' (Martin M. Tweedale, 'Logic (i) To the Time of Abelard', in *A History of Twelfth Century Western Philosophy* [ed. P. Dronke; Cambridge: Cambridge University Press, 1988], p. 297). See also, in the same volume, D.E. Luscombe, on 'Peter Abelard': 'Abelard applied to the content of faith procedures of interpretation and explanation which were tested in another domain' (p. 297).

2.   John of Salisbury considered that logic provided 'a schooling in the arts of thinking, reasoning and speaking': an argument I apply to the implications of the poetic debate. By the later twelfth century, after Abelard, logicians were more concerned with understanding the wider question of 'how language functions' and how the world is perceived through language. The shift from what we would now recognize as a humanities to a scientific approach is striking (Klaus Jacobi, 'Logic (ii) The Later Twelfth Century', in Dronke [ed.], *History*, pp. 250, 239).

3.   J.W.H. Atkins (ed.) sees the debate poem as influenced directly by Abelard's insistence on the importance of dialectic argument; *The Owl and the Nightingale* (Cambridge: Cambridge University Press, 1922), pp. xlviii-xlix. Even the connected form of the dialogue works on the principle of analysis and argument, of the employment of logic in *every* sphere. Thus Abelard's fascinating *Dialogue between a Philosopher, a Jew and a Christian* marks not only the employment of rational argument but the entry of the 'philosopher' into the the world of religious difference. (The comparison with the conservative position—the reference to a separate realm of nature and the emotional manipulation of the anxious reader—in the text by Fulbert of Charters discussed in the previous chapter is very striking.)

4.   Caroline Walker Bynum argues that the twelfth century saw the emergence of 'a kind of work unknown in the early Middle Ages', in attempts 'to catalogue and categorize the full range of human roles in society'. In line with her research interests Bynum is discussing the contemporary classification of religious groups. Moore points to similar classification principles at work at a wider level, looking at the conceptualization of clearly defined groups as scapegoats—Jews, heretics, lepers, male homosexuals, female prostitutes—and in the corresponding spatial subdivisions of urban areas—ghettos, red light districts, social outcasts (*Jesus as Mother: Studies in the Spirituality of the High Middle Ages* [Berkeley/Los Angeles: University of California Press, 1982], p. 90. Moore, *Persecuting Society*, especially ch. 2, 'Classification').

5.   See p. 255 n. 44 above.

6.   Richard Niccols, *The Cuckow*, 1607, draws on *The Cuckoo and the Nightingale* (in R. Niccols, *Selected Poems* [ed. Glyn Pursglove; Salzburg: Institut für Anglistik und Amerikanistik, 1992]).

7.   Milton's first sonnet, 'O, Nightingale', draws on both *The Cuckoo and the Nightingale* and Niccols's *Cuckow*. See Jeni Williams, 'The Voice out of Darkness: Milton and the Nightingale', *Swansea Review* 7 (December 1990), pp. 10-31.)

8.   Dryden translates *The Floure and the Leaf* as one of his *Fables*: 'The Flower and the Leaf'.

9.   Wordsworth translates *The Cuckoo and the Nightingale*.

10.   Barrett Browning's 'The Lost Bower' rewrites *The Floure and the Leaf*. (See Chapter 5.)

11.   E.G. Stanley takes issue with Atkins's more rigidly legal reading of the text by claiming that, because of the shortage of specialized legal terminology, the poem invokes the atmosphere of the legal dispute rather than being conducted as one (*The Owl and the Nightingale* [Manchester: Manchester University Press, 1972], pp. 27-30). Janet Coleman, however, considers that the poem is structured according to the narrower remit of *ecclesiastical* law ('*The Owl and the Nightingale*', 517-68). My argument is unaffected in any case.

12.   Maurice Keen suggests that 'knights and clerks sprang from the same stock and understood each other's worlds, better than is often thought' (*Chivalry* [New Haven and Yale University Press, 1984], p. 32). But 'understanding' does not mean shared values. Keen uses Abelard as a useful example but Abelard chose to separate himself from the norms of his knightly origins—perhaps a reason for his unceasingly controversial arguments: transposing aggression from a physical and anti-intellectual arena to one rooted in intellectual activity involves a huge shift in values.

13.   The debate seems the perfect form for such analysis, in line with Bynum's assessment of the thorny and much-discussed question of whether the twelfth century 'discovered' the individual: '…twelfth-century efforts do not stop at accepting the self-description of a given group; they create new categories and reanalyze existing ones' (*Jesus as Mother*, p. 91).

14.   Respectively: Keen, *Chivalry*, p. 3; Peter S. Noble, 'Knights and Burgesses in the Feudal Epic', in C. Harper-Bill and Ruth Harvey (eds.), *The Ideals and Practice of Medieval Knighthood* (Woodbridge: Boydell Press, 1986), 104-10; Patterson, *Chaucer*, p. 15.

15.   Lee Patterson, 'On the Margin: Postmodernism, Ironic History, and Medieval Studies', *Speculum* 65 (1990), pp. 87-108 (99).

16.   See Utley, *The Crooked Rib*.

17.   C.S. Lewis, *The Allegory of Love* (Oxford: Clarendon Press, 1936), p. 248.

18.   Patterson considers that the aristocracy found it difficult to discriminate between its own class values and those of religion: '…chivalric piety is a blend of sacred and secular values, in particular the desire for fame in this world and salvation in the next, that can be easily distinguished and ranked

by nonchivalric writers but that in chivalric discourse remain undiscrimi-
nated' (*Chaucer*, p. 176-77); see Keen for a less critical discussion of 'the place
of religion in this ethic for secular men' (*Chivalry*, chapter 3, 'Chivalry, the
Church and the Crusade', pp. 44-63).

19.   Stephen G. Nichols discusses 'linguistic code-switching', and the
multiple levels of interpretation that it can provide. See also Robert Hodge's
excellent discussion of the different values attached to the languages within a
medieval macaronic poem ('An Intellectual Anthropology of Marriage', in
The New Medievalism [ed. Marina Brownlee *et al.*; Baltimore: The Johns
Hopkins University Press, 1991], p. 89); Hodge, *Literature as Discourse*, pp.
37-39).

20   Derek Pearsall considers that the dream framework 'not only
[provided] a means of surmounting reality, but also gave unlimited flexibility
to a narrative, doing away with the need for trivialities like sequence and
coherence' (*Introduction to* The Floure and the Leaf [ed. D.A. Pearsall,
London/Edinburgh: Thomas Nelson, 1962], p. 57). Stephen G. Nichols sees
it as *extending* reality instead: 'Oneiric narratives—dream-visions—can be
seen...as an attempt to penetrate the boundaries of the known'. (Nichols,
'The New Medievalism: Tradition and Discontinuity in Medieval Culture', in
Brownlee *et al.* [eds.], *The New Medievalism*, p. 3). It is an argument that
suggests an exploration of interiors.

21.   See Nichols, 'The New Medievalism', p. 23.

22.   See William Henry Jackson's discussion of the German tournament.
He sees one of its functions to be the provision of an arena in which transgressions of a class code could be punished within the class—and amongst
those transgressions are cross-class marriage. Although cross-class marriages
certainly took place and the prohibitions that Jackson notes belong to a
specific group of German nobility, because he bases his argument on the
structural relation of the nobility to an increasingly wealthy merchant class,
more general conclusions about aristocratic attitudes towards lineage may be
drawn from this example ('The Tournament and Chivalry in German Tournament Books of the Sixteenth Century, in Harper-Bill and Harvey [eds.],
Ideals and Practice, pp. 54-56.)

23.   This participation takes the form of pleasure in the text—a response
rigorously policed in the determined rationalism of earlier debates.

24.   'The golden age for careerism in the schools... began with the
twelfth-century'; '...law was rational, related to the *bonum commune*. A man
ready to give his efforts to the service of that common good could hope for
personal advancement from the new institutions' (Murray, *Reason and Society*,
pp. 220, 271).

25.   *Reason and Society.*, p. 271.

26.   Atkins summarizes many of the arguments in his introduction (*The
Owl and the Nightingale*, pp. lv-lvii), though *he* sees the debate as an argument
between different kinds of poets and poetry, between religious didactic
poetry (owl) and the new love poetry of the troubadours (nightingale): an

assessment, however, which divorces the text from its political context.

27.   Coleman argues that the poem stages a debate between the Cistercians and the Cluniacs; the birds representing Bernard and Abelard respectively.

28.   Ferrante, *Woman as Image*, pp. 99-100.

29.   Warner, *Alone of All her Sex*, pp. 134-35.

30.   M. Harley 2253 (*English Lyrics of the Thirteenth Century* [ed. Carleton Brown; Oxford: Clarendon Press, 1932], p. 154).

31.   Carleton (ed.), *English Lyrics*, p. 145.

32.   Carleton (ed.), *English Lyrics*, p. 101; full text, pp. 101-107.

33.   The particular 'tunge' of the troubadour poet, according to Atkins (*The Owl and the Nightingale*, p. lii): an argument very much in line with my class-interested reading of the text.

34.   'The goal of erotic partners is union in *joie*, and not separation in death, and the science of love is by and large a science of mediation and exchange within a framework of implied reciprocity. In combat... the process of material exchange is conceived negatively: blows are "good" and bargains are "bad"' (Vance, 'Love's Concordance', p. 46).

35.   Murray, *Reason and Society*, devotes a whole chapter, 'The University Ladder', specifically to clerkly careerism, and two others to the relation of an emergent intellectual élite to peasants and aristocrats.

36.   For an example: see 'The Husbandman and the Clerk', in Robbins (ed.), *Secular Lyrics*, pp. 180-81.

37.   Murray, *Reason and Society*, p. 244.

38.   *Reason and Society*, p. 271.

39.   Patterson, *Chaucer*, p. 192.

40.   See Chaucer's *Parliament of Fowls*. Also M. Emslie, 'Codes of Love and Class Distinctions', *Essays in Criticism* 5 (1955), pp. 1-17; see also the critical responses and reply in the same volume, pp. 205-18; and D.S. Brewer, 'Class Distinction in Chaucer', *Speculum* 43 (1968), pp. 290-305; esp. the pages dealing with 'gentles and churls' (pp. 297-302).

41.   Murray, *Reason and Society*, refers to substantial speculation on the equation of nobility with virtue, noting with H. Köhler that the idea 'could occasionally be used by the nobility itself to ward off rivalry from *nouveaux riches* who lacked aristocratic virtues' (p. 273): a usage clearly pertinent to my reading of this debate. See also Keen's point on the relation of the ideal of chivalry with 'nobility of life' and 'good lineage' (*Chivalry*, p. 16).

42.   Patterson points out that 'for chivalric theorists like Ramon Lull and Christine de Pisan, there are not good and bad knights but only true and false ones, knights and non-knights' (*Chaucer*, pp. 177-78).

43.   *Chaucer*, pp. 178-79.

44.   Warner, *Alone of All her Sex*, p. 137.

45.   *Alone of All her Sex*, p. 147.

46.   Ferrante, *Woman as Image*, pp. 12, 99-100.

47.   *Woman as Image*, p. 100.

48. Sandison, *'Chanson d'Aventure'*.

49. The realm of the aesthetic serving as a substitute: an argument valid for the function of writing in both *The Cuckoo and the Nightingale* and *The Floure and the Leaf.* Lacan's commment that 'the symbol manifests itself first of all through the murder of the thing' is pertinent (quoted in Elizabeth Grosz, *Jacques Lacan: A Feminist Introduction* [Routledge, 1990], p. 61).

50. Wishing to emphasize the poem's undeniable quality as debate and its affinities with earlier nightingale debates, rather than its status as an individual utterance, I choose to continue to use the name by which it was formerly known. On the other hand, Lee Patterson's meticulous and intelligent reading of the poem rests in part on the 'correct' title, *The Boke of Cupide.* It draws him to concentrate on the historical situation of the courtier, by setting the dreamer in problematic relation to an absolute lord ('Court Politics and the Invention of Literature: The Case of Sir John Clanvowe', in David Aers [ed.], *Culture and History, 1350–1600: Essays on English Communities, Identities and Writing* [Harvester Wheatsheaf, 1992], pp. 9-41).

51. Lee Patterson, 'Historical Criticism and the Claims of Humanism', in *Negotiating the Past* (Madison, WI: University of Wisconsin Press, 1987), p. 74.

52. Patterson, *Chaucer*, p. 170.

53. As to be expected within an ideology that rested on an avoidance of rationality as a key quality in its self-identity, chivalry is a very slippery term which not only changes between the twelfth and fifteenth centuries but also varies according to region. Richard Mortimer discusses the vexed question of the status of knights and knighthood: 'Knighthood as a cultural concept emerges in force in Germany during the 1180's, and this kind of knighthood has been described as "primarily an ideological phenomenon," poetic, metaphoric, a programme of education even, while in the view of one historian, knighthood simply is the noble lifestyle' ('Knights and Knighthood in Germany in the Central Middle Ages', in Harper-Bill and Harvey [eds.], *Ideals and Practice*, p. 98; quoting from Joachim Bumke, *The Concept of Knighthood in the Middle Ages* [trans. W.T.H. and Ericka Jackson; New York: AMS Press, 1982], pp. 131-32). Though Mortimer refers to a specific situation in Germany, Bumke's claims embrace the situation in general. Text for *Cuckoo and the Nightingale* in *The Works of John Clanvowe* (ed. V.J. Scattergood; Cambridge: D.S. Brewer, 1965).

54. Lewis, *Allegory*, p. 244.

55. Patterson claims that 'every courtly poem is in effect a debate, whether it be between a nightingale and a cuckoo or, as is more commonly the case, between feeling and form, love and the language of love' ('Court Politics', p. 28). He follows unconsciously the gendered associations of the feminine nightingale with feeling and love, of the masculine cuckoo with form and language—and without recognizing the role of gender he does not recognize the way the birds are marked by class. His narrator is a courtier subjected to the capricious power of an earthly/regal 'Cupid', and wrestling with 'self-identity and dispersion'—not with conflicting identities. This is in

some way to occlude the class origins of the specific debate genre, a form which foregrounds and thus contains those conflicts in a particular way which is *different* to other courtly writing. Patterson discusses Clanvowe's life ('Court Politics', pp. 12-13, 25-30).

56.   Patterson refers to French literary historians' discussion of court poetry as part of a desire to 'create a cultural *hortus conclusus* where the aristocratic "culte égocentrique" can find a fulfillment impossible in the difficult historical world of the late Middle Ages' ('Court Politics', p. 15). It is a familar argument, however, from New Historicist critics of the early modern court: see, for example, Louis Montrose, '"Eliza, Queene of Shepheardes" and the Pastoral of Power', *English Literary Renaissance*, 10 (1980), pp. 153-82; Arthur F. Marotti, '"Love Is not Love": Elizabethan Sonnet Sequences and the Social Order', *English Literary History* 49 (1982), pp. 396-428; Daniel Gavitch, 'The Impure Motives of Elizabethan Poetry', *Genre* 15 (1982), pp. 225-38; Gary Waller, *English Poetry of the Sixteenth Century* (London/New York: Longman, 1986). (But see note 60 below, p. 27.)

57   'Court Politics', pp. 14-15.

58.   Patterson, *Chaucer*, p. 230.

59.   V.J. Scattergood (ed.), *Works*, discussed pp. 9-10.

60.   Patterson writes of a 'twofold audience—one engaged in mere dalliance, another capable of reading ironically' ('Court Politics', p. 29).

61.   As my last chapter demonstrates, I take Christianity very seriously: see David Aers's comment that 'One simply cannot write the history of the subject in a culture where Christian beliefs and practices are pervasive without taking Christianity extremely seriously' ('A Whisper in the Ear of Early Modernists; or, Reflections on Literary Critics Writing the "History of the Subject"', in Aers, *Culture and History*, pp. 177-202). In this case one of the aspects of Lollardy that I think important is the significance of the vernacular Bible with its implication of a community defined by a shared national language—hence *not* primarily by class: though of course the early Lollards were aristocrats from areas distant to the potent centre of the court.

62.   'Court Politics', p. 21.

63.   'Court Politics', p. 25.

64.   Patterson, *Chaucer*, p. 168.

65.   *Chaucer*, p. 169.

66.   Murray notes the hostility between clerk and peasant as well as between clerk and aristocrat, and aristocrat and peasant (see *Reason and Society*, chapter 10, 'The Intellectual Elite', pp. 244-46).

67.   A significant part of the courtly life rested on the conscious creation of leisured and formal patterning, on dancing, jousting and poetry. Patterson sees this as not merely an arena to practise the arts of manipulation (compare note 55 above) but a space to mediate the irreconcilable demands on the courtier. Again a New Historicist reading provides a useful paradigm. Frank Whigham's comments on 'Sexual and Social Mobility in *The Duchess of Malfi*', though drawing on Marx to discuss the play in terms of Bosola's 'alienated

labour', are yet more suggestive for the unstable and dependent position of the courtier: 'It may be argued [that] aestheticizing can restore a felt unity or wholeness to actions by decontextualising them, separating them from the context that displays one's fragmentation...as it were, alienating them from their alienation' (*PMLA* 100 [1985], pp. 167-86 [178]).

68.   Scattergood, *Works*, 55, 82n. Patterson stresses the *literary* background to the date by referring to *Troilus and Criseyde* (2, 1. 56), rather than seeing it as colloquially 'unlucky'—yet this oral tradition may have provided the rationale for its appearance in Chaucer ('Court Politics', p. 22).

69.   David Lampe, 'Tradition and Meaning', pp. 49-62.

70.   A.C. Spearing, *Medieval Dream Poetry* (Cambridge: Cambridge University Press, 1976), pp. 176-81; Patterson, 'Court Politics', p. 23).

71.   Scattergood (ed.), *Works*, p. 84; Patterson, 'Court Politics', p. 10.

72.   There is no need to refer to Scattergood's proverb (*Works*, p. 85), this action by itself conveys the similarities between the two characters.

73.   See G.L. Marsh on the cult of the daisy, 'Sources and Analogues of *The Flower and the Leaf*', *Modern Philology* 4 (1906–1907); pp. 37-40, 121-69, 281-329.

74.   A perfect example of the role of the aesthetic in reconstituting identity (compare Whigham, 'Sexual and Social Mobility', note 67, above).

75.   Patterson, 'Court Politics', p. 29.

76.   V.J. Scattergood, *Politics and Poetry in the Fifteenth Century* (1971).

77.   Bynum's discussion is extremely useful here in view of the current argument over subjectivity between the new medievalists and New Historicists/cultural materialists. She points out that 'A sense of models or types, a sense of proliferating groups and structures and of the necessity to choose among them, and a sense of relationship are characteristics of the twelfth-century at least as salient as a new sense of self,' and that 'The twelfth-century person did not "find himself" by casting off inhibiting patterns but by adopting appropriate ones' (*Jesus as Mother*, pp. 88, 90). See also the meticulous arguments which include Chaucer's *Criseyde* in Anne Ferry, *The Inward Language* (Chicago/University of Chicago Press, 1983).

78.   As implicit in this discusssion, prefigured in the resolutions of this Lollard text and in its kind of writing.

79.   Patterson, 'Court Politics', p. 28.

80.   'Court Politics', p. 29.

81.   'Court Politics', p. 28.

82.   'A Defence of Poetry', p. 109.

83.   Style being perceived as intimately associated with gender. See the unsigned review in *The Anti-Jacobean Review and Magazine* which opens: 'Had not the title page informed us that this curious "Romance" was the product of "a gentleman," a freshman of course, we should certainly have ascribed it to some "Miss" in her teens; who, having read the beautiful and truly poetic descriptions in the unrivalled romances of Mrs Ratcliffe [*sic*], imagined that to admire the writings of that lady, and to imitate her style were one and the

same thing' (in *Shelley: The Critical Heritage* [ed. James E. Barcus; Routledge & Kegan Paul, 1975], p. 51).

84. E.g. Tillotama Rajan, 'The Web of Human Things: Narrative and Identity in *Alastor*', in *The New Shelley* (ed. Kim G. Blank; Macmillan, 1991), p. 85.

85. Timothy Clark, *Embodying Revolution: The Figure of the Poet in Shelley* (Oxford: Clarendon Press, 1989); G.M. Matthews, 'A Volcano's Voice in Shelley' (1957), in *Shelley: Modern Judgements* (ed. R.B. Woodings; Macmillan, 1968). Specifically on the nightingale, John F. Schell, 'The Nightingale Figure in Shelley's *Defence*', *English Language Notes* 17 (1980), pp. 265-68.

86. Shelley, 'The Woodman and the Nightingale', in *Complete Works*, III. See Jeni Williams, 'Interweaving Poetry and the "Origin of Man": Shelley and the Transforming Nightingale', in *Shelley, 1792–1992: A Bicentenary Conference* (ed. James Hogg; Institut für Anglistik und Amerikanistik, 1993), pp. 58-77.

87. Paul de Man, 'Shelley Disfigured', in *The Rhetoric of Romance* (New York: Columbia University Press, 1984), pp. 93-123 (122).

88. Compare Erasmus Darwin's conception of evolution (rooted in delight) to that of his grandson, Charles Darwin, who focuses on aggressive competition and the survival of the fittest individual (Desmond Hele-King, 'Shelley and Erasmus Darwin', in Kelvin Everest [ed.], *Shelley Revalued* [Leicester: Leicester University Press, 1983]).

89. Patterson, 'Historical Criticism and the Claims of Humanism', in *Negotiating the Past*, pp. 3-39 (9-13).

90. William Hazlitt, *Lectures on English Poets and the Spirit of the Age* (Everyman, 1910), p. 27.

91. Walter Skeat, quoted in Pearsall (ed.), *The Floure and the Leaf*, p. 1.

92. Very evident in Victorian art where realism frequently slides into moral tale, sentiment, or visions of death—see especially the paintings of Landseer. Those of the 'Pre-Raphaelite Brotherhood' stress instead the escapism of a medieval 'mysticism'.

93. Lewis, *Allegory*, p. 249.

94. *Allegory*, p. 248.

95. And indeed Lewis sees it as expressing 'the morality of modern life' (*Allegory*, p. 248).

96. Pearsall (ed.), *The Floure and the Leaf*, pp. 34-36. Text used is Pearsall's.

97. Lewis, *Allegory*, p. 248.

98. Patterson, *Chaucer*, p. 168.

99. See Patterson, *Chaucer*, pp. 26-27; especially the quotation from H. Marshall, Leicester: 'A text of this sort may be said to be *about* its speaker... The tales...concentrate not on the way preexisting people create language but on the way language creates people.'

100. Pearsall (ed.), *The Floure and the Leaf*, p. 48.

101. Rosamund Tuve, *Seasons and Months* (Paris: Folcroft Press, 1933), pp. 25-26.

102 *Seasons and Months.*, p. 25.

103. *Seasons and Months*, p. 59.

104. As in Rilke's 'call-note / of depth-dark sobbing' (First Duino Elegy, in R.M. Rilke, *Duino Elegies* [trans. J.B. Leishman and Stephen Spender; Chatto & Windus, 1975], p. 25).

105. Chaucer, *Complete Works* (ed. W.W. Skeat; Oxford: Clarendon Press, 1912).

106. Lewis, *Allegory*, p. 248.

107. Perhaps the reason for the absence of that aspect of the conventional spring opening in which the assocation of the natural with the feminine is made clear by representing Nature as a desirable woman to whom the (male) poet responds, while the female nightingale triggers his symbolic song. See the opening of Lydgate's 'Reson and Sensualyte' for a superb example.

108. Lewis responds unconsciously to this when he claims that 'we may detect a ladylike ignorance of the heights and the depths' (*Allegory*, p. 248).

109. Pearsall points out that colour has emblematic importance in medieval poetry: red conveys excitement, richness and heraldry, and green—the colour of nature—ambiguously calls up the regeneration of spring as well as the instability of threatened change. See also Marsh, 'Sources', pp. 301-302.

110. This seems equally to be the case for critics who speak on the two companies as 'contrasting ways of conducting the aristocratic life' referring to contemporary courtly games about flowers and leaves. It is very difficult to make any *ethical* pronouncements on these grounds and yet—as Lewis points out (*Allegory*, p. 248)—this is what the poem attempts to do via the Leaf maiden's concluding pronouncement. In this process however it lays bare the constructed nature of those ethics.

111. Pearsall (ed.), *The Floure and the Leaf,* pp. 35-36; quoting Bell's *Chaucer*, iv, p. 235.

112. Pearsall, on the other hand, considers the introduction of Flora as 'very much an afterthought' (*The Floure and the Leaf,* p. 65).

113. Pearsall points out not only the courtly game of the flower and the leaf (see the introduction to *Charles of Orleans: The English Poems* (ed. Robert Steele; Early English Text Society, 1941), but biblical exegesis indicates the significance of the symbols of the leaf and flower. I believe that this makes it all the more significant that the *text* itself demonstrates to the reader the attraction of integration, of the Flower company.

114. The meaning of the passage is not clear. Pearsall quotes Skeat's gloss 'in order to joust with them afterwards', but claims it makes no sense as the jousting has already finished and the companies ride off without taking part in more. He suggests, with Manly (1940), that 'joustes' may be a 'mechanical scribal error' for 'lustes' (*Floure*, p. 146). I believe, however, that the difference between the two companies rests on this very activity and that the fact that jousts are introduced here points to the knights' acquisition of 'proper' gendered roles.

115. For magnificent examples see *Les très riches heures du Duc de Berry* (Musée Condé, Chantilly: Miller Graphics, 1979).

116. M. Vale links the two more directly, commenting that jousting remained a practical training for warfare in the late fifteenth century (*War and Chivalry: Warfare and Aristocratic Culture in England, France and Burgundy at the End of the Middle Ages* [Duckworth, 1981]). See pp. 78, 118, 128.

117. See its striking impression in the obituary notice on Barrett Browning in *The Dublin University Magazine*: '...the rarer and stronger and more passionate Sappho of our times... [but women should take note that] the function of women is—not to write, not to act, not to be famous—but to love'.

Chapter 4
Fragmentation and Alienation: Victorian Nightigales

1. *The Poems of Gerard Manley Hopkins* (ed. W.H. Gardner and N.H. McKenzie; Oxford: Oxford University Press, 1970), pp. 133.

2. Ruskin, 'Love's Meinie' (Keston Kent, 1973). Quoted in Gillian Beer, *Darwin's Plots: Evolutionary Narrative in Darwin, George Eliot, and Nineteenth Century Fiction* (Routledge, Kegan & Paul, 1983).

3. Hicks (ed.), *Selected Poems.*

4. Heather Glen suggests that 'the easy clichés and untroubled regularity of all magazine verse', found in both conservative and radical magazines, from *The Gentleman's Magazine* to *The Monthly Magazine* sought 'at a deep level, to reassure the reader that even these threatening subjects can be incorporated by the polite rational consciousness, that all reasonable men share the same basic values and points of view'. But this enlightenment claim for universally shared experience became suspect by the end of the century. Marilyn Butler notes that 'even to write in a style meant for mankind became a divisive and inflammatory gesture' (Heather Glen, *Vision and Disenchantment: Blake's 'Songs' and Wordsworth's 'Lyrical Ballads'* [Cambridge: Cambridge University Press, 1983], p. 37); Marilyn Butler, *Romantics, Rebels and Reactionaries* [Oxford: Oxford University Press, 1981], p. 68). It is clear that Hopkins would have disapproved of the democratic undercurrents of sentimental verse.

5. Isobel Armstrong, *Victorian Poetry: Poetry, Poetics, Politics* (Routledge: 1993), pp. 6-7.

6. *Victorian Poetry*, p. 6.

7. Linda Shires, 'Ideology and the Subject as Agent', in *Rewriting the Victorians: Theory, History, and the Politics of Gender* (ed. Linda M. Shires; Routledge, 1992), pp. 185.

8. Spivak suggests that her readings may 'incite a degree of rage against the imperialist narrativisation of history, that it should produce such an abject script for [the female writer]'—in this case Charlotte Brontë ('Three Women's Texts and a Critique of Imperialism', in *The Feminist Reader* [ed. Catherine Belsey and Jane Moore; Macmillan, 1989], p. 176).

9.   The policy followed in S. Gilbert and S. Gubar, *The Madwoman in the Attic: The Woman Writer and the Nineteenth Century Imagination* (New Haven and Yale University Press, 1979). Sandra Gilbert has written specifically on 'Bianca' in 'From *Patria* to *Matria*: EBB's Risorgimento', *PMLA* 99 (1984), pp. 194-211.

10.   W. Irvine and P. Honan, *The Book, the Ring and the Poet* (New York: Bodley Head, 1974), pp. 253-54.

11.   Peter Dally, *Elizabeth Barrett Browning: A Psychological Portrait* (Macmillan, 1989), p. 190. More recently Germaine Greer dismisses Barrett Browning as an anorexic junkie in *Slipshod Sybils: Recognition, Rejection and the Woman Poet* (New York: Viking, 1995), p. 396.

12.   Brian Doyle, 'The Hidden History of English Studies', in *Re-reading English* (ed. Peter Widdowson; Methuen, 1982), p. 24.

13.   Armstrong, *Victorian Poetry*, p. 1.

14.   Armstrong, *Victorian Poetry*, p. 28.

15.   Shires, 'Ideology', p. 185.

16.   Shires, 'Ideology', p. 186.

17.   Patterson, 'Historical Criticism', p. 74.

18.   Johnson's *Alien Vision of Victorian Poetry*, for example, sees the relation of poet to community as one of fracture and alienation that is actively incorporated into the text, while Langbaum's *Poetry of Experience* considers that the dramatic monologue explores alien and alienated subjectivities in response to a crisis in ethical standards, seeing them as dramatizing tension between the opposing poles of sympathy and judgement. (E.D.H. Johnson, *The Alien Vision of Victorian Poetry* [Hampden, CT: Archon Books, 1963]; Robert Langbaum, *The Poetry of Experience: The Dramatic Monologue in Modern Literary Tradition* [Chatto & Windus, rev. edn, 1972 [1957]]).

19.   A common assumption in many feminist readings of Victorian women's writing. Angela Leighton, for example, considers that the garden —which I see as a medieval figure—'was always a place of lost childhood gladness in Barrett Browning's early poems' (*Elizabeth Barrett Browning* [Brighton, Sussex: Harvester, 1986]). But I think that the image is far more ambivalent. More often than not medievalism does not even merit discussion. See, for example, Dorothy Mermin, *Godiva's Ride: Women of Letters in England, 1830–1880* (Bloomington and Indianapolis: Indiana University Press, 1993), or the rather schematic readings of Gilbert and Gubar, *Madwoman in the Attic*. As Beer points out, however, 'escape is not necessarily a form of retreat or failure. Escape can mean freedom and the trying out of new possibilities after imprisonment.' Though Beer is responding to Elaine Showalter's unhappiness with Woolf's retreat from realism, her comment is useful for any rejection of the dominant mode of realism (*Arguing with the Past* [Routledge], p. 127).

20.   Patterson sees a clear political division between conservative and Romantic medievalists ('The Development of Chaucer Studies', *Negotiating the Past*, esp. pp. 9-11). I select only two interpretations of the pervasive medi-

evalism of Victorian culture, focusing on gender and class respectively. There are clearly many others but there is no space to discuss those at length here.

21.   'We are getting back to the world of the fifteenth century,' Norman Stone said on *The New Middle Ages*, a BBC documentary that suggests that the twentieth century is returning to 'a time ruled by robber barons and plagued by disease...not so much a "modern" world as a "medieval" one'. It is clear that this formulation of the medieval as a 'Dark Age' has little in common with the Middle Ages as an 'age of faith' whose passing is mourned by Arnold and others. As with Macaulay and Mill, the 'medieval' is opposed to the science and reason which characterize the 'modern' age. This dichotomy emerged during the nineteenth century and is clearly visible in the poetry of the time, where, once again, the poetic nightingale serves as an index of changing boundaries.

22.   Armstrong, *Victorian Poetry*, p. 39.

23.   Dorothy Mermin argues that the use of silent auditors within the dramatic monologue was both a way of integrating poetry with the world of fiction and an approach which questioned the possibility of communicating the inner self with the external public world (*The Audience in the Poem: Five Victorian Poets* [New Brunswick, NJ: Rutgers University Press, 1983], p. 11). E. Warwick Slinn takes issue with her, claiming that the genre actively investigates the relation of self and other: '...intrasubjective perception is also an intersubjective structure. But Mermin's formulation tends to privilege an epistemological subjectivism, maintaining private feelings and social world as separate realms, whereas it is through tying both private and public to the mediations of discourse that Victorian poetry...develops its social and intellectual critique' (*The Discourse of Self in Victorian Poetry* [Macmillan, 1991], p. 7). See U.C. Knoepflmacher for a discussion of the dramatic monologue which foregrounds gender: 'Projection and the Female Other: Romanticism, Browning and the Victorian Dramatic Monologue', *Victorian Poetry* 22 (1984), pp. 139-59. Armstrong goes as far as to claim that women poets 'invented' the monologue, an approach which stresses the genre's active investigation of relations between self and other: '...by using a mask a woman writer is in control of her objectification and at the same time anticipates the strategy of objectifying women by being beforehand with it and circumventing masculine representation' (*Victorian Poetry*, p. 326).

24.   Richard Holt Hutton in the *North British Review* (1858, p. 474) excludes women from writing poetry altogether because their 'fancy deals directly with *expression*', quoted Ina Ferris, 'From Trope to Code: The Novel and the Rhetoric of Gender in Nineteenth Century Critical Discourse', in Shires, *Rewriting the Victorians*, p. 27.

25.   Beer, *Darwin's Plots*, p. 127.

26.   Shelley, *Complete Works*.

27.   Beer comments that a major premise of Darwin's theory was the importance of happiness—which complicates a theory popularly based on a vicious struggle for survival (*Darwin's Plots*, 68). Elswhere she quotes Darwin

on the subject: 'Pain or suffering of any kind, if long continued, causes depression and lessens the power of action; yet is well adapted to make a creature guard itself against any great or sudden evil. Pleasurable sensations, on the other hand, may long be continued without any depressing effect; on the contrary, they stimulate the whole system to increased action' (*The Autobiography of Charles Darwin* [Collins, 1958], pp. 51-52).

28.   The lost Romantic dream, expressed most powerfully in Wordsworth's *Prelude*.

29.   Mermin argues that 'the Victorian interest in the primitive is the idea of evolution, or progress, turned on its head to become an obsession with origins' ('Browning and the Primitive', *Victorian Poetry* 25 [1982], p. 216).

30.   The artist Landseer is a case in point: famous for his portraits of pet dogs with melting eyes, he also painted images of extraordinary cruelty and violence—an example being the nightmarish painting of the fate of the polar expedition torn to pieces by polar bears in 'Man Proposes, God Disposes'. See Richard Ormond, *Sir Edwin Landseer* (Thames & Hudson, 1981), p. 207, plate 151. Ormond notes the 'dark and fatalistic' imagery of the last works in particular where 'death and destruction are inevitable; there are always predators and victims' (p. 201).

31.   Fred Randel sees Coleridge's poem as a sustained reinterpretation of Milton's nightingale figure, and—by extension—his poetry as a whole. For example, referring to ll. 40-43, he considers that by making 'two males and a female, the latter related by sisterhood, discourse on the farthest reaches of their learning while out in a dark forest', Coleridge is deliberately echoing *Comus* (Milton refers to his lady as a 'poor hapless nightingale' [l. 66]). In this poem about poetry and relationships 'no-one is at risk… but however relaxed the atmosphere, no-one is prepared to settle for the prophane' ('The Contentiousness of Romantic Nightingales', *Studies in Romanticism* 21 [1982], pp. 33-55 [41, 42]). Coleridge of course draws attention to the association with Milton through his disingenuous disclaimer.

32.   See also 'The Woodman and the Nightingale' which sets the nightingale/poet against the materialist—and destructive—Woodman.

33.   Beer, *Darwin's Plots*, 127.

34.   '… and be no more.' (*Idylls of the King*, 'The Last Tournament', l. 125). Tennyson's interest in the idea is demonstrated by the recurrence of the phrase in 'The Passing of Arthur', where the despairing king laments the collapse of the Round Table: '… all my realm / Reels back into the beast and is no more' (ll. 124-25) (*A Variorum Edition of Tennyson's 'Idylls of the King'* [ed. John Pfordresher; New York: Columbia University Press, 1973]).

35.   'It's queer how out of touch with truth women are. They live in a world of their own, and there had never been anything like it, and never can be… if they were to set it up it would go to pieces before the first sunset. Some confounded fact we men have been living contentedly with ever since the day of creation would start up and knock the whole thing over' (*Heart of Darkness* [ed. Paul O'Prey; Harmondsworth: Penguin, 1983], p. 39). Yet it is

women who engineer Marlow's entry into the heart of darkness—the aunt, the fateful secretaries, the intended—and the voice of the wilderness is expressed through Kurtz's mistress. Nina Auerbach's *Woman and the Demon* (Cambridge, MA: Harvard University Press, 1982) examines the ambivalent masculine attitude towards the secluded female in Victoran culture (see particularly chapter 3, 'Angels and Demons').

36. Edward W. Said, *Orientalism* (Harmondsworth: Penguin, 1985) See particularly 'Imaginative Geography and its Representations: *Orientalising the Orient*', pp. 49-73. Said notes the association of the orient with 'the escapism of sexual fantasy', at a time of increasing puritanism in the West (p. 190).

37. Milton's associations with the nightingale were mentioned in the previous chapter. Armstrong extensively discusses Arnold's fascination with Keats, a fascination which she claims was so overpowering that he abandoned poetry—a reading in line with 'Dover Beach' as a poem built on belatedness and loss—particularly with the *Ode to the Nightingale* in mind.

38. Armstrong, *Victorian Poetry*, p. 7.

39. The work ethic famously associated with Carlyle. Browning's magnificent 'Childe Harold to the Dark Tower Came' sets work against nature in a wholly destructive way. His knight forces his way through a meaningless landscape, forced on by his task, knowing it to be pointless. When he thrusts his spear into the only element of fecundity in the poem—the fetid stream— he thinks that he hears 'a baby's shriek': a sound that voices the destructiveness of military action and the unquestioning obedience it demands, on future generations.

40. Jacob Burckhardt's famous statement that, prior to the Renaissance, 'man was conscious of himself only as a member of a race, people, party, family, or corporation—only through some general category' (*The Civilisation of the Renaissance in Italy* [repr.; Phaidon Books, 1965], p. 81), quoted in, Patterson, 'Historical Criticism', p. 10.

41. English Gothic was seen very much as an indigenous style. See Kevin L. Morris's somewhat partisan arguments about *The Image of the Middle Ages in Romantic and Victorian Literature* (Croom Helm, 1984), particularly chapter 3, 'Anti-Medievalism'. Ruskin wrestled with his ambivalent attraction to medieval art throughout his life, justifying it on many levels. In 1853 he argued the medieval cathedral testified to 'the unconstrained labour of its individual makers', working co-operatively to create an 'organic' artifact, to which alienated modern workers could look back and see their forebears ('The Nature of the Gothic', in *Works* [ed. E.T. Cooker and Alexander Wedderburn; George Allen, 1904], X, p. 88).

42. The rose has long been associated with divine and courtly love and therefore with religious, romantic and erotic poetry, but the nightingale is associated with poetry *itself*. See Barbara Seward, *The Symbolic Rose* (New York: Columbia University Press, 1960) for an interesting traditional account of the topos of the rose.

43. Gilbert and Gubar, *Madwoman in the Attic*, p. 43.

44. Armstrong, *Victorian Poetry*, p. 85.

45. Delores Rosenblum, 'Face to Face: Elizabeth Barrett Browning's *Aurora Leigh* and Nineteenth Century Poetry', *Victorian Studies* 26 (1982–3), pp. 321-38.

46. 'Face to Face', p. 322.

47. Mermin argues that 'the social and psychological dangers of writing, the anomalousness of the positions they forged for themslves, and the effort of staking out new ground gave an impulsion of energy and excitement to [Victorian women writers'] work'. Similarly she notes that 'even in their most conservative forms… the ideas about women's role and nature that made them afraid to write also enabled them to do so'. She is discussing women writers from 1830 to 1880. (*Godiva's Ride*, pp. xviii, 59).

48. 'As the female individualist, not-quite/not-male, articulates herself in shifting relation to what is at stake, the "native female" as such (*within* discourse, *as* a signifier) is excluded from any share in this emerging norm' (Spivak, 'Three Women's Texts', p. 177).

49. 'Three Women's Texts', pp. 175-76.

50. Such as the radical feminism of writers such as Mary Daly who 'employs deliberately "non-theoretical" methodology with self-conscious rectitude'. Yet, as Gillian Beer points out, 'our thinking is often at the mercy of our communal metaphors' which take for granted that images are static. The relevance of this argument lies in my own interest in the nightingale's significance as an *index* of ideological change, rather than an unchanging symbol ('Representing Women: Re-presenting the Past', in Belsey and Moore [eds.], *The Feminist Reader*, p. 70).

51. In particular those concerning 'the history of the subject': see David Aers, 'Whisper'.

52. Spivak sees the temptation to identify with the figure of Jane Eyre as a non-imperialist feminist 'heroine'; likewise the re-labelling of the 'Renaissance' as the 'Early Modern Period' indicates a desire to look forward, almost as if there was nothing before which relegates the medieval period to limbo.

53. D. Mermin, *Elizabeth Barrett Browning: Origins of a New Poetry* (Chicago/University of Chicago Press, 1989).

54. 'In cultivating the young boy's ability to speak Latin, women, not being part of the Latin speaking world, were commonly of no use to a [boy] child after the age of seven' (W.J. Ong, 'Latin Language Study as a Renaissance Puberty Rite', *Studies in Philology* 56 [1939], pp. 103-25 [110]). Ong's more recent work sets up the distinction between mother-tongue (*materna lingua*) and father-tongue (*patrius sermo*), between the vernacular and classical languages, a distinction he sees arising towards the end of the Middle Ages (*Fighting for Life: Contest, Sexuality and Consciousness* [Ithaca, NY: Cornell University Press, 1981]). His argument suggests the possibility that *reading* the vernacular/mother-tongue literature of the medieval period could have been associated with reading 'feminine' writing.

55. Mermin, *Origins*, p. 19. Beer (among others) questions the 'claimed homology of "women" and "nature"... since nature is so socialised a category ('Representing Women', p. 71).

56. Beer, *Arguing with the Past*, p. 62.

57. In addition to making the supporter of the 'moderns' a woman, Richardson makes the supporter of the 'ancients' the classically educated Walden who has studied at Oxford.

58. Beer, *Arguing with the Past*, p. 62.

59. The most infamous being the Peterloo massacre of 1819 at St Peter's Field, Manchester.

60. Most famously in Matthew Arnold's *Culture and Anarchy* (1869). Representative quotations include: 'Everywhere we see the beginnings of confusion, and we want a clue to some sound order and authority'; 'Through culture seems to lie our way, not only to perfection, but even to safety' (ed. J. Dover Wilson; Cambridge: Cambridge University Press, 1960), pp. 144, 202.

61. It was not until the Cambridge Tripos instituted during the 1920s that English literature 'shook off much of what had been its role (as one aspect of the "national character")' (Doyle, 'Hidden History', p. 28).

62. This is not to deny the hidden issue of class relations, but I want to draw attention to the fact that many medieval texts openly discuss the place of women.

63. Butler, *Romantics*, p. 121.

64. *Romantics*, p. 123.

65. She comments that after the 1820s 'the religious revival prevailed, the Goths of the North swept in, and a change occurred in the spirit as well as in the style of the arts far more absolute than the variations of nuance between Grecian and Gothic in the previous century' (*Romantics*, p. 121).

66. Where Leighton suggests that 'Barrett Browning repudiates the habit of nostalgia which tempts the Victorian poet with the glamour of the past, and from this new sense of the present, she develops a crusading female poetics' (*Browning*, p. 115), I consider that Barrett Browning's poetry is 'modern' by engaging with the past as *part* of its commitment to the present.

67. 'No woman could take the classics for granted. Starting Latin or Greek was a journey into alien territory and for some women the sense of strangeness never entirely wore off'; 'The classics sometimes eluded women, sometimes infuriated them, but were inevitably both a symbol and an instrument of their rebellion' (R. Fowler, '"On Not Knowing Greek": The Classics and the Woman of Letters', *Classical Journal* 78 [1983], pp. 337-49).

68. *Blackwoods Magazine* wrote in 1844 that her powers extended 'over a wider and profounder range of thought and feeling, than ever before felt within the intellectual compass of the softer sex' (no. 56, pp. 621-39, quoted in D. David, *Intellectual Women and Victorian Patriarchy* [Macmillan, 1987], p. 101).

69. David discusses her classicism and notes that her learning was frequently commented on by contemporary reviewers; my final chapter claims

that her medieval learning was equally significant.

70.   With the world of women's novels. Interestingly, not French novels, which were exciting and—in the racy example of the cross-dressed George Sand—challenged gender stereotypes.

71.   David does not discuss the plurality of history as providing possible sites of resistance within a patriarchal system.

72.   David, *Intellectual Women*, p. 98.

73.   *Intellectual Women*, p. 97.

74.   Morris, *Image of the Middle Ages*, pp. 82-83. (*LM* = *Charles Kingsley: His Letters and Memories of his Life* [ed. Fanny Kingsley; 2 vols., 1878].)

75.   Mermin discusses Barrett Browning's innovation and influence: 'It was as if she held in suspension all the elements of Victorian poetry, all its potential voices' (*Origins*, p. 2).

Chapter 5
Bitter Confusions: Barrett Browning among the Nightingales

1.   *Poems* (3 vols; Chapman & Hall, 1856), III, pp. 49-50.

2.   James Thorpe, 'Elizabeth Barrett's Commentary on Shelley: Some Marginalia', in *Modern Language Notes* 66 (1951), pp. 455-58.

3.   'His *Comus*, and *Samson*, and *Lycidas*—how are we to praise them? His epic is the second to Homer's, and the first in sublime effects... [But] If we hazard a remark which is not admiration, it shall be this—that with all his heights and breadths... with all his rapt devotions and exaltations towards the highest of all, we do miss something—we, at least, who are writing, miss something—of what may be called, but rather metaphysically than theologically, *spirituality*' ('The Book of the Poets' [repr.; Hertfordshire: Wordworth Editions, 1994]), pp. 647-48.

4.   As demonstrated in her Preface to the 1844 edition of her *Poems*, where she discusses how the 'subject' of *A Drama of Exile* 'rather fastened on me than was chosen'. She writes tortuously and at great length of how she does not wish to compete with Milton: 'I had promised my own prudence to shut close the gates of Eden between Milton and myself, so that none might say that I dared to walk in his footsteps... It would not do' (p. 102).

5.   See 'The Book of the Poets' (p. 635). See also Barrett Browning's letter to Mary Russell Mitford in which she equates poetry with light and nightingales: 'I shd. as soon say do not look at the sun—do not listen to the nightingale—as do not read the poets!' (*Women of Letters: Selected Letters of Elizabeth Barrett Browning and Mary Russell Mitford* [ed. Meredith B. Raymond and Mary Rose Sullivan; Boston: Twayne, 1987]), letter of 27–28 March 1842, p. 75.

6.   *Women of Letters*, p. 75.

7.   'I should tremble to oppose any one scene in *Prometheus* to the Cassandra scene in *Agamemnon*' (Preface to *Prometheus Bound* [repr.; Hertfordshire: Wordsworth Editions, 1994]), p. 139.

8.   Marian's father is drunken and violent; Aurora's was beloved but had forsaken the fatherland for the motherland when he fell in love with Aurora's mother and stayed in Italy. Yet even this father is a restrictive influence: Angela Leighton points out that it is 'not the realisation that she has loved and lost Romney, but that she has loved and lost her father, which tests and educates her imagination'. Only when Aurora is free from his shadow can she make a new home (*Browning*, pp. 136, 137-39).

9.   Preface to *Prometheus Bound and Other Poems* (1833), p. 138.

10.   'The Book of the Poets', p. 628.

11.   Armstrong, *Victorian Poets*, chapter 12, 'A Music of Thine Own', p. 318.

12.   '*Sonnets from the Portuguese* inaugurated both the nineteenth-century revival of the amatory sonnet sequence, and also (with *In Memorium*, published a few months earlier) a major Victorian innovation: the long poem telling a story through a series of individual lyrics' (Mermin, *Origins*, p. 129).

13.   Armstrong, *Victorian Poets*, p. 356.

14.   Mermin, 'The Female Poet and the Embarrassed Reader', *ELH* 48 (1981), p. 351-67. (Expanded in *Origins*, chapter 5.)

15.   Mermin, *Origins*, p. 114.

16.   *Origins*, p. 2.

17.   Mermin, *Origins*, pp. 78-79.

18.   'The Female Poet', p. 361.

19.   'The Female Poet'.

20.   The Rossetti brothers were passionately fond of Barrett Browning's poetry. W.M. Rossetti commented that 'we revelled in them in profuse delight' (quoted in Mermin, *Origins*, p. 114). See discussion in Lionel Stevenson, *The Pre-Raphaelite Poets* (Chapel Hill: University of North Carolina Press, 1972), pp. 130, 201, and Florence Saunders Boos, *The Poetry of Dante G. Rossetti* (The Hague: Mouton, 1976), pp. 279-81. Ruskin associates Barrett Browning with the Pre-Raphaelites ('Things to be Studied' [1856], *Complete Works*, XV, p. 224).

21.   I am influenced by R.B. Wilkenfeld's striking analysis of vertical and horizontal movement in *Comus*, 'The Seat at the Centre', *ELH* 33 (1966), pp. 170-97. Clearly the 'enclosed space' had uncomfortable connotations to a bedridden invalid—no matter how hard she struggled to sublimate the fact of enclosure—but these connotations should not be reduced to repression alone.

22.   Mermin, *Origins*, p. 152.

23.   *Origins*, p. 152.

24.   *Origins*, p. 153.

25.   *Origins*, p. 154.

26.   *The New Larousse Encyclopedia of Mythology* (ed. R. Graves; Hamlyn, 1968), p. 143.

27.   Barrett Browning made a clear choice to use the daisy, arguing with Richard Horne, the editor of a literary magazine to which she contributed

reviews and articles, and who thought the flower too humble to be used in poetry: '*You* say, to Wordsworth alone, it is [allowable but] if anyone else calls a daisy noble, he is an imitator by that sign... in which you are wrong... because the daisy under the heel of a clown has a lesson, if sought for...' (quoted in Alethea Hayter, *Mrs Browning: A Poet's Work and its Setting* [Faber & Faber, 1962], pp. 88-89).

28.   See Morris's discussion of the relative values accorded to the classics and medieval writers: almost without exception qualified by their relation to Christianity. See particularly the last chapter on Ruskin.

29.   In line with her own non-conformism, Barrett Browning rejected the Catholicism of the Middle Ages.

30.   The active child is primarily related to horizontal movement, and the physically constricted adult is related to vertical spiritual movement: the stillness of the child is thus a precursor of the adult creativity. (See again the arguments of Wilkenfeld, 'The Seat at the Centre'.)

31.   Mermin, *Origins*, p. 101.

32.   *Origins*, p. 101. Yet the reference to God need not only be taken as a return to patriarchy. When Ruskin described her as 'spiritual' in his 'Stones of Venice' he sees her as refusing a modern and materialist world: the world seen by Kingsley as 'masculine' in contrast to the 'effeminate' Middle Ages. An editorial footnote gives earlier variations which emphasize this aspect: 'wild, bright spirituality', 'bright spirituality', 'disembodied spirituality' (*Works*, XI, p. 228 and n.). Once again it is possible to make links between the feminine and the medieval; Ruskin characterizes the art of the Middle Ages in exactly the same terms: 'ancient art was religious art; modern art is profane art' (*Works*, XII, p. 143). Barrett Browning's religious poetry is thus aligned with medieval art.

33.   See also the nightingales at Colonus. Possibly also significant here because it is through the agency of his daughter that Oedipus arrives at Colonus.

34.   Goldberg's rhetorical question, quoted previously, continues to be apt: 'What is to be made of loss? Perhaps that is every poet's question.'

35.   Again a previous reference is relevant: Lacan's view that the death of the thing (in this case the bower) allows the symbol with its wider resonance to come into being.

36.   E.g. 'The Lay of the Early Rose', 'A Flower in a Letter' (*Poems*, III, pp. 40, 78).

37.   Quoted in Leonid Arinstein, '"A Curse for a Nation": A Controversial Episode in Elizabeth Barrett Browning's Political Poetry', *Review of English Studies* NS 20 (1969), pp. 33-42 (38).

38.   See the discussion and Barrett Browning's reponse to the accusations in Mermin, *Origins*, pp. 114-15.

39.   When LEL was attacked in the *Westminster Review* 3 (1825), pp. 537-39, Barrett Browning defended her with lukewarm praise, commenting that she would be 'the best of women poets if she would cultivate her powers of

execution and write about something besides love' (quoted in Mermin, *Origins*, p. 32). Her own poems range far more widely.

40. Barrett Browning defended the success of Harriet Beecher Stowe's *Uncle Tom's Cabin* and suggested that a woman uninterested in such questions 'had better subside into slavery and concubinage herself...as in the times of old, shut herself up with the Penelopes in the "women's apartment", and take no rank among thinkers and speakers' (quoted in Kaplan [ed.], p. 10): the Greeks—and Greek literature—being clearly associated with female 'slavery and concubinage'.

41. Auerbach, *Woman and the Demon*. Mary Poovey goes further than Auerbach by claiming the the 'dizzying ascent [of women]...from metaphorical agent of damnation to literal agent of salvation' is a *result* of contemporary religious doubt, rather than part of it (*The Proper Lady and the Woman Writer: Ideology as Style in the Works of Mary Wollstonecraft, Mary Shelley and Jane Austen* [Chicago: University of Chicago Press, 1984], p. ix).

42. Rosenblum, 'Face to Face', p. 324.

43. Mermin, *Origins*, p. 104.

44. The insistence on the common humanity through a heterosexual love which slaves and masters feel alike, together with the insistence of Christ as a paradigm of virtue, recall the patterns of the sentimental novel, in particular *Uncle Tom's Cabin*, which Barrett Browning had read. Jane P. Tompkins's argument that the sentimental novel was 'a political enterprise, halfway between sermon and social theory, that both codifies and attempts to mold the values of its time' is very pertinent to this reading of 'The Runaway Slave' ('Sentimental Power: *Uncle Tom's Cabin* and the Politics of Literary History', in *The New Feminist Criticism* [ed. Elaine Showalter; Virago, 1989], pp. 84-85).

45. David, *Intellectual Women*, p. 100.

46. Beverly Taylor discusses Aurora's movement away from the 'masculine' art represented by the Danaë myth: 'The woman-poet's labors yield living poetry only when they infuse with Jovian "hot fire-seeds" of artistic and physical passion not only the ecstacies of Danaë but also the struggle for survival of mute Io and the anguish of individuals composing the tormented social body' ('"School-Miss Aldred" and "Materfamilias": Female Sexuality and Poetic Voice in "The Princess" and *Aurora Leigh*', in Antony H. Harrison and Beverly Taylor [eds.], *Gender and Discourse in Victorian Literature and Art* [De Kalb: Northern Illinois University Press, 1992], pp. 5-29).

47. Kaplan (ed.), *Aurora Leigh*, p. 5.

48. Re Kingsley's attack on the Franciscans.

49. Hayter, *Mrs Browning*, p. 164.

50. Instead she associates it with the thin 'bird-like' figure of Barrett Browning herself (*Mrs Browning*, p. 164).

51. Links with Christian redemption, peace and the new world. The nightingale is contrasted with the dove in Wordsworth's short lyric, 'O, Nightingale! thou surely art'. Wordsworth was seen as the great Romantic, originator of a new poetry; Coleridge as the genius who had failed, so Fred

Randel's speculation that 'Coleridge is the nightingale... overmatched by the less ostentatious stock-dove which is Wordsworth himself' ('Romantic Night-ingales', p. 50) suggests that Barrett Browning's choice of the dove rather than the nightingale marks her desire for success: for Wordsworth rather than Coleridge.

52.   Or Richard Niccols, *The Cuckow*, 1607, itself based on Clanvowe.

53.   H. Bloom, *The Anxiety of Influence: A Theory of Poetry* (Oxford University Press, 1975).

54.   Mermin's argument in *Godiva's Ride*.

55.   See Arinstein, 'A Curse for a Nation'.

56.   Gilbert and Gubar consider that poetry *per se* was seen as 'unfemi-nine' ('Shakespeare's Sisters', in *Feminist Literary Theory* [ed. Mary Eagleton; Oxford: Oxford University Press, 1986], pp. 106-12). Kaplan believes that the 'male stronghold' consists of particular *kinds* of poetry: 'epic and dramatic verse are associated with the Classicists, and with Shakespeare, Milton, Shelley and Tennyson, and later, Browning... women's voice, as in life, should be confined to the lyric' (*Aurora Leigh*, p. 8). It hardly needs adding that the split between classics and medieval is implicit in this distinction— and Chaucer certainly does not appear in the list of major (male) poets.

57.   Julia Markus draws attention to the political astuteness of *Casa Guidi Windows* in the introduction to her edition of the poem (New York: Browning Institute, 1977).

58.   Arinstein, 'A Curse for a Nation', p. 38.

59.   'A Curse for a Nation', p. 38.

60.   Arinstein quotes from Barrett Browning's letter to Isa Blagden, (?July/August 1859): '*I* will never forgive England the most damnable part she has taken on Italian affairs, never.'

61.   Gilbert, 'From *Patria* to *Matria*', p. 196.

62.   'From *Patria* to *Matria*', p. 197.

63.   The echoes are definately medieval, whether religious/erotic (as in the cult of images of St Sebastian, who was shot through with arrows), or courtly/erotic as in the nightingale-filled garden of the *Romaunt of the Rose* where the first bird to be mentioned is a nightingale, and Cupid is depicted as having nightingales flying around his head as he shoots the lover with the arrows of desire (Fragment A, 909-11, from *Complete Works*).

64.   *The Routledge Dictionary of Historical Slang* (ed. Eric Partridge; abr. J. Simpson; Routledge, Kegan & Paul, 1973).

Appendix 1
Nightingales in Classical Literature

1.   Unless otherwise stated, all texts taken from the Loeb Classical Library.

2.   For a fuller listing of the 'innumerable poetic references' to the nightingale see Thompson, *Glossary*, pp. 10-14.

3. Unclear as to date but following *Cambridge History of Classical Literature:* vol. I, part 1, 'The Hellenistic Period and the Empire' (ed. P.E. Easterling and B.W. Knox; Cambridge: Cambridge University Press, 1989).

4. Thompson, *Glossary,* p.11.

Appendix II
Christian Latin Poems

1. *The Oxford Book of Medieval Latin Verse* (ed. F.J. Raby; Oxford: Oxford University Press, 1959) no. 26, p. 33.

2. *Medieval Latin Verse,* no. 62, p. 82.

3. A.J. Wyatt, *Old English Riddles* (Boston and Heath, 1912), pp. 69-70.

4. Raby, *SLP,* I, p. 184.

5. Raby, 'Philomena Praevia', p. 437.

6. Waddell, *MLL,* p. 118.

7. Raby, 'Philomena Praevia', p. 437.

8. Raby, *CLP,* p. 262 (bracketed and indented passages omitted in translation).

9. Raby, *SLP,* I, p. 288.

10. Translated by Dr Adrian Wilmott and Dr Siân Lewis.

11. Fleur Adcock, *The Virgin and the Nightingale* (Newcastle-upon-Tyne: Bloodaxe, 1983), p, 19.

12. Translated by Dr Adrian Wilmott and Dr Siân Lewis.

13. Waddell, *MLL,* p. 89.

14. Translated by Dr Siân Lewis.

15. Waddell, *MLL,* p. 119.

16. Dr Wilmott suggests that this may be a reference to the shift from monophonic to polyphonic song.

17. Though the bird *appears* to be a sparrow, the description of its song quite clearly marks it out as a nightingale.

18. Dr Lewis comments that these lines appear to refer to the bird, not to God, but, as the grammar of the passage is somewhat idiosyncratic and it does not make sense otherwise, it may be a fault in the original.

19. Translated by Dr Adrian Wilmott and Dr Siân Lewis.

20. Waddell, *Morell,* bracketed and indented in original, p. 229 (verses missing).

21. Adcock, *The Virgin and the Nightingale,* pp. 10-14 (first stanza omitted).

Bibliography

Unless otherwise stated, place of publication is London, and classical texts are taken from the Loeb Classical Library (London: Heineman; Cambridge, MA: Harvard University Press).

Primary Sources

Classical

Aeschylus, *The Suppliant Maidens*, I (1922).
—*Agamemnon*, in *Aeschylus*, II (trans. Herbert Weir Smyth, 1926).
Aesop, *Subtyll Historyes and Fables of Esope* (Westminster, 1483).
Aristophanes, *The Birds*, in *Aristophanes*, II (trans. B.B. Rogers, 1924).
—*Lysistrata*, in *Aristophanes*, III (1924).
Aristotle, *Historia Animalium*, in *Aristotle*, II (trans. A.L. Peck, 1970).
Callimachus, 'Epigram ii' (trans. William Cory), in *Greek Literature: An Anthology* (Michael Grant, 1976).
Catullus, *The Poems of Catullus* (ed. and trans. Peter Whigham; Harmondsworth: Penguin, 1966).
Euripedes, *Hecuba*, in *Euripedes*, I (trans. Arthur S. Way, 1912).
Hesiod, *The Homeric Hymns and Homerica* (trans. Hugh G. Evelyn-White, 1914).
Homer, *The Odyssey*, II (trans. A.T. Murray, 1919).
Martial, *Epigrams*, II (trans. Walter C.A. Ker, 1920).
Ovid, *Heroides*, in *Ovid*, I (trans. Grant Showerman, 1921); *Amores*, II.
—*Metamorphoses* (trans. Frank Justus Miller, 1916).
Pausanias, *Pausanias's Description of Greece*, I (6 vols.; trans. J.G. Frazer; Macmillan & Co., Ltd, 1913).
Plato, *Phaedo*, in *Plato*, I (trans. H.N. Fowler, 1914).
—*The Republic*, in *Plato*, II (trans. Paul Shorey, 1935).
—*The Republic* (trans. Desmond Lee; Harmondsworth: Penguin, rev. edn, 1974).
Pliny, *Natural History*, IX, Books 33–35 (trans. H. Rackham, 1952).
Sappho, fragments in *Greek Lyric*, I (trans. David A. Campbell, 1982).
Sophocles, *Oedipus at Colonus*, in *Sophocles*, I (trans. F. Storr, 1912).
—*Ajax; Trachiniae*, in *Sophocles*, II (1913).
Theocritus, Idyll XV: 'The Women at the Adonis Festival', *The Greek Bucolic Poets* (trans. J.M. Edmonds, 1912).
Thucydides, *The Peloponnesian War*, I (trans. C. Foster Smith, 1919).
Virgil, *Eclogues; Georgics*, in *Virgil*, I (trans. H. Rushton Fairclough, 1935); 'Ciris', *Virgil*, II (1934).

Anthologies/Collections

Adcock, Fleur, *The Virgin and the Nightingale* (Newcastle-upon-Tyne: Bloodaxe, 1983).

Anthology of Troubadour Lyric Poetry (ed. and trans. Alan R. Press; Edinburgh: Edinburgh University Press, 1971).

Bithell, Jethro, *The Minnesingers. I. Translations* (New York: Longman, Greene & Co., 1909).

Chants d'Auvergne (orch. Canteloube).

The Early English Carols (ed. R.L. Greene; Oxford: Clarendon Press, 1935).

Early English Lyrics (ed. E.K. Chambers and F. Sedgewick; A.H. Bullen, 1907).

English Lyrics of the Thirteenth Century (ed. Carleton Brown; Oxford: Clarendon Press, 1932).

English Verse between Chaucer and Surrey (ed. Eleanor Prescott Hammond; Durham, NC: Duke University Press, 1927).

Medieval English Lyrics (ed. R.T. Davies; Faber, 1963).

Medieval English Verse (ed. and trans. Brian Stone; Harmondsworth: Penguin, 1964).

Mediaeval Latin Lyrics (trans. Helen Waddell; Constable, 1929).

More Latin Lyrics from Virgil to Milton (trans. Helen Waddell; Gollancz, 1976).

The Oxford Book of Medieval English Verse (ed. Celia and Kenneth Sisam; Oxford: Clarendon Press, 1970).

The Oxford Book of Medieval Latin Verse (ed. F.J.E. Raby; Oxford: Oxford University Press, 1959).

Political, Religious, and Love Poems (ed. F.J. Furnivall; Early English Text Society, 1903).

The Rattle Bag (ed. Ted Hughes and Seamus Heaney; Faber, 1982).

Secular Lyrics of the XIVth and XVth Centuries (ed. Russell Hope Robbins; Oxford: Clarendon Press, 1952).

Wine, Women and Song (trans. J.A. Symonds; Chatto & Windus, 1907).

Individual Texts

Browning, Elizabeth Barrett, Aurora Leigh *and Other Poems* (ed. Cora Kaplan; The Women's Press, 1978).

—*Casa Guidi Windows* (ed. Julia Markus; New York: Browning Institute, 1977).

—*Poems* (3 vols.; Chapman & Hall, 1856).

—*Selected Poems* (ed. Malcolm Hicks; Manchester: Carcanet/Fyfield, 1983).

—'The Book of the Poets' (repr.; Hertfordshire: Wordsworth Editions, 1994 [review in *The Athenaeum*, Feb./March, 1842]).

—Preface to the 1844 edition of *Poems* (repr.; Hertfordshire: Wordsworth Editions, 1994).

—Preface to *Prometheus Bound and Other Poems* (repr.; Hertfordshire: Wordsworth Editions, 1994 [1833]).

—'Some Account of the Greek Christian Poets' (repr.; Hertfordshire: Wordsworth Editions, 1994 [*The Athenaeum*, Feb./March, 1842]).

Le Chant de Roussigneul (ed. E. Walberg; Lund: C.W.K. Gleerup, 1942).

Charles of Orleans: The English Poems (ed. Robert Steele; Early English Text Society, 1941).

Chaucer, *Complete Works* (ed. W.W. Skeat; Oxford: Clarendon Press, 1912).

Clanvowe, John, *The Works of Sir John Clanvowe* (ed. V.J. Scattergood; Cambridge: D.S. Brewer, 1965).

Condé, Jean de, *La Messe des Oiseaux*, in B.A.Windeatt (ed.), *Chaucer's Dream Poetry: Sources and Analogues* (Cambridge: Cambridge University Press, 1982).

Conrad, Joseph, *Heart of Darkness* (ed. Paul O'Prey; Harmondsworth: Penguin, 1983).

Drummond of Hawthorden, William, *Poetical Works* (ed. L.E. Kastner; Manchester: Manchester University Press, 1913).

Dryden, *The Poems and Fables of John Dryden* (ed. James Kinsley; Oxford: Oxford University Press, 1962).

The Floure and the Leaf (ed. with introduction D.A. Pearsall; London/Edinburgh: Thomas Nelson, 1962).

France, Marie de, *The Lais of Marie de France* (trans. with an intro. by Glyn S. Burgess and Keith Busby; Harmondsworth: Penguin, 1986).

Hafiz, *Fifty Poems* (ed. and trans. A.J. Arberry; Cambridge: Cambridge University Press, 1953).

'The Harmony of Birds', in *Two Early Renaissance Bird Poems* (ed. M. Andrew; Washington, DC: Folger Shakespeare Library; Associated University Presses, 1984).

Hopkins, Gerard Manley, *Poems* (ed. W.H. Gardner and N.H. McKenzie; Oxford: Oxford University Press, 1970).

Lydgate's Minor Poems: The Two Nightingale Poems (ed. O. Glauning; Early English Text Society, 1900).

Milton, *The Complete Shorter Poems* (ed. John Carey; Longman, 1968).

Niccols, Richard, *Selected Poems* (ed. Glyn Pursglove; Salzburg: Institut für Anglistik und Amerikanistik, 1992).

The Owl and the Nightingale (ed. and trans. J.W.H. Atkins; Cambridge: Cambridge University Press, 1922).

The Owl and the Nightingale (ed. E.G. Stanley; Manchester: Manchester University Press, 1972).

Pecham, John, *Philomena*, in Walberg (ed.), *Chant de Roussigneul.*

Rilke, R.M., *Duino Elegies* (trans. J.B. Leishman and Stephen Spender; Chatto & Windus, 1975).

Shelley, 'A Defence of Poetry', in *The Complete Works of Shelley* (ed. R. Ingpen and W.E. Peck; New York: Gordian Press, 1965), VII.

Tennyson, Alfred, *A Variorum Edition of Tennyson's 'Idylls of the King'* (ed. John Pfordresher; New York: Columbia University Press, 1973).

Wordsworth, *Poetical Works* (ed. Thomas Hutchinson; Oxford: Oxford University Press, 1936).

Secondary Sources

Aers, David, 'A Whisper in the Ear of Early Modernists', or Reflections on Literary Critics Writing the "History of the Subject"', in *idem* (ed.), *Culture and History, 1350–1600: Essays on English Communities, Identities and Writing* (Harvest-Wheatsheaf, 1992), pp. 177-202.

Altieri, Charles, 'Ovid and the New Mythologists', *Novel* (Fall 1973), pp. 31-40.

Arinstein, Leonid, '"A Curse for a Nation": A Controversial Episode in Elizabeth Barrett Browning's Political Poetry', *Review of English Studies*, NS 20 (1969), pp. 33-42.

Armstrong, Isobel, *Victorian Poetry: Poetry, Poetics, Politics* (Routledge, 1993).

Arnold, Matthew, *Culture and Anarchy* (ed. J. Dover Wilson; Cambridge: Cambridge University Press, 1960 [1869]).

Auerbach, Nina, *Woman and the Demon* (Cambridge, MA: Harvard University Press, 1982).

Barcus, James E. (ed.), *Shelley: The Critical Heritage* (Routledge & Kegan Paul, 1975).

Beer, Gillian, *Arguing with the Past* (Routledge, 1989).

—*Darwin's Plots: Evolutionary Narrative in Darwin, George Eliot, and Nineteenth Century Fiction* (Routledge & Kegan Paul, 1983).

—'Representing Women: Re-presenting the Past', in Belsey and Moore (eds.), *Feminist Reader*.

Belsey, Catherine and Jane Moore (eds.), *The Feminist Reader* (Macmillan, 1989).

Bloom, Harold, *The Anxiety of Influence: A Theory of Poetry* (Oxford: Oxford University Press, 1975).

Boase, Roger, *The Troubadour Revival* (Routledge & Kegan Paul, 1978).

Boos, Florence Saunders, *The Poetry of Dante G.Rossetti* (The Hague: Mouton, 1976).

Brewer, D.S., 'Class Distinction in Chaucer', *Speculum* 43 (1968), pp. 290-305.

Bromwich Rachel, *Writers of Wales: Dafydd ap Gwilym* (Cardiff: University of Wales Press, 1974).

Brownlee, Marina *et al.* (eds.), *The New Medievalism* (Baltimore: Johns Hopkins University Press, 1991).

Butler, Marilyn, *Romantics, Rebels and Reactionaries* (Oxford: Oxford University Press, 1981).

Bynum, Caroline Walker, *Jesus as Mother: Studies in the Spirituality of the High Middle Ages* (Berkeley/Los Angeles: University of California Press, 1982).

Cargo, Robert T., 'Marie de France's *Le Laustic* and Ovid's *Metamorphoses*', *Comparative Literature* 18 (1966), pp. 162-66.

Carson, Anne, *Eros the Bittersweet* (Princeton: Princeton University Press, 1986).

Chandler, A.R., 'The Nightingale in Greek and Latin Poetry', *Classical Journal* 30 (1934), pp. 78-84.

Clark, Timothy, *Embodying Revolution: The Figure of the Poet in Shelley* (Oxford: Clarendon Press, 1989).

Coleman, Janet, 'The *Owl and the Nightingale* and Papal Theories of Marriage', *Journal of Ecclesiastical History* 38.4 (October 1987), pp. 517-68.

Collins, Roger, *Early Medieval Europe* (Macmillan, 1991)

Cottrell, R.D., 'Le Lai de Laustic: From Physicality to Spirituality', *Philological Quarterly* 47 (1967), pp. 499-505.

Dally, Peter, *Elizabeth Barrett Browning: A Psychological Portrait* (Macmillan, 1989).

David, Deirdre, *Intellectual Women and Victorian Patriarchy* (Macmillan, 1987).

De Man, Paul, 'Shelley Disfigured', *The Rhetoric of Romance* (New York: Columbia University Press, 1984).

Derrida, Jacques, *Of Grammatology* (trans. Gayatri Chakravorty Spivak; Baltimore/London: Johns Hopkins University Press, 1976).

A Dictionary of Historical Slang (ed. Eric Partridge; abr. J. Simpson; Harmondsworth: Penguin, 1972).

Dorst, Jean, *The Migrations of Birds* (trans. Constance Sherman; Heinemann, 1962)

Doyle, Brian, 'The Hidden History of English Studies', in *Re-reading English* (ed. Peter Widdowson; Methuen, 1982).

Dronke, Peter, *Medieval Latin and the Rise of the European Love Lyric.* I. *Problems and Interpretations* (2 vols.; Oxford: Clarendon Press, 1965).

—*The Medieval Lyric* (Hutchinson, 1968).

—*The Medieval Poet and his World* (Rome: Edizioni di Storia e Letteratura, 1984).

—*Women Writers of the Middle Ages* (Cambridge: Cambridge University Press, 1984),

Dronke, Peter (ed.), *A History of Twelfth Century Western Philosophy* (Cambridge: Cambridge University Press, 1988).

Emslie, M., 'Codes of Love and Class Distinctions', *Essays in Criticism* 5 (1955), pp. 1-17; critical responses and reply, pp. 205-18.

Everest, Kelvin (ed.), *Shelley Revalued: Essays from the Gregynog Conference* (Leicester: Leicester University Press, 1983).

Ferrante, Joan, *Woman as Image in Medieval Literature* (New York: Columbia University Press, 1975).

Ferris, Ina, 'From Trope to Code: The Novel and the Rhetoric of Gender in Nineteenth Century Critical Discourse', in Shires (ed.), *Rewriting the Victorians.*

Ferry, Anne, *The Inward Language* (Chicago/London: University of Chicago Press, 1983).

Forbes Irving, R.M.C., *Metamorphosis in Greek Myth* (Oxford: Clarendon Press, 1990).

Fowler, R., ' "On Not Knowing Greek": The Classics and the Woman of Letters', *Classical Journal* 78.4 (1983), pp. 337-49.

Garrod, H.W., 'The Nightingale in Poetry', *The Profession of Poetry and Other Lectures* (Oxford: Clarendon Press, 1929).

Gavitch, Daniel, 'The Impure Motives of Elizabethan Poetry', *Genre* 15 (1982), pp. 225-38.

Gilbert, Sandra and Susan Gubar, *The Madwoman in the Attic: The Woman Writer and the Nineteenth Century Imagination* (New Haven/London: Yale University Press, 1979).

—'Shakespeare's Sisters', in *Feminist Literary Theory* (ed. Mary Eagleton; Oxford: Blackwell, 1986).

Gilbert, Sandra, 'From *Patria* to *Matria*: EBB's Risorgimento', *PMLA* 99 (1984), pp. 194-211.

Glen, Heather, *Vision and Disenchantment: Blake's 'Songs' and Wordsworth's 'Lyrical Ballads'* (Cambridge: Cambridge University Press, 1983).

Glier, Ingebor, 'Troubadours and Minnesang', in *The New Pelican Guide to English Literature* (gen. ed. Boris Ford; 5 vols.; Harmondsworth: Penguin, 1982), I, part 2, *The European Inheritance.*

Goldberg, Jonathan, *Voice Terminal Echo: Postmodernism and English Renaissance Texts* (Methuen, 1986).

Goldhill, Simon, *Reading Greek Tragedy* (Cambridge: Cambridge University Press, 1986).

Gray, Douglas, *Themes and Images in the Medieval English Religious Lyric* (Routledge & Kegan Paul, 1972).

Greenblatt, Stephen, *Renaissance Self-Fashioning* (Chicago/London: University of Chicago Press, 1984).

Greer, Germaine, *Slipshod Sybils: Recognition, Rejection and the Woman Poet* (New York: Viking, 1995).

Grosz, Elizabeth, *Jacques Lacan: A Feminist Introduction* (Routledge, 1990).

Halliday, W.R., *Indo-European Folk-Tales and Greek Legend* (Cambridge: Cambridge University Press, 1933).

Harper-Bill, C., and Ruth Harvey (eds.), *The Ideals and Practice of Medieval Knighthood* (Woodbridge, Surrey: Boydell Press, 1986).

Hartman, Geoffrey, 'The Voice of the Shuttle: Language from the point of view of Literature', *Beyond Formalism, Literary Essays 1958–1970* (New Haven: Yale University Press, 1970), pp. 337-55.

—'Evening Star and Evening Land', in *The Fate of Reading and Other Essays* (Chicago: University of Chicago Press, 1975), pp. 147-78.

Hatto A.T. (ed.), *EOS: An Inquiry into the Theme of Lovers' Meetings and Partings at Dawn in Poetry* (London, The Hague, Paris: Mouton, 1965), 'Appendix I: "The Nightingale"', pp. 792-80.

Hayter, Alethea, *Mrs Browning: A Poet's Work and its Setting* (Faber & Faber, 1962).

Hazlitt, William, *Lectures on English Poets and The Spirit of the Age* (Everyman, 1910).

Hele-King, Desmond, 'Shelley and Erasmus Darwin', in Everest (ed.), *Shelley Revalued.*

Herzfeld, Michael, 'Ritual and Textual Structures: The Advent of Spring in Rural Greece', in R.K. Jain (ed.), *Text and Context: The Social Anthropology of Tradition* (Philadelphia: Institute for the Study of Human Issues, 1977).

Hodge, Robert, *Literature as Discourse* (Cambridge: Polity Press, 1991).

Hollander, J., *The Untuning of the Sky* (Princeton: Princeton University Press, 1961).

Irvine, W. and P. Honan, *The Book, the Ring and the Poet* (London, Sidney, Toronto: Bodley Head, 1974).

Jackson, Kenneth, *Studies in Early Celtic Nature Poetry* (Cambridge: Cambridge University Press, 1935).

Jackson, William Henry, 'The Tournament and Chivalry in German Tournament Books of the Sixteenth Century', in Harper-Bill and Harvey (eds.), *Ideals and Practice.*

Jacobi, Klaus, 'Logic (ii) The Later Twelfth Century', in Dronke (ed.), *History.*

Johnson, E.D.H., *The Alien Vision of Victorian Poetry* (Hampden, CT: Archon Books, 1963)

Joplin, Patricia Klindiest, 'The Voice of the Shuttle is Ours', *Stanford Literature Review* 1 (1984), pp. 25-53.

Keen, Maurice, *Chivalry* (New Haven and London: Yale University Press, 1984).

Keuls, Eva C., 'Attic Vase-Painting and the Home Textile Industry', in Warren G. Moon (ed.), *Ancient Greek Art and Iconography* (Madison, WI: University of Winsconsin Press, 1983), pp. 209-30.

Knoepflmacher, U.C., 'Projection and the Female Other: Romanticism, Browning and the Victorian Dramatic Monologue', *Victorian Poetry* 22 (1984), pp. 139-59.

Koestler, Arthur, *The Sleepwalkers: A History of Man's Changing Vision of the Universe* (Arkana, 1989).

Langbaum, Robert, *The Poetry of Experience: The Dramatic Monologue in Modern Literary Tradition* (Chatto & Windus, rev. edn, 1972 [1957]).

Lampe, David, 'Tradition and Meaning in *The Cuckoo and the Nightingale*', *Papers in Language and Literature* 3 (1967), pp. 49-62.

Lears, J.T. Jackson, 'The Concept of Cultural Hegemony', *American Historical Review* 90 (1985), pp. 567-94.

Lehrman, Sara, 'The Education of Women in the Middle Ages', *The Roles and Images of Women in the Middle Ages and Renaissance* (ed. D. Radcliff-Umstead; Pittsburgh: University of Pittsburgh Publications on the Middle Ages and the Renaissance, 1975).

Leighton, Angela, *Elizabeth Barrett Browning* (Brighton: Harvester, 1986).

Lewis, C.S., *The Allegory of Love* (Oxford: Clarendon Press, 1936).

Luscombe, D.E., 'Peter Abelard', in Dronke (ed.), *History*.

Marenbon, John, *From the Circle of Alcuin to the School of Auxerre: Logic, Theology and Philosophy in the Early Middle Ages* (Cambridge: Cambridge University Press, 1981).

Marotti, Arthur F., ' "Love Is Not Love": Elizabethan Sonnet Sequences and the Social Order', *ELH* 49 (1982), pp. 396-428.

Marsh, G.L., 'Sources and Analogues of *The Flower and the Leaf*', *Modern Philology* 4 (1906–1907), pp. 121-69, 281-329.

Matthews, G.M., 'A Volcano's Voice in Shelley' (1957), in R.B. Woodings (ed.), *Shelley: Modern Judgements* (Macmillan, 1968).

McDonnell, Ernest W., *The* Béguines *and Beghards in Medieval Culture* (New York: Octagon Books, 1954).

Mermin, Dorothy, *The Audience in the Poem: Five Victorian Poets* (New Brunswick, NJ: Rutgers University Press, 1983).

—'Browning and the Primitive', *Victorian Studies* 25 (1982), pp. 211-37.

—*Elizabeth Barrett Browning: Origins of a New Poetry* (Chicago/London: University of Chicago Press, 1989).

—'The Female Poet and the Embarassed Reader', *ELH* 48 (1981), pp. 351-67.

—*Godiva's Ride: Women of Letters in England, 1830–1880* (Bloomington and Indianapolis: Indiana University Press, 1993)

Mizruchi, Ephraim H., *Regulating Society* (Chicago/London: University of Chicago Press, 1983).

Montrose, Louis, ' "Eliza, Queene of Shepheardes", and the Pastoral of Power', *English Literary Renaissance* 10 (1980), pp. 153-82.

Moore, R.I., *The Formation of a Persecuting Society* (Oxford: Blackwell, 1990).

Morris, Kevin L., *The Image of the Middle Ages in Romantic and Victorian Literature* (Croom Helm, 1984)

Mortimer, Richard, 'Knights and Knighthood in Germany in the Central Middle Ages', in Harper-Bill and Harvey (eds.), *Ideals and Practice*.

Murray, Alexander, *Reason and Society in the Middle Ages* (Oxford: Clarendon Press, 1978).

The New Larousse Encyclopedia of Mythology (ed. R. Graves; Hamlyn, 1968).

Nichols, Stephen G., 'An Intellectual Anthropology of Marriage', in Brownlee *et al.* (eds.), *New Medievalism.*

—'The New Medievalism: Tradition and Discontinuity in Medieval Culture', in Brownlee *et al.* (eds.), *New Medievalism*

Noble, Peter S., 'Knights and Burgesses in the Feudal Epic', in Harper-Bill and Harvey (eds.), *Ideals and Practice.*

Ong, W.J., *Fighting for Life: Contest, Sexuality and Consciousness* (Ithaca, NY: Cornell University Press, 1981).

—'Latin Language as a Renaissance Puberty Rite', *Studies in Philology* 56 (1959), pp. 103-24.

Ormond, Richard, *Sir Edwin Landseer* (Thames & Hudson, 1981).

Parry, Thomas, *Hanes Llenyddiaeth Gymraeg hyd 1900* (Cardiff: University of Wales Press, 1945).

Patterson, Lee, *Chaucer and the Subject of History* (Routledge, 1991).

—'Court Politics and the Invention of Literature: The Case of Sir John Clanvowe', in David Aers (ed.), *Culture and History, 1350–1600: Essays on English Communities, Identities and Writing* (Harvester Wheatsheaf, 1992).

—'Historical Criticism and the Claims of Humanism', in *Negotiating the Past* (Madison, WI: University of Winsconsin Press, 1987), pp. 3-39.

—'On the Margin: Postmodernism, Ironic History, and Medieval Studies', *Speculum* 65 (1990), pp. 87-108.

Pollard, J.R.T., *Birds in Greek Life and Myth* (Thames and Hudson, 1977).

—'*The Birds* of Aristophanes: A Source Book for Old Beliefs', *American Journal of Philology* 69 (1948), pp. 353-76.

Poovey, Mary, *The Proper Woman and the Woman Writer: Ideology as Style in the Works of Mary Wollstonecraft, Mary Shelley and Jane Austen* (Chicago: University of Chicago Press, 1984).

Raby, F.J.E., *Christian Latin Poetry* (Oxford: Clarendon Press, 1927).

—'Philomena Praevia Temporis Amoeni', in *Mélanges Joseph de Ghellinck, S.J.* (Gembloux: J. Ducolot, 1951), pp. 435-48.

—*Secular Latin Poetry in the Middle Ages* (2 vols.; Oxford: Clarendon Press, 1934).

Randel, Fred, 'The Contentiousness of Romantic Nightingales', *Studies in Romanticism* 21 (1982), pp. 33-55.

Raymond, Meredith B., and Mary Rose Sullivan (eds.), *Women of Letters: Selected Letters of Elizabeth Barrett Browning and Mary Russell Mitford* (Boston, MA: Twayne, 1987).

Rosenblum, Delores, 'Face to Face: Elizabeth Barrett Browning's *Aurora Leigh* and Nineteenth Century Poetry', *Victorian Studies* 26 (1982–83), pp. 321-38.

Rowland, Beryl, *Birds with Human Souls: A Guide to Bird Symbolism* (Knoxville, TN: University of Tennessee Press, 1977).

Ruskin, John, *Works* (ed. E.T. Cooker and Alexander Wedderburn; George Allen, 1904), X, XI.

Said, Edward W., *Orientalism* (Harmondsworth: Penguin, 1985).

Sandison, Helen E., *The 'Chanson d'Aventure' in Middle English* (Bryn Mawr, PA: Bryn Mawr College, 1913).

Scattergood, V.J., *Politics and Poetry in the Fifteenth Century* (Blandford Press, 1971).

Schell, John F., 'The Nightingale Figure in Shelley's *Defence*', *English Language Notes* 17 (1980), pp. 265-68.

Seward, Barbara, *The Symbolic Rose* (New York: Columbia University Press, 1960).

Shippey, T.A., 'Listening to the Nightingale', *Comparative Literature* 22 (Winter 1970), pp. 46-60.

Shires, Linda, 'Ideology and the Subject as Agent', in Shires (ed.), *Rewriting the Victorians*.

Shires, Linda M. (ed.), *Rewriting the Victorians: Theory, History, and the Politics of Gender* (Routledge, 1992).

Sienert, Edgar, *Les Lais de Marie de France: Du conte merveilleux à la nouvelle psychologique* (Paris: Librairie Honoré Champion, 1978).

Slimm, E. Warwick, *The Discourse of Self in Victorian Poetry* (Macmillan, 1991).

Snyder, Jane McIntosh, 'The Web of Song: Weaving Imagery in Homer and the Lyric Poets', *Classical Journal* 76 (1981), pp. 193-96.

Spearing, A.C., *Medieval Dream Poetry* (Cambridge: Cambridge University Press, 1976).

Spivak, Gayatri Chakravorty, 'Three Women's Texts and a Critique of Imperialism', in Belsey and Moore (eds.), *Feminist Reader*.

Stevenson, Lionel, *The Pre-Raphaelite Poets* (Chapel Hill: University of North Carolina Press, 1972).

Swainson, Charles, *The Folklore and Provincial Names of British Birds* (repr.; E. Stock, 1956 [1886]).

Taylor, Beverley, '"*School-Miss* Aldred" and "Materfamilias": Female Sexuality and Poetic Voice in "The Princess" and *Aurora Leigh*", in Antony H. Harrison and Beverley Taylor (eds.), *Gender and Discourse in Victorian Literature and Art* (DeKalb: Northern Illinois University Press, 1992), pp. 5-29.

Taylor, E., *Lays of the Minnesingers* (Longman, 1825).

Thompson, D'Arcy Wentworth, *A Glossary of Greek Birds* (Oxford: Clarendon Press, 1895).

Thorpe, James, 'Elizabeth Barrett's Commentary on Shelley: Some Marginalia', *Modern Language Notes* 66 (1951), pp. 455-58.

Tompkins, J.P., 'Sentimental Power: *Uncle Tom's Cabin* and the Politics of Literary History', in Elaine Showalter (ed.), *The New Feminist Criticism* (Virago, 1989).

Les très riches heures du Duc de Berry (text by Demond Pognon; trans. David Macrae; Musé Condé, Chantilly: Miller Graphics, 1979).

Tuve, Rosamund, *Seasons and Months* (Paris: Folcroft Press, 1933).

Tweedale, Martin M., 'Logic (i) To the Time of Abelard', in Dronke (ed.), *History*.

Utley, F.L., *The Crooked Rib* (Columbus: Ohio State University, 1944).

Vale, M., *War and Chivalry: Warfare and Aristocratic Culture in England, France and Burgundy at the End of the Middles Ages* (Duckworth, 1981).

Vance, Eugene, 'Love's Concordance: The Poetics of Desire and the Joy of the Text', *Diacritics* 5 (1975), pp. 40-52.

Waddell, Helen, *The Wandering Scholars* (Constable, 1927).

Waller, Gary, *English Poetry of the Sixteenth Century* (London/New York: Longman, 1986).

Warner, Marina, *Alone of All her Sex: The Myth and Cult of the Virgin Mary* (Picador, 1985).

Whigham, Frank, 'Sexual and Social Mobility in *The Duchess of Malfi*', *PMLA* 100 (1985), pp. 167-86.

Wilkenfeld, R.B., 'The Seat at the Centre', *ELH* 33 (1966), pp. 170-97.

Williams, Ifor, *Lectures on Early Welsh Poetry* (ed. Rachel Bromwich; Cardiff: University of Wales Press, 1972).

Williams, Jeni, 'Interweaving Poetry and the "Origin of Man": Shelley and the Transforming Nightingale', in *Shelley, 1792–1992: A Bicentenary Conference* (ed. James Hogg; Salzburg: Institut für Anglistik und Amerikanistik, 1993).

—'The Voice out of Darkness: Milton and the Nightingale', *Swansea Review* 7 (December 1990), pp. 10-31.

Wimberley, L.C., *Folklore in the English and Scottish Ballads* (New York: Dover, 1965 [Chicago: University of Chicago Press, 1928]).

Woolf, Rosemary, *The English Religious Lyric in the Middle Ages* (Oxford: Clarendon Press, 1968).

Wyatt, A.J., *Old English Riddles* (Boston/London: Heath, 1912).

Index of Names and Titles

...all I have brought back
From that long night are the fixed stars reeling.
It is the poet's bird, they say. Perhaps I took it home.
For here I am, raising my voice, scraping my throat raw again.

—(Leslie Norris, 'Nightingales', 3. 13-15)